Snapshots of the Mind

Snapshots of the Mind

Gary Klein

The MIT Press
Cambridge, Massachusetts
London, England

© 2022 Massachusetts Institute of Technology

All rights reserved. No part of this book may be reproduced in any form by any electronic or mechanical means (including photocopying, recording, or information storage and retrieval) without permission in writing from the publisher.

The MIT Press would like to thank the anonymous peer reviewers who provided comments on drafts of this book. The generous work of academic experts is essential for establishing the authority and quality of our publications. We acknowledge with gratitude the contributions of these otherwise uncredited readers.

This book was set in Stone Serif and Stone Sans by Westchester Publishing Services. Printed and bound in the United States of America.

Library of Congress Cataloging-in-Publication Data

Names: Klein, Gary A., author.
Title: Snapshots of the mind / Gary Klein.
Description: Cambridge, Massachusetts : The MIT Press, [2022] | Includes
    bibliographical references and index.
Identifiers: LCCN 2021051212 | ISBN 9780262544429 (paperback)
Subjects: LCSH: Cognition. | Decision making. | Naturalism.
Classification: LCC BF311 .K6254 2022 | DDC 153—dc23/eng/20220601
LC record available at https://lccn.loc.gov/2021051212

10 9 8 7 6 5 4 3 2 1

For Jacob, Ruth, Jonathan, and Harold
and
For Helen

Contents

1 Introduction: Learning to See Cognition   1

2 The Cognitive Dimension   9
     2.1 The Cognitive Dimension   13
     2.2 Mapping the Sources of Power   17
     2.3 The Naturalistic Decision Making Approach   21
     2.4 The Mental Model Matrix   25
     2.5 The RPD Model: Criticisms and Confusions   29
     2.6 ShadowBox   33
     2.7 Tower of Hanoi: Surprising Lessons from a Classic Puzzle   37
     2.8 Reflections   41

3 Rationalist Fever Dreams   43
     3.1 Hopelessly Irrational or Wonderfully Creative?   47
     3.2 Can We Trust the Decision Researchers?   49
     3.3 Positive Heuristics   53
     3.4 The Myths of *Moneyball*   57
     3.5 Getting Crunched by the Numbers   61
     3.6 The Curious Case of Confirmation Bias   65
     3.7 Escaping from Fixation   73
     3.8 The Substitution Trap   81
     3.9 Costly Mistakes?   85
     3.10 Playing to Win   87
     3.11 Stealth Decisions   91
     3.12 Reflections   95

4   Smarter Machines or Machines That Make Us Smarter?—Information Technology versus Expertise   99

    4.1   Playing to Our Strengths   103
    4.2   Failure of Imagination   107
    4.3   Derailing Yourself   111
    4.4   Data versus Insights   115
    4.5   The Second Singularity   121
    4.6   The Invention of Hyperlinks   127
    4.7   Small Data   131
    4.8   Improv Chess   137
    4.9   AIQ: Artificial Intelligence Quotient   141
    4.10 Reflections   145

5   Seeing the Invisible—Expertise   149

    5.1   The Flea   153
    5.2   From Chimps to Champs   157
    5.3   The War on Expertise   161
    5.4   Anomaly Detection: The Art of Noticing the Unexpected   165
    5.5   Anticipation   169
    5.6   Missing Pieces   173
    5.7   Leverage   177
    5.8   The Skill Portfolio Account of Expertise   181
    5.9   How Can We Identify the Experts?   185
    5.10 The Art of Being Stupid   189
    5.11 Reflections   193

6   Making Discoveries—Speculative Thinking   197

    6.1   The Insight Test   203
    6.2   The Second Wave of Critical Thinking   207
    6.3   The Different Forms of Insight   211
    6.4   Scientific Insights   215
    6.5   Cognitive Roadblocks   217
    6.6   Popular Advice for Achieving Insights   221
    6.7   Dreamy Insights   225
    6.8   Different Tactics for Making Discoveries   229

Contents

- 6.9 The Insight Stance 233
- 6.10 Getting Unstuck 239
- 6.11 The Discovery Platform 243
- 6.12 Reflections 247

7 Getting Stronger—Training 249

- 7.1 Common Confusions about Teaching 253
- 7.2 Training versus Evaluation 257
- 7.3 Is Teaching Overrated? 259
- 7.4 Training as if Your Life Depended on It 263
- 7.5 Cognitive Coaching 267
- 7.6 Teaching through Insights 273
- 7.7 The Cognitive Audit 279
- 7.8 Cognitizing a Scenario 283
- 7.9 Mindsets 285
- 7.10 How to Harness Curiosity 289
- 7.11 Getting Smarter 293
- 7.12 Bring It On! 299
- 7.13 Changing the Mindset of the Marines 301
- 7.14 Reflections 305

8 Other Minds—Teamwork 307

- 8.1 The Power to Read Minds 313
- 8.2 Can We Train Perspective-Taking Skills? 317
- 8.3 The Camera Grip 321
- 8.4 Switch! 325
- 8.5 Don't Decide Like Martians 327
- 8.6 Cutting Down on Confusion 331
- 8.7 How to Defuse a Dispute 335
- 8.8 Is COVID-19 a Black Swan Event? 339
- 8.9 Insights versus Organizations 343
- 8.10 Reflections 347

9 Making Waves—Tools and Tactics for Improvement 349

- 9.1 Naturalistic Decision Making Tools 353
- 9.2 When to Consult Your Intuition 355

9.3 Know Yourself   359
9.4 Are You Pursuing a Pipe Dream?   361
9.5 The Causal Landscape   365
9.6 Why Did Hillary Lose the Election?   371
9.7 Is Wanting to Change Enough?   379
9.8 The Pre-mortem Method   385
9.9 The Decision Scorecard   389
9.10 Management by Discovery   391
9.11 The Nine Levers Organizations Can Use for Better Performance   395
9.12 Turning Policy into Practice   399
9.13 The Difference-Makers   403
9.14 Reflections   407

Afterword   411
Acknowledgments   413
References   417
Index   427

1 Introduction: Learning to See Cognition

The most important thing I want to accomplish with this book is to help you, the reader, become more skilled at "seeing" cognition. Seeing it in work settings, seeing it all around you, gaining an edge over others who are oblivious, becoming more successful in partnering with others, and guiding others who have become confused.

The word "cognition" may sound academic, but I am using it as a blanket term to capture everyday activities such as decision-making, detecting and solving problems, making sense of confusing situations, and managing risks and uncertainty. These are the capabilities we'll be examining. Cognition is about thinking, but we're not going to review the kinds of cognitive processes found in most introductory psychology textbooks. Instead, we'll be exploring the kinds of cognition that matter to decision-makers—the aspects of cognition that can make a difference in life-and-death situations.

And when I describe my goal of helping you "see cognition," I mean enabling you to quickly spot qualities that most people often miss—for example, the mindset of the decision-maker, the flaws in a person's mental model that can explain a poor choice, the experience that lets one person detect subtle signs that are invisible to others. I don't simply want you to better understand these aspects of cognition. I want you to become more attuned to them so that you recognize them as events are unfolding and can build on them rather than being oblivious to them. As you get better at seeing cognition, you may find yourself noticing the subtle ways that experts are different from the rest of us.

Here's an example provided by a geologist, Peter Kamstra, from a project he did in graduate school in Australia, see figure 1.1.

Peter is a Canadian, and before he started his project, he had never heard of rock fishing, which is one of the most dangerous sports in Australia,

Figure 1.1
Rock fishers casting off a ledge.

drowning more than ten fishers a year. The idea is that you stand on a rock shelf or a rock outcropping that extends into the ocean, so the water is very deep, giving you a chance to catch much larger fish. You don't have to rent a seat on a fishing boat. You just drive to a promising location and cast your line into the waves. And that's the rub—those waves. If a freak wave washes over the rock ledge, it can knock you off balance and into the sea.

The Australian national safety group had studied the statistics and determined that a major risk was an overlapping wave, perhaps a freak wave, so they mandated practices, such as wearing life jackets and monitoring the weather conditions to see if the ocean swells might be too high that day. In high-risk zones, rock fishers could be fined if the police found they weren't wearing a life jacket. However, Peter got the sense that no one on the safety group had examined how rock fishers actually entered the sea. No one seems to have asked rock fishers what they thought the risks were. No one had tried to contrast experienced versus inexperienced rock fishers.

Peter decided to make this his research project and conducted 52 interviews with rock fishers. Not traditional interviews, sitting around a desk in a quiet office but what he called "walk-along interviews" out on the rock ledges while the people he interviewed continued to fish. To gain their confidence, Peter purchased his own fishing gear and learned to fish, usually arriving at a promising location at 4:00 a.m. so that when the real rock fishers arrived, he was already there.

Peter found that the official analyses were at best incomplete and at worst misguided because they were missing the cognitive dimension. For example, the official recommendation was to check weather conditions to see if the ocean swells that day were too high, but Peter learned that the experienced fishers really paid attention to which way the waves were running and which direction the winds were blowing because in protected locations, they would still be safe even though the waves were crashing just around the bend.

And while the official analyses pointed to inexperience as a cause of drowning, Peter uncovered the ways that inexperience worked: your line might get snagged on the rock shelf and you'd go out to the edge to retrieve it rather than just being smart and cutting it loose.

Even worse, if you did fall in, you'd do the natural thing and swim back to the ledge to climb back up. Big mistake. Once you were in the water you didn't want to go near that rocky shelf covered in slippery algae. You didn't want the waves pounding you against the rocks, perhaps knocking you out, perhaps sucking you underneath the rock shelf. Instead, you needed to swim away from the shelf and to a nearby sandy beach that you had identified in advance as a safe landing zone.

If you did catch a big fish, how would you land it? Inexperienced fishers often just tried to pull it out of the water, standing at the edge of the shelf, maybe getting knocked off balance by the thrashing of their prize, being vulnerable to a wave that might wash over the shelf. In contrast, the experienced fishers would call for help from others. If they were alone, they'd wait for a wave to waft it onto the shelf, which meant they were watching the waves, looking for a helpful one, and being alert to ones that might pose a hazard.

The whole issue of life jackets annoyed the experienced fishers because the jackets were uncomfortable. Worse, the rock fishers would be fined if caught without one. The experienced fishers acknowledged that life jackets were a good idea for people who weren't good swimmers. But the jackets wouldn't help you if you were stupid enough to swim back to the ledge after getting swept off it. The life jacket mentality came from settings where you had nearby life services and emergency services, not the isolated rock ledges favored by the fishers. The experienced rock fishers felt that life jackets were much less useful than nonslip rock cleats (which weren't even mentioned in the official reports).

Peter had found that the actual causes of drowning were very different from the causes listed in the official documents, which relied on statistical analyses rather than on observation and interviews. He found a more powerful set of safety practices than the official recommendations.

He captured the cognitive dimension of staying safe during a high-risk activity: anticipating problems (noting any nearby sandy beaches to swim to), managing risks (cutting a line that gets snagged instead of trying to recover it), making sense of situations (gauging whether a location is safe, given the current and wind directions), making tough decisions (inhibiting the impulse to swim back to the ledge after being swept off it), anticipating opportunities (waiting for a friendly wave to wash your fish onto the ledge), managing attention (scanning the wave patterns while looking for that friendly wave in case a freak wave is approaching).

Instead of fixating on unsafe *behaviors* and offering solutions like mandatory life jackets to improve those behaviors, Peter zeroed in on the cognitive dimension—what *decisions* the fishers were making and how they were making them. What signals and patterns the experienced fishers had learned to monitor. What were the flaws in the thinking and decision-making of the inexperienced fishers—the flaws that were getting them killed.

We'll be covering many examples like this to help you notice and appreciate the kinds of things experts can pick up on. People don't learn to "see" cognition just by reading or hearing that it's important. Seeing cognition is not a set of facts for us to learn and remember. Rather, it's a skill we gain like any other skill, through repeated practice.

Why does this matter? Because people so often miss the cognitive challenges of a task or a policy or a system. They think all they have to do is set up the mechanism and the rest will take care of itself. Except that it doesn't. If you can learn to anticipate the cognitive challenges, you could achieve much greater success when you introduce interventions.

A book cannot give you the ideal training with feedback, but it can offer lots of examples. By the time you come to the end, I expect that you'll be in a different place. You'll be noticing things you might have ordinarily missed. You'll be asking questions that might not have previously occurred to you. You will have become sensitized to the cognitive dimension.

Some of you are already attuned to cognition, and I want to help you get better. Others don't (yet) have much awareness of the cognitive dimension, and I want to get you started. You may find that once you begin seeing cognition, it becomes self-reinforcing, each discovery preparing the way for the next.

However, I don't want to over-promise. I have encountered a number of people who don't resonate with the idea of seeing cognition, the way some people are color-blind, and others don't have a good sense of smell (especially if, like me, they've recovered from COVID-19). Some people claim to grasp what the cognitive dimension is all about, but then a few weeks later, they need to have it explained to them again. So not everyone can become attuned to the primary aspects of expert cognition—the mindsets, the mental models, the perceptual sensitivity.

Most people do enjoy the discoveries and revelations as they gain strength and confidence in unpacking how tough decisions were actually made, how ambiguous events really were decoded, how critical clues were noticed and appreciated. I hope that's the outcome in store for you as you read this book.

And that raises the question of how I came to prepare this book.

Writing a book without writing it

After I published my last book on the nature of insights, *Seeing What Others Don't* (2013), I announced to friends and colleagues that this was, in fact, my last book. I had no intention of ever writing another one.

Then my resolve was dented by my oldest daughter, Devorah. Following my 2013 book, the editors at *Psychology Today* had invited me to host a blog, and I had been posting about one essay a month ever since, more than a hundred essays to date. At first, the entries followed the theme of gaining insights, but soon I branched out and wrote essays on whatever interested me at the moment.

In 2020, Devorah mentioned to me that several of my essays were kind of good (which coming from her is very high praise), and I should think about collecting the best ones and publishing them. Being a dutiful father, I approached Phil Laughlin, my editor at the MIT Press, and asked him if he'd be interested in such a collection, and a few months later I had a contract to deliver that book—the book you are now holding.

You can see, therefore, that I have *prepared* this book without writing it. All I had to do was collect the essays I had already written. This process sounded so simple at the time and let me preserve some self-respect because I wasn't going back on my proclamation of not *writing* another book.

That simple plan didn't stay simple for very long. Once I started to organize the essays, I realized what an opportunity I had to help readers gain the skill of detecting cognitive aspects of their own behaviors and the actions of others. I could sensitize readers to the cognitive dimension.

Furthermore, the preparation of the book was coming at an important time. One of the forces behind the cognitive dimension is the way we gain expertise and use it and disseminate it. Unfortunately, the value of expertise is coming under assault by communities that want to promote artificial intelligence (AI) and machine learning, and by the widespread assumption that people, even experts, are hopelessly biased. The longer these assaults continue unchecked, the more established they become as common knowledge, and the harder it will be to appreciate our human capacity for speculative thinking and insights. Therefore, I was feeling some urgency to help readers see cognition and the expertise underlying it. This book is my chance to invite readers to celebrate the sources of our cognitive power.

That is how the activity of preparing this book changed shape. The end goal was no longer the collection of essays. Instead, it was about arranging those essays and—inevitably—revising them in order to reach my goals.

I used three primary criteria to choose the essays I included in this book. First, I selected the essays that received the strongest reactions from my *Psychology Today* audience (measured in page views), usually in the thousands, sometimes 10,000 or 20,000, and in one case more than 50,000 hits. Second, I also picked essays that I felt would excite readers. For an essay to be included in this book, it had to have at least one idea or example that, in my opinion, would leave you feeling that your time reading that essay was well spent. That meant that I dropped some popular essays that struck me as too fluffy, and I added some essays that I thought you would enjoy reading, even if they didn't capture a large audience when I posted them. The third criterion I used in selecting essays was that they should help strengthen your ability to see cognition—in one way or another, the essays had to elaborate on the cognitive dimension.

Also, I revised the essays to make them work better. Books that collect previously published articles and materials usually contain a lot of redundancy because each article was written to stand alone. Many of the articles provide the same kind of background. Therefore, I decided to revise the essays to remove a lot of that redundancy, especially within a part, to make the book more readable. In a few cases, I renamed an essay to make its contribution clearer to readers. I also did some updating where appropriate. For example, one essay dating from June 2017 mentions that MIT Press was going to issue a twentieth-anniversary issue of my first book, *Sources of Power* (1998). Now I revised that sentence to state that the new edition is available.

The *Psychology Today* blogs are deliberately short and have been getting shorter. The current maximum length is only 1,000 words. In the past, I had been able to argue my way around that word limit, but the editors have tightened up. One advantage of a word restriction is that it usually improves the quality of the essays—I am forced to drop extraneous material and keep the essay sharply focused. One disadvantage is that the word restriction discourages stories and examples. In revising the essays for this book, I have added some stories back in. I couldn't help myself.

I organized the essays into nine parts. This introduction is the first part. Part 2 is **The Cognitive Dimension** and sets out the central and unifying theme of the book. Part 3 is **Rationalist Fever Dreams**. These essays contrast a cognitive approach with a mechanical one that assumes that difficult tasks can be broken down into steps and procedures and that thinking can be replaced by analysis. Part 4 takes up the most powerful evolution of rationalist fever dreams, the belief that AI will soon take over decision-making. This part is titled **Smarter Machines or Machines That Make Us Smarter?—Information Technology versus Expertise**. As you can imagine, I am advocating for the latter—machines that expand our expertise, and expertise is the topic of part 5, **Seeing the Invisible—Expertise**, the ways that experts perceive elements and relationships that the rest of us miss. But it's not just about deploying expertise—we also need to understand speculative thinking, so part 6 is titled **Making Discoveries—Speculative Thinking**.

How can we help people gain expertise more quickly and achieve more insights? Part 7, **Getting Stronger—Training**, tackles these challenges and examines training approaches for the cognitive dimension. Of course, we can't just think about ourselves. We must consider how to coordinate with team members and how to thwart adversaries. Part 8, **Other Minds—Teamwork**, widens our perspective from the individual to the team and the organization.

The book concludes with part 9, **Making Waves—Tools and Tactics for Improvement**, which includes several essays presenting tactics for taking action. Thus, the book starts with the theoretical, moves on to the central theme of cognition, and ends with the practical methods and techniques for implementing the cognitive dimension.

Setting up the parts was easy. Deciding which essay went into which part was much harder because many of the essays cross boundaries. The essay "Teaching through Insights" (July 28, 2015) could easily fit into the part on teaching (**Getting Stronger**), the part on insights (**Making Discoveries**), the part on expertise (**Seeing the Invisible**), or the part on tools and techniques to put into action (**Making Waves**). I did the best I could in placing the essays into the parts, but I am sure there will be times when you question my judgment.

Now you know how this book came into existence and what topics it covers. You'll probably have some skepticism while reading the essays because my approach is to make the most extreme claims that I can defend. I am not trying to be deliberately contrarian. Rather, I think we make better progress by taking strong positions rather than trying to be safe and uncontroversial, and sometimes I go over the line—or go over your line. Therefore, I don't expect you will agree with me on everything. Still, I hope you agree on most things, or at least many things, and that you will find the disagreements usefully thought-provoking. You may not find many disagreements at all.

Most of all, what I think you will find is a set of discoveries and insights about the cognitive dimension, expanding your perspective, and enriching your perceptions.

2 The Cognitive Dimension

Overview

When I interview people, I usually want to learn what makes them so good, if they have lots of experience, and one of the most effective tactics is to ask them about tough cases and how they made difficult decisions. I've found that most people tell me about the actions they took or what they should have done.

That's not good enough. I want to know what is behind the decisions and behind their actions. I want to get below the surface and into the things they noticed, the things that, with hindsight, they wished they had been watching more carefully, the ways they were interpreting the event and how this interpretation changed the more they learned.

This is the cognitive dimension. It is found below the surface, below the actions and behaviors that are easily seen and remembered. Most people don't volunteer information like this and may have trouble even recalling these kinds of information.

Part 2 begins with essay 2.1, "The Cognitive Dimension," to provide you with a deeper understanding of what the cognitive dimension is and how it plays out.

The cognitive dimension can be studied in a laboratory using standard laboratory tasks, but you will find it most rewarding to explore it in real-world settings—settings that are a bit chaotic, messy, and ambiguous. That's part of the excitement.

When we explore the cognitive dimension in real-world settings, we gain respect for the strengths and capabilities that decision-makers have developed—the sources of power that they can draw upon. Essay 2.2 in this part, "Mapping the Sources of Power," suggests how we can become attuned to these sources of power and examine them more deeply.

This type of exploration calls for special methods and strategies, and a community has formed to exchange lessons about methods and discoveries. The third essay, 2.3, "The Naturalistic Decision Making Approach," describes that community.

The Naturalistic Decision Making (NDM) community tries to learn why people make mistakes or why the situations in which they work may influence them to make bad decisions, but NDM researchers are also very interested in learning what makes experts so good—what are the sources of cognitive power that experts have acquired.

One of the prime sources of power is the mental models we develop as we gain experience with a task or a setting. Essay 2.4, "The Mental Model Matrix," captures different aspects of our mental models and shows the limitations of most typical attempts to describe mental models.

We believe that our mental models affect the way we make rapid and high-stakes decisions, but how does that happen? My first book, *Sources of Power* (1998/2017) described a Recognition-Primed Decision (RPD) strategy. Somewhat surprisingly, this decision-making model has held up very well over the years since it was first published, in 1986. Yet inevitably some confusion and mistaken interpretations have crept in. Essay 2.5, "The Recognition-Primed Decision (RPD) Model: Criticisms and Confusions," seeks to correct those problems.

Given that the RPD model provides a pretty good idea of how people make decisions, how can we train people to become better decision-makers? Ever since I described the RPD model, I've been searching for a way to train decision-making, and finally in 2010, I learned about a strategy I could use to apply the RPD model—ShadowBox. The essay describing ShadowBox (2.6) might belong in part 6 on building stronger mindsets and other training issues, but I decided to include it as the sixth essay in part 2 because it so closely follows the essay on the RPD model.

Part 2 concludes with an essay on a study of the Tower of Hanoi puzzle (2.7). This is the kind of laboratory task that the NDM community avoids, and my essay defensively explains why we did that project. Of greater interest is why I am including it in this book. The answer is that the project provides a nice illustration of the cognitive dimension and the kinds of discoveries you can make even with a task that has received such intense research for over a half-century.

Plus, there is an epilogue. After I posted this essay on my *Psychology Today* blog, I received sharp criticism on social media from a computer scientist who said, "Actually we do know everything there is to know about this puzzle. Klein thinks that he has discovered some simple facts that every student of CS [computer science] learns when they first encounter recursion."

This news didn't cheer me up. My immediate reaction was that I was found out, activating all my impostor syndrome emotions. I feared that I hadn't done a sufficient literature search. That's always a worry because I work on so many topics in so many domains. It's inevitable that I'll miss something important.

But as is often the case, when I investigated further, the criticism didn't hold up. I was aware of the work in computer science and AI on the Tower of Hanoi, and the recursion strategy. But my essay pointed out several other things that, as far as I can tell, have never been mentioned in the research literature, such as the difficult decisions facing people working on the puzzle and, more important, the flaws people have in their mental model. We found people correctly solving the puzzle while complaining that "this feels wrong" because they didn't understand how they have to build interim towers. And then I realized that my computer science critic was only aware of the algorithms that can solve the puzzle. He seemed oblivious to the way the decisions were experienced or the confused mental model people held. My critic was describing how computers solve the problem (which might be the right way), not trying to understand how humans approach these problems. He was unaware of the cognitive dimension, even when my essay highlighted it. To the extent that he is representative of computer scientists and AI specialists—he develops advanced systems for people to use in the future—that's a cause for worry. This story is an example of why I feel such urgency in preparing this book.

2.1 The Cognitive Dimension

Searching for the Basis of Expert Performance

Recently, a large company asked my group to work on a one-year demonstration project of cognitive skills training using the ShadowBox approach we have been developing. But what content area should we use for this demonstration? The company works on a wide range of military activities. However, the company wanted to keep the project unclassified, which ruled out the top contenders.

The company decided that we should focus the training on the engineering specialty of systems integration, which made a lot of sense, except that I don't know anything about systems integration, nor did my team members. Over the years, we have gotten used to jumping into a totally new specialty area. Yet we were very uncomfortable with working on systems integration because it seemed to be very technical and likely to require engineering experience and sophistication far more complex than anything we had done before. Despite our uneasiness, we agreed to give it a try.

We showed up for a week of in-depth cognitive interviewing and discovered that the company already had a training program for systems integration. Moreover, it had a thick manual detailing the phases and steps of systems integration. We thumbed through the manual, and it seemed extremely comprehensive, covering every part of the systems integration process. If we felt inadequate before, we felt even less confident now.

What in the world could we add?

And then, as we thumbed through the manual, we realized what was missing:

- What are the tough decisions here?
- What makes situations difficult?
- What can go wrong?
- Where do systems engineers get confused?
- What kinds of mistakes do new systems engineers make?
- How can you recover from mistakes?
- How does the mindset of a new systems engineer change with experience?
- What are the difficult trade-offs in a systems engineering project?
- What tactics have experienced engineers learned for managing risks?
- What do highly experienced systems engineers see and understand that their less-experienced colleagues miss?

None of these topics were covered in the manual. They are examples of the cognitive challenges that are so important—challenges that people usually miss.

By the end of the week, after conducting eight in-depth cognitive interviews, we had identified a set of 15 cognitive training requirements, including some critical mindset shifts. These included diagnosing problems that inevitably arose, making trade-offs between goals, managing risks, and taking the perspective of other team members. One of the mindset shifts was to be open to adapting the initial goals as the project proceeded—too many engineers believed they needed to lock into the initial goals, even when these were becoming impractical and even when exciting opportunities were opening up. In addition, we had sketched out several ideas for cognitive training scenarios.

Before we started our interviews, the sponsor had made it clear that he wanted a rigorous evaluation of our training program at the end of the project. On Friday afternoon, at the end of the week of interviews, we showed him and his team the cognitive training challenges we had identified and asked which one to select for the training and evaluation. We explained that we needed to concentrate the training on just one or at the most two of the challenges in order to have a reasonable evaluation. The sponsor stopped us. "I want the training scenarios to cover all of them," he said. "We need everything on your list." We pushed back—that kind of unsystematic approach would prevent us from doing the careful evaluation he wanted. He told us to forget the evaluation and to craft the richest scenarios we could.

We ultimately worked with the company to formulate six scenarios and tested three of them, showing that the cognitive training could potentially substitute for some of the expensive instructor-led training they were currently using.

Afterward, I was struck by the changes in attitude, my own attitude and that of the sponsor, regarding what we might contribute. The sponsor was justifiably proud of the manual on how to do systems integration—it captured the processes and procedures. Yet it was clear to everyone what was missing—the cognitive dimension. The questions listed earlier illustrate the cognitive dimension but you shouldn't assume that all it takes is to ask these questions.

Moving into the cognitive dimension takes experience and a mindset shift, from believing that complex tasks can be performed by carrying out the steps, to a mindset that appreciates the subtleties and the ways that context affects which steps you perform, how you perform them, and how to adapt beyond the steps when necessary. The cognitive dimension is a mindset that is centered around curiosity—to ask the next question and the question after that, excited to learn more about the tacit knowledge that underpins expertise.

The cognitive dimension is what makes humans able to think so differently from machines. Sometimes we're not as good, sometimes we're better, but to design better machines, or support systems, or training programs, it helps to understand HOW we think.

—April 6, 2019

2.2 Mapping the Sources of Power

The Knowledge and Abilities That Come with Experience

I published *Sources of Power* in 1998, intending it as a counterpoint to all the publicity about how biased people are, how irrational, how overconfident. Lost in the arguments about biases and irrationality was an appreciation for how skillful people can be, how well we can apply our expertise, how effective we are at making difficult decisions under time pressure and uncertainty. This positive message in *Sources of Power* resonated with many people.

Nevertheless, the critiques of human decision-making that seemed so one-sided in 1998 have continued in the past 20 years and are possibly even more strident today. The popular media have picked up on the theme of biases and irrationality, and that is why the message of *Sources of Power* continues to be relevant. MIT Press issued a 20th-anniversary edition of *Sources of Power* in September 2017, with a new introduction.

At the end of the 1998 book, I included a whimsical map of the sources of power discussed in the previous chapters. I sketched out a crude version of this map and the artist David Sweeney created the version that appeared in the book and is shown in figure 2.1.

In 2016, my wife Helen asked me what, if anything, I would change about this map. As I reviewed the page proofs of the anniversary edition, I was struck by how well the map has held up.

All the entries seem very relevant to the field of Naturalistic Decision Making (see Klein 2008). I would add a few additional ones, such as sensemaking and curiosity and anticipatory thinking. I also would add the

Figure 2.1
Mapping the sources of power.
Source: Gary Klein, *Sources of Power* (MIT Press, 1998).

capacity for speculative thinking, which goes farther than the map entry for imagining. I would tone down the emphasis the map gives to intuition/pattern matching and mental simulation. These are shown as the centerpiece of the 1998 map because together they make up the RPD model that was the primary discovery described in the book.

Still, these modifications are minor. The depiction of the sources of power seems as relevant today as in 1998.

However, in reviewing the 1998 map, I found myself making a distinction between the types of knowledge people have and the abilities that their experience enables. The 1998 map doesn't make this distinction, and I think it might be important.

So here is an updated map (figure 2.2), 20 years later, rendered by the graphic artist Michael Fleishman. The sources of power stem from six types of knowledge: *mind reading* (essentially, the knowledge of other people that

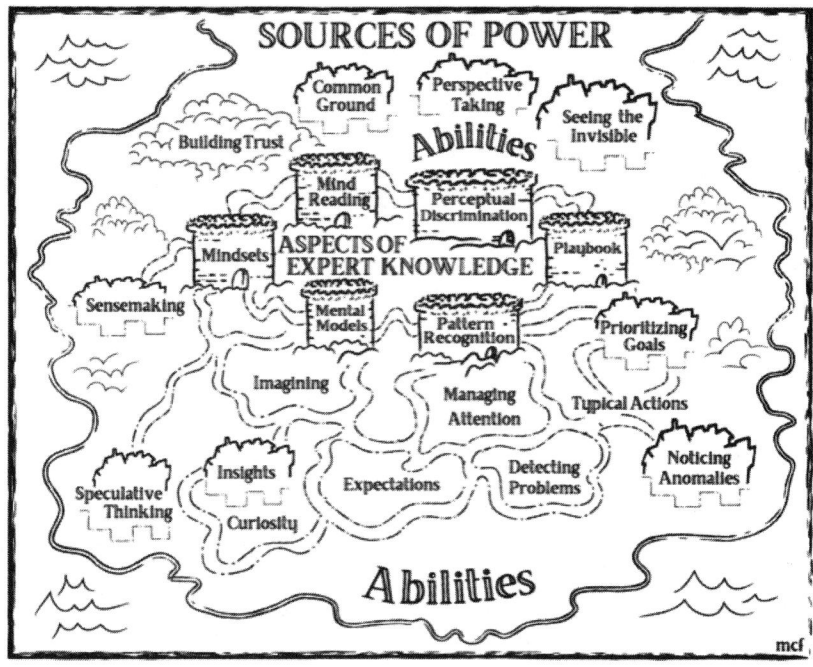

Figure 2.2
Mapping the sources of power, version 2.

allows us to take their perspective), *perceptual discriminations*, the playbook of *procedures* for getting things done, *pattern recognition*, the *mental models* of how things work, and the *mindsets* that we acquire.

These types of knowledge give rise to a variety of abilities that are the sources of power we can use to handle complex and ambiguous situations.

—*June 8, 2017*

2.3 The Naturalistic Decision Making Approach

What We Have Learned by Studying Cognition in the Wild

What is Naturalistic Decision Making (NDM)?

NDM is the research tradition begun in the 1980s to study how people actually make decisions—people such as firefighters, military commanders, nurses, design engineers, pilots, and petrochemical unit managers. NDM examines the kinds of decisions they make in the course of their work and how they use their experience to cope with challenging conditions, such as time pressure, uncertainty, vague goals, high stakes, organizational constraints, and team coordination requirements. Thus, the NDM approach is a contrast to judgment and decision paradigms that use predefined tasks given to naive subjects under controlled laboratory conditions (see figure 2.3).

How NDM got started

In the late 1980s, Judith Orasanu, working in the Basic Research Group at the Army Research Institute, assembled a cadre of researchers who were investigating decision-making in natural settings using cognitive ethnographic methods. Orasanu and Gary Klein, one of these researchers, convened a small workshop in 1989 to bring this community together to share ideas. One outcome of this workshop was an edited book, *Decision Making in Action* (1993). Since that time, more than a dozen NDM conferences have been held at roughly two-year intervals, alternating between the United States and Europe. Many of the conferences have generated edited volumes. In addition, the Cognitive Engineering and Decision Making Technical

Figure 2.3
Conditions of decision-making.

Group was established in 1995 to provide an annual opportunity for NDM researchers to exchange ideas; it quickly grew to become one of the largest Technical Groups within the Human Factors and Ergonomics Society.

What has the NDM movement achieved?

Many people are excited by the NDM approach and the possibilities it opens up. But other people are skeptical about whether we can learn anything without carefully controlled experiments. The way to assess NDM research is to see what it has discovered. Here is a summary taken from some recently published articles.

We used to believe that the only way to make good decisions was to generate several options and pick the best one. NDM studies found that experienced decision-makers recognize patterns and don't compare options. They evaluate an option by imagining how it would play out.

We used to believe that expertise depends on learning rules and procedures. NDM research demonstrated that expertise primarily depends on tacit knowledge.

We used to believe that projects had to start with a clear description of the goal. NDM researchers saw that challenging projects involve wicked problems and ill-defined goals that cannot be specified in advance. The goals become clarified while they are being pursued.

We used to believe that people make sense of events by building up from the data to information to knowledge and finally to understanding. NDM studies showed that experienced decision-makers use their mental models to define what counts as data in the first place. And as discoveries are made about the nature of a situation, different aspects of the data are revealed.

We used to believe that insights arise by overcoming mental sets that lock us into tactics that have worked in the past. NDM research discovered that insights also arise by detecting contradictions and anomalies and by noticing connections.

We used to believe that we could reduce uncertainty by gathering more information. NDM researchers found that performance seems to suffer when too much information is gathered and that uncertainty can result from inadequate framing of data, not just the absence of data.

We used to believe that we could improve performance by fostering critical thinking practices, such as listing assumptions. NDM researchers noted that flawed assumptions are often unconscious and thus could never get listed.

Where is NDM heading?

As you can see from the preceding part, we NDM researchers have broadened our investigations. We are not just interested in decision-making. We study other cognitive processes, such as situation awareness, sensemaking, problem detection, and anticipatory thinking. We use naturalistic inquiry methods to explore a range of macrocognitive phenomena (as opposed to microcognitive phenomena studied under controlled laboratory conditions).

In addition to trying to understand more aspects of thinking in complex settings, NDM researchers are also seeking ways to improve performance: better decision-making, better sensemaking, quicker and more accurate problem detection. In contrast to the behavioral decision-making community, which focuses on human limitations and tries to reduce biases, NDM researchers try to understand human capabilities.

While reducing mistakes is important, good performance is not just the absence of mistakes—it consists of discoveries and achievements. Performance depends on the strengths of decision-makers. Unlike research approaches that seek to debunk experts, NDM practitioners are impressed by experts, whether they are expert firefighters or physicians or pilots or military commanders. And so NDM practitioners are seeking ways to bring people up to speed more quickly and effectively.

—*February 1, 2016*

2.4 The Mental Model Matrix

Important Aspects of Mental Models Often Get Ignored

The simple definition of a mental model is a description of how something works. We all have mental models for different types of systems and machines and organizations and even protocols for social interactions. Our mental models provide us with a blueprint for how the device or the interaction produces its results. They let us describe a system's form, explain how it functions, and predict its future states (Rouse & Morris, 1986).

But maybe our simple definition is too simple. Maybe it misses some of the most important features of our mental models. That's the conclusion my colleagues Joseph Borders and Ron Besuijen and I reached after we conducted a field study sponsored by the Center for Operator Performance (Borders, Klein, & Besuijen, 2019). This post is a continued collaboration between the three of us.

We observed and interviewed eight qualified panel operators in a petrochemical plant as they responded to upset scenarios on a high-fidelity training simulator of a distillation unit separating ethylene and ethane. Some of the operators had more than a decade of experience but most had less than three years and one had only six months; they averaged 4.5 years on the panel. The scenarios were very demanding; no two operators approached them in the same way.

How the system works. As expected, we found that the operators relied on a set of beliefs about how the system worked. Sometimes these beliefs were limited in ways the operators didn't appreciate, and sometimes they were flawed, but generally, they were accurate and the operators usually were able to diagnose their own confusions.

How the system fails. We also found that operators understood ways that the system could fail—its limitations and its vulnerabilities to break down. These "negative" beliefs were a very important aspect of the operators' mental models—providing them with ideas about what might be going wrong.

Being able to consider and anticipate system limitations and failures is obviously important for troubleshooting. It is also a very important aspect of system design—imagining how a system might fail rather than just considering how it is supposed to work. Too many designers fixate on delivering a system that meets the requirements and don't stop to imagine where the system might break down, the conditions under which a system, say a commercial airliner, might crash. Mumaw et al. (2000) found that workers monitoring a nuclear power plant couldn't just rely on the schematics. They had to appraise the plant's performance against a noisy background. They had to be alert to recent developments, such as valves sticking or sensors acting up.

Workarounds. The operators had beliefs about how to do workarounds to overcome limitations and failures. These workarounds were important for recovering from upsets. Knowing how to perform workarounds is obviously valuable for adapting to unexpected situations. The more experience operators had, the more sophisticated their ideas were for keeping the system running.

Confusions. Finally, the concept of a mental model should include beliefs about the limitations of people, such as the users of a system—the ways they can become confused.

	Capabilities	**Limitations**
System	How the system works: Parts, connections, causal relationships, process control logic	How the system fails: Common breakdowns and limitations (e.g. boundary conditions)
User	How to make the system work: Detecting anomalies, appreciating the system's responsiveness, performing workarounds, and adaptations	How users get confused: The kinds of errors people are likely to make

Figure 2.4
The mental model matrix.
Source: Adapted from a chart by Joseph Borders.

For example, someone might direct us to a location (e.g., go two blocks, turn left). But a person with a stronger mental model of the route and of our navigation abilities might anticipate where we might get confused or mistaken and annotate the directions accordingly (e.g., go two blocks and turn left; it's a narrow street, and there's no street sign, so it might look like a driveway, but there's a little antique store on the far corner). Here, the mental model is about our limitations and potential failures, not those of a system. It's really impressive when people can anticipate how others might get confused and make the appropriate adjustments.

Figure 2.4 illustrates this mental model matrix account.

The initial concept of a mental model, a set of beliefs about how a system works, is not wrong. But it is incomplete. This initial concept misses the kinds of beliefs gained through experience that underpin an expert's mental model.

—*February 5, 2021*

2.5 The RPD Model: Criticisms and Confusions

Six Challenges to the Recognition-Primed Decision (RPD) Model

---

Is it time to retire the Recognition-Primed Decision (RPD) model? The model initially attracted little attention (Klein, Calderwood, & Clinton-Cirocco, 1986). Only when I published *Sources of Power* (Klein, 1998) did the RPD model come onto peoples' radar. That was 20 years ago, long enough for it to have become outdated.

Yet the model keeps chugging along, gaining general acceptance as the way people actually make decisions. I am grateful and surprised by the RPD model's longevity and acclaim; I hope this post doesn't provoke a backlash.

My goal here is simply to correct some minor confusions and misrepresentations that have emerged over the decades.

Description

The RPD model explains how fireground commanders can make good decisions within seconds. Researchers at the time thought that effective decisions depended on generating a set of options and then comparing them on evaluation dimensions. But what if you don't have much time or if an uncertain situation prevents careful evaluation? The RPD model shows how experienced decision-makers can do a good job even with minimal time (see figure 2.5).

The RPD model combines two processes: pattern matching to match the current situation to ones encountered in the past, which identifies reasonable courses of action, and then an evaluation process using mental

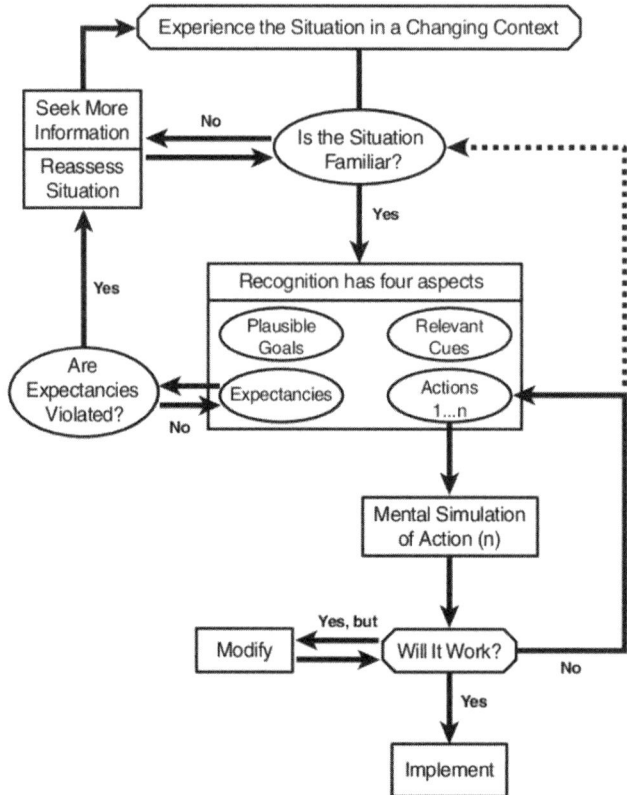

Figure 2.5
The RPD model.

simulation to imagine how that option would play out and to see if it is going to work. Thus, people can make rapid decisions without generating alternative courses of action and without doing any comparisons.

Misunderstandings of the RPD model

1. It is a model of gut feelings, as opposed to analysis. This misunderstanding is unfortunately common and ignores the fact that the RPD model has two components: a fast, nonconscious, intuitive pattern matching and a slower, deliberate, conscious mental simulation to do the analysis/evaluation. These two components map well to the System 1/System 2 account (e.g., Kahneman, 2011).

2. It's easy to build a computer simulation of the RPD model. This process is only easy if you ignore the mental simulation portion and just address the pattern-matching part. Even then, artificial intelligence simulations typically rely on reinforcement learning, strengthening and weakening connections based on their success. However, people don't just weaken connections. We diagnose what went wrong in order to build stronger mental models.

3. The RPD model only applies to time-pressured situations. Initially, I thought this might be the case, but I found that people use the RPD tactic even in slower-paced conditions.

4. The RPD model isn't scientific—it isn't testable or falsifiable. I have tested it by studying inexperienced decision-makers. Predictably, they use the RPD tactic less than half the time. I also studied experienced chess players (Klein et al., 1995). If the first option they generated was of random quality, it would falsify the RPD model. The results supported the RPD model. As the model predicts, the first option the skilled chess players consider is of high quality.

Also, the research supporting the RPD model has been replicated several times.

5. The evidence base is fairly thin. Some decision researchers have complained that there aren't many studies conducted under controlled conditions. A government research sponsor once commented that she would never fund field studies. After someone reminded her that Darwin had relied on field studies, she replied, "And I wouldn't have funded him, either."

However, our field studies have shown their value for uncovering dynamics of decision-making such as the role of experience. The RPD model describes how people use 10 or 20 years of experience. It is impractical to run controlled studies, employ unfamiliar tasks, and provide that amount of experience. And it is worth noting that decision researchers relying on controlled laboratory conditions failed to grasp the importance of large amounts of experience for making effective decisions.

6. The model isn't useful. I worried about its value when I first started publishing about it, but practitioners are clear that the RPD model has freed them from trying to apply rational choice techniques that don't fit with complex and ambiguous situations. The RPD model guides a variety of training approaches for effective decision-making.

Recently, Gigerenzer (2019) stated that "on its 20th anniversary, 'Sources of Power' continues to offer relevant directions and corrections of current research on decision-making" (p. 479).

—*March 17, 2021*

2.6 ShadowBox

Seeing the World through the Eyes of Experts

How can we improve decision-making skills? My colleagues and I kept asking ourselves that question after we published our findings about the RPD model in 1986. Frustratingly, we never could find an answer. Decades passed.

Then in 2008, I got lucky. I was in New York City for a conference and some FDNY firefighters asked if we could meet for lunch. One of the group members was a battalion chief, Neil Hintze. The lunch went well, and we all exchanged contact information with no real expectation that we would collaborate on anything.

But not long afterward, I was invited to put on a two-day, decision-making workshop for the Seattle Fire Department in 2010. I decided to ask Hintze to help me develop the materials and to accompany me to Seattle. After we had arrived at an overall design for the workshop, Hintze asked if he could have a slot, perhaps just a half-hour, to try out an exercise based on the master's thesis he had just completed. I didn't fully understand how the exercise would work but I agreed to let him try.

His exercise was the origin of ShadowBox.

In the exercise, Hintze presented a challenging scenario with a series of multiple-choice decision points interspersed throughout. The firefighters in the workshop had to rank the options for each decision point and write down the reasons for their ranking, and then Hintze would tell them what a panel of experts had chosen and why. He had found that this training—specifically, the reflection on the expert feedback after three practice scenarios—resulted in about an 18 percent closer match in responses between the trainees and the experts compared to a control group, who did not receive expert feedback.

Because Hintze was running the exercise, I could sit back and watch the group. I saw how captivating this exercise was—everyone was involved, everyone wanted their rankings to match the experts. I also realized that Hintze's method looked like a way to improve decision-making skills—the approach I had been seeking for so long. Plus Hintze was capturing the judgment of the panel of experts without bringing in the panel itself. He had shown the experts the scenario and recorded their choices and reasons and synthesized all of this so that the experts were no longer needed. This was significant because one of the bottlenecks of training is getting access to the experts when you need them, and Hintze had eliminated that bottleneck. He had the experts' responses, so he didn't have to involve the experts any longer.

As my team and I used and modified Hintze's method in the following years, we worried about the effort and expense needed to build the scenarios. My colleague (and daughter) Devorah Klein came up with a streamlined approach. Instead of a scenario, she just prepared statements and had trainees and experts identify what they agreed with and what aspects of the statements they didn't accept. We call this the "ShadowBox Lite" version to contrast it with the "scenario" version Hintze had developed. And we expanded it to cover different types of materials: a single spreadsheet in financial settings or a chart of vital signs in medical settings. We contrast what the trainees notice in these vignettes versus what the experts noticed.

We also worked out a third ShadowBox format: the Expert-Eyes™ approach that we have patented. Here, we show trainees a video and let the trainees click on anything they find noteworthy or relevant to a mission. The trainees record their reasons for clicking on any specific cue. Then they see what the experts clicked on and why. This method is the same format as the scenario version and the ShadowBox Lite version, using a video instead of a text scenario or a single page with a statement or chart. With this open-ended format, the trainees truly are learning to see the world through the eyes of experts.

We have developed software versions of ShadowBox, and these have come in handy during the pandemic to allow us to conduct online training without requiring face-to-face interaction. These versions run on desktop computers, laptops, and tablets, and we are thinking about a smartphone version of the Expert-Eyes format. We are currently using the software version of ShadowBox to train child protective services workers in Ohio and law enforcement officers in California.

Regardless of the format, the ShadowBox work has shown its effectiveness in bringing people up to speed more quickly and strengthening decision-making (Klein & Borders, 2016). We are still discovering new types of applications for it.

—*February 22, 2021*

2.7 Tower of Hanoi: Surprising Lessons from a Classic Puzzle

A Cognitive Analysis Demonstrates Its Power

The Tower of Hanoi puzzle is exactly the type of artificial, laboratory-based task that my Naturalistic Decision Making (NDM) community has avoided. There is no expertise. No context, no uncertainty.

And yet, several decades ago, I did a small study of how people try to solve the Tower of Hanoi puzzle. This essay is the first time I am telling that story.

Why did I do that study? Greed.

I had been included as a subcontractor on a larger effort to develop a cognitive test battery for railroad engineers and others to detect signs of impairment, such as alcohol or drug use or lack of sleep (O'Donnell, Moise, & Schmidt, 2004). Once the project was underway, the program manager steered it in a different direction than I expected and there was little need for my company's involvement. However, the program manager was still obligated to fulfill the financial commitment to bring us on board. But what could we add?

The manager had decided to use the Tower of Hanoi puzzle as part of this cognitive test battery and hit upon the idea that I could do a cognitive task analysis of how people did the task. He rejected all my alternative suggestions, so it was either study the Tower of Hanoi puzzle or wave goodbye to $25,000.

With severe misgivings, I decided to give it a shot.

However, after agreeing, I ran into a big problem. I had no intention of doing these interviews on such an artificial task, and I couldn't find anyone on my technical staff who was willing to do it either. Therefore, I turned my attention to other projects my company was working on.

Then, as the cognitive test battery project was ending, the program manager reminded me of this Tower of Hanoi deliverable that I had never even started to work on. Fortunately, my company had very recently hired a new research assistant, Andrew Mills. I called Andy into my office and told him that I had the perfect training project to help him come up to speed with doing cognitive interviews: he could do cognitive interviews with the Tower of Hanoi puzzle under my supervision.

Andy enthusiastically agreed.

Of course, after our meeting, Andy told other people in the company about this arrangement, and they told him, "Gary has finally found his sucker." As a result, Andy's excitement was considerably reduced when he started on this project.

For those unfamiliar with the Tower of Hanoi puzzle, the diagram in figure 2.6 shows three pegs. Your task is to move all the doughnut-shaped disks from the peg on the left, we'll call it Peg A, to the peg on the right, Peg C. You move the disks one at a time. You can never put a larger disk on a smaller one. The task is difficult, and it gets harder the more disks you start with on Peg A.

Here I suggest that before you read further in this essay, you go online and attempt the puzzle yourself so you can see how it works. Try the MathIsFun site, https://www.mathsisfun.com/games/towerofhanoi.html. And see if you can get up to five or six disks.

Andy and I agreed that he would interview seven people in my company, one at a time. He'd watch them doing the task and ask them to talk out loud, so he knew what they were trying to do. He could inject questions if he was unsure how they were making decisions.

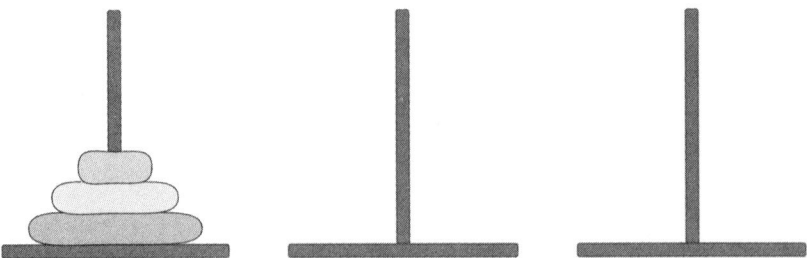

Figure 2.6
Tower of Hanoi example.

Andy expected that everyone would solve the puzzle in the same way—the way he solved it. To his surprise, no two people used the same strategy. And some were better than others. Some could only do four or five rings, while others could manage seven or eight or nine rings.

With the seven interviews completed, it was time to review our findings from Andy's notes.

Our first discovery: The primary decision people wrestled with was where to move the top disk in a stack. Once you moved that disk, the rest of the sequence followed naturally, and you built what we called an "interim tower." And then you had the same decision—where to move the top disk of that interim tower.

Our second discovery was that to solve the puzzle, you had to build interim towers—partial towers on other pegs. Also, the people in our sample relied on mental simulation: "If I move this disk there, then the next disk goes there . . ." and so on. This mental simulation tactic wasn't a real discovery because we assumed as much from our own experience with the game. Herbert Simon (1975) refers to these interim towers as pyramids and describes the approach as a goal recursion strategy.

The third discovery, not really a discovery because it was already well-known in the literature, was that the strategy created a major difficulty—keeping track of the disks as you did the mental simulation. That tactic chewed up working memory and differentiated the people who could handle a lot of disks versus those who could only do a few. See Kotovsky, Hayes, & Simon (1985) for a masterful analysis of the memory requirements for different versions of the Tower of Hanoi problem.

Our fourth discovery was that even when people were solving the puzzle successfully, they often felt they were doing it wrong! The only way to solve the puzzle was to build interim towers on the different pegs, but people would say, "This can't be right. I'm building this tower on the wrong peg, not the peg I want all the rings to wind up on." Therefore, we could see that people didn't have a good mental model of how these interim towers played out. We also noted that even when performance is successful, it doesn't mean that the person really understands what s/he is doing.

Our fifth discovery was that there was a simple strategy that pretty much eliminated the memory struggles. *You start at the bottom, not the top!* Here's how it works. If all the disks are on Peg A at the left, and you need to move them all to Peg C on the right, then you need to move the bottom disk, the largest one, to Peg C. Obviously.

To do that, you need to build an interim tower on Peg B with the next largest disk at the bottom. And to do that, you need to build an interim tower on Peg C with the next largest disk. And so forth. You still need to do some analysis, but the memory burden is greatly reduced, and so are the errors.

You might want to go back to the Tower of Hanoi website and try the puzzle using this bottom-up strategy.

Our takeaway from this project was that by studying the cognitive challenges of the task, we could make a series of discoveries about the key decisions people faced, what made the task difficult, and what were the weaknesses in their mental models. Plus, a bonus discovery of the bottom-up strategy.

As far as we can tell, no one has previously reported several of these five discoveries.

If a cognitive perspective can yield so many discoveries for a puzzle that has been around for over a century, imagine the payoff for new tasks and requirements.

—*March 8, 2021*

2.8 Reflections

Now you are oriented to the perspective of this book. The remaining parts deepen on these themes, so let's take stock of the major takeaways thus far.

One primary theme is the cognitive dimension—the thinking that goes on beneath the surface. It's easy to fixate on the behavioral dimension, the actions people take that are easy to observe, or the procedural dimension, the rules and steps people are supposed to follow. The cognitive dimension is invisible. It affects our behaviors, and it affects the way we carry out procedures or modify them or even discard them. The cognitive dimension ties into expertise and the ways that experts notice things that the rest of us miss.

A related theme is our ability to see cognition. Not just intellectually understand it but to spot various aspects of cognition as they come into play. One of the goals of this book is to help you develop skills at seeing cognition. Part 1 provided you with the example of the rock fishers, and part 2 has provided other examples such as the Systems Integration course and the Tower of Hanoi problem. Examples like these make the idea of "seeing cognition" more concrete, and they make the concept of cognitive challenges more vivid.

The cognitive dimension rests on the sources of power that underlie our expertise. Part 2 showed you how to map these sources of power, such as pattern recognition, perspective taking, curiosity, speculative thinking, and sensemaking. Part 2 also explored a few of these sources of power in more detail, the mental models we acquire, and our ability to make rapid decisions.

You won't encounter these kinds of sources of power in most college courses in psychology, even courses in cognitive psychology. You won't encounter them very often in media coverage of cognition. That coverage is dominated by weaknesses and flaws and biases in our thinking abilities.

This book is about the strengths in our thinking, the sources of power. To investigate these strengths, it helps to become curious about how people actually think, how people actually make decisions, especially in complex and ambiguous settings, and that is the perspective taken by the Naturalistic Making (NDM) community.

Sometimes NDM researchers use controlled laboratory studies, but for the most part, we investigate real-world settings and real-world decision-makers. That means giving up precision in order to gain a broader comprehension. NDM researchers accept that trade-off. However, we know that it makes our laboratory-centered colleagues uncomfortable. It may make some readers uncomfortable but if it is any consolation, studying complex phenomena in tightly controlled environments with artificial tasks and naive participants makes us NDM researchers uncomfortable.

Because you can now appreciate this NDM perspective and the trade-offs it entails, you are prepared to better understand the different facets of expertise and cognition that will be covered in the rest of the book. You might also be thinking about the implications of the NDM perspective—the kinds of tools and tactics that it opens up, such as ShadowBox.

And yet there is still a barrier to engaging with the sources of power and seeing cognition. You have long been exposed to different perspectives, such as the Heuristics and Biases approach that run counter to the sources of power and the NDM approach covered in parts 1 and 2. You are likely to wonder how we can celebrate the cognitive dimension in the face of all the evidence showing that we are defective thinkers. Therefore, we might as well confront that perspective directly in part 3.

3 Rationalist Fever Dreams

Overview

The title for this part comes from a 2018 article by Devorah Klein, Dave Woods, Shawna Perry, and me about the belief that complex decisions can be handled by analytical tools: plans, procedures, algorithms, automation, checklists, and standards such as best practices—a conviction that the only criterion for rational behavior is compliance with these tools and standards. We argued that it is a delusion to believe that these tools and standards could be adequate to help people perform complex tasks and make decisions in ambiguous settings, with incomplete information, and with many contextual/causal factors operating in parallel. Those who have the goal of someday replacing expertise with these tools and standards appear to be gripped by a "rationalist fever dream."

We stated, "As the fever worsens, the pressures to conform to rules grow . . . the rationalist fever dream is a kind of oversimplification that affects managers, researchers, and practitioners in many domains . . . the fever is manifested by the strength of exhortations to rely just on procedures, principles, rules, algorithms, and standards" (p. 227). One of the major problems with rationalist approaches is that they are so brittle; organizations that are very rule-bound struggle to adapt in the face of surprising events. They are likely to rigidly adhere to standards and techniques that no longer apply. In short, organizations are blind to the cognitive challenges of getting the work done. "Organizations can be designed for adaptability that builds on plans rather than be constrained to just comply with plans" (p. 229).

Because this rationalist fever dream has taken hold so strongly and in so many communities, it is important to confront it. I attempted to do that in the essays I have included in this part.

Please note that I am *not* claiming that plans, procedures, algorithms, checklists, and standards are useless. Obviously, they have great value in many settings. My claim is that they are not sufficient and that you can't proceduralize expertise in complex and ambiguous situations. Yet even with this disclaimer, I expect that I will be attacked for advocating for irrational methods, which I am not. I expect that for some, any attempt to point out the limits of analytical tools will be treated as a red flag and provoke outrage. We can view the existence of that outrage and its intensity as a sign of how deeply the rationalist fever has taken hold, so deeply that its proponents cannot countenance any disagreement or attempt at debate.

The Heuristics and Biases (HB) community is one of the most vocal and influential advocates for the rationalist fever dreams. Despite my admiration for many members of the HB community, I have strong misgivings about its assumptions and claims. In my 1989 article "Do Decision Biases Explain Too Much?" I showed that if a decision-maker chose one option and it turned out badly, you could explain it by invoking one decision bias, but if he chose the opposite option and that one turned out badly, you could invoke a different decision bias. Therefore, if decision biases could explain everything, they were explaining nothing. The claim that biases cause decision errors is therefore meaningless.

Even worse, the HB movement seems fixated on reducing errors and ignores the importance of seeking ambitious achievements. It generally downplays expertise and questions its existence. Several essays in part 3 criticize these tendencies on the part of the HB community and raise questions about the so-called biases.

Because the Naturalistic Decision Making (NDM) community has questioned many of the HB positions, some researchers within the HB and the judgment and decision-making (JDM) community have concluded that NDM is nothing more than a reaction to HB's and JDM's work. This conclusion is telling—it ignores the major thrust of NDM researchers to identify the sources of power that enable skilled decision-making—the positive side of the equation. This conclusion ignores the development of accounts such as the Recognition-Primed Decision model, which explains how people actually make decisions, a finding that the HB and JDM researchers never achieved even after so many decades of laboratory experiments.

Essay 3.1 in part 3, "Hopelessly Irrational or Wonderfully Creative?," contrasts the positive and negative views of human cognition. This was the very first essay I posted when I started the *Psychology Today* blog in May 2013. In some ways, it is a foundational essay for my *Psychology Today* materials and a foundational essay for this book.

Essay 3.2, "Can We Trust the Decision Researchers?," expands on some of the themes from my initial May 2013 blog and lists eight questionable assumptions that conventional decision researchers typically make—eight biases that they have. These biases can help us to assess their research findings and the claims of the HB community.

The HB community has shown the ways that cognitive heuristics can lead to poor performance, but I think that in most cases, these heuristics are very valuable. Essay 3.3, "Positive Heuristics," explains the benefits of some of the most-studied heuristics/biases.

In his book, *Moneyball*, Michael Lewis offered a vivid example of the hopelessly irrational viewpoint, one of the biases of the HB researchers. Lewis documented the cluelessness of baseball scouts. However, I don't agree with him. Essay 3.4, "The Myths of *Moneyball*," argues that his analysis is off base.

And while Lewis wants us to put our trust in hard numbers rather than subjective impressions, just how meaningful are those numbers? We know we can't completely trust subjective impressions, but essay 3.5, "Getting Crunched by the Numbers," explains why we should also be skeptical about the numbers.

Part 3 then shifts into a higher gear. Essay 3.6, "The Curious Case of Confirmation Bias," is a critique of perhaps the best-known and most widely cited decision bias. This essay explains why it may be time to retire the concept of confirmation bias because of problems it leads to. Fortunately, there is a better way to think about these issues: fixation errors. Essay 3.7, "Escaping from Fixation," explains how fixation errors arise and, more importantly, offers some ideas for reducing these errors.

Essay 3.8, "The Substitution Trap," expands on the critique of confirmation bias and presents several examples of how decision researchers claim to be studying a complex and interesting phenomenon but then, almost by sleight of hand (sleight of mind), substitute a simpler and simplistic formulation instead.

The rationalist fever dreams mentality is heavily directed at reducing errors. Checklists, procedures, best practices, all of these are ways to cut the chances that we will make mistakes. We can see this preoccupation with mistakes in televised sports events. The commentators pounce on any mistakes as the reason a team lost and blame the player who made that mistake. Essay 3.9, "Costly Mistakes?" provides an example—a football game in which a quarterback threw a "costly" interception near the end of a tight game. However, a close inspection shows that this mistake really didn't make much difference.

This example may seem trivial, but the sensationalizing of mistakes in sports may bleed over to professional and even personal matters, discouraging people from taking risks. In my work with investment managers, I find that they often talk about downside risks—the risks of losing money on a stock they purchase. But I am also finding that they're realizing they need to worry about upside risks—the risks of failing to purchase a stock that then increases in value. Essay 3.10, "Playing to Win," explains why we shouldn't be too defensive. Life is more than avoiding mistakes.

The final essay in part 3, essay 3.11, "Stealth Decisions," discusses an inconvenient feature of decision-making: even if we are determined to make perfect decisions and avoid mistakes, the toughest decisions may come down to a coin toss. Or they'll come down to minor considerations that were never part of our careful analyses. Calculations only get us so far.

3.1 Hopelessly Irrational or Wonderfully Creative?

Warnings about Biases Should Be Balanced with Celebrations of Insights

Insights often appear magical, popping into our mind without any warning. New ideas are unexpectedly created. In contrast to controlled, logical thinking, insights don't follow any formal rules for rational reasoning.

This accidental quality of insights makes them exciting, but it also makes them unreliable and untrustworthy. Proponents of rational reasoning and critical thinking tend to regard insights with suspicion—as a potential source of biases.

The field of Heuristics and Biases (HB) was started over 40 years ago. Initially, Danny Kahneman and Amos Tversky just wanted to show that people use heuristics—simple strategies—for making judgments and decisions and didn't behave in a perfectly logical way (Tversky & Kahneman, 1974). Economists had assumed that people were rational and relied on perfect reasoning strategies, but Kahneman and Tversky demonstrated that this wasn't the case. People used heuristics. Fair enough.

However, the field of HB has evolved into a gleeful collection of examples purporting to show that people are irrational. Books such as *Predictably Irrational* (Ariely & Jones, 2008), *Blind Spots* (Van Hecke, 2009), *Think Twice* (Mauboussin, 2012), *Sway* (Brafman & Brafman, 2008), and *Everyday Irrationality* (Dawes, 2001) go too far. We use heuristics because they generally are useful. They're not perfect but in a complex and uncertain world, they get the job done.

We would be immobilized if we only made judgments using perfect reasoning strategies. The conditions for perfect reasoning strategies aren't often met outside the laboratory. Neither Bayesian statistics nor forms of deductive inference are very robust or very practical in natural settings. That's why we have to rely on our experience and the heuristics we've learned.

Unfortunately, too many researchers in the HB tradition continue to propagate the message that because we use heuristics, we are flawed. Even experts come under suspicion. The message is that we can't be trusted to make important judgments. That's a pretty depressing message.

What's missing from the HB work is an appreciation for how smart we can be. How we can use our experience so well. And how we can form insights.

Martin Seligman and Mihaly Csikszentmihaly (2000) ushered in the field of positive psychology by suggesting that psychotherapists and other practitioners look for ways to promote happiness and well-being instead of just trying to reduce the miseries of depression, anxiety, or neurosis. Similarly, I think we need a positive *cognitive* psychology that appreciates the sources of power people use to make sense of complex and dynamic situations. We need to take insights more seriously. Improving performance depends on reducing errors but it also depends on increasing insights. If we eliminate all errors, we still haven't generated any new and innovative ideas.

I think that insights provide a complement to the HB worldview. Insights don't arise through careful analytical reasoning. They spring to our minds unexpectedly. Sure, we need to worry about making bad judgments. But we also should celebrate our capacity for insights.

—*May 31, 2013*

3.2 Can We Trust the Decision Researchers?

Eight Biases of the Heuristics and Biases Community

This essay holds up a mirror to one of the most influential movements in psychology—the Heuristics and Biases (HB) framework initiated by Danny Kahneman and Amos Tversky around a half-century ago (Kahneman & Tversky, 1972; Tversky & Kahneman, 1971, 1974).

The HB community can boast many important accomplishments, many discoveries, many counterintuitive demonstrations. It has spawned the field of behavioral economics, with its record of nudging people to make wise choices.

I have no intent to denigrate the HB framework. I simply want to describe the tendencies and inclinations of the members of the HB community. That's how I am defining bias in this essay. Not errors, but tendencies, like we might describe a bias for action or a bias for justice.

Any community of practice is bound together by attitudes, preferences, and reactions. Often these inclinations become so automatic that the members of the community don't even notice them. I think that the biases, tendencies, and reactions, are part of the makeup of the HB community no less than formal axioms and a body of research.

By holding up a mirror, this essay can help those outside the HB community coordinate with them. And it can help those inside the community understand themselves.

I have assembled a list of eight biases found in the HB community.

1. Eliminate errors. Obviously, we all want to reduce if not eliminate errors, no argument there. However, there can be a downside to this bias: it's necessary but not sufficient. We also need to make discoveries. An overemphasis on errors can potentially reduce the chance to gain insights. That's why it's a balancing act, taking actions that cut down on mistakes but not going overboard to the extent that performance suffers. Because of their tendency to fixate on errors, HB researchers are troubled by one of the causes of errors—the use of heuristics.

2. Discourage heuristics. The HB community has convincingly shown that we use heuristics. The researchers set up conditions in which the heuristics result in suboptimal performance and demonstrate that people use the heuristics anyway. The heuristics aren't perfect—they're not algorithms. They open the door for making errors. However, the HB community hasn't done cost/benefit analyses to gauge how much we gain and how much we lose by using heuristics. The community hasn't examined the value of heuristics. Without heuristics, none of us would be able to function very well in complex settings. Even Tversky & Kahneman (1974) stated, "In general, these heuristics are quite useful, but sometimes they lead to severe and systematic errors" (p. 1124). Yet HB researchers only look at the disadvantages of heuristics. The researchers conclude that because people rely on heuristics, they will necessarily exhibit cognitive weaknesses.

3. Look for the flaws in cognitive performance. There is nothing wrong with this skeptical mindset that has helped the HB community generate a long list of cognitive limitations. However, HB researchers are generally insensitive to the strengths of cognitive performance. Their glass is half-full. Instead of appreciating our ability to make difficult decisions under time pressure and uncertainty, HB researchers catalog the ways that our intuitions—based on heuristics—can get us in trouble.

4. Distrust intuitive judgments. When can you trust intuition? The HB community would say, "Never," and I agree because intuition isn't infallible. But in most settings, it works well enough and is the best we have. Even if we shouldn't put total trust in intuitions, we should at least listen to our intuitions because they are reflecting our experience. Kahneman and Klein (2009) identified conditions under which we can develop skilled intuitions: a sufficiently stable environment and the chance to get timely and accurate feedback. Nevertheless, many if not most of the HB community have a deep-seated antipathy toward intuitions, even the intuitions of experts.

5. Distrust experts and expertise. Experts aren't infallible, and they sometimes fall into the traps that HB researchers set in their experiments. But in very many domains, experts do an impressive job. Ericsson et al. (2018) have documented the varieties of expertise that have been demonstrated. What concerns me is the pleasure that members of the HB community take in stories of expert comeuppance. The HB community happily cites work by Paul Meehl (1954) and others showing that expert judgments do worse than statistics, omitting the fact that the statistics are based on the factors identified by the experts. The primary advantage of the statistical methods is to provide consistency in the use of these factors. How important is consistency?

6. Maximize consistency. The HB community holds this bias very strongly, and consistency is definitely a virtue. Noise—random variation—detracts from performance. But is consistency more important than accuracy? Further, some variation, some inconsistency, may help individuals and teams explore alternatives and become less rigid. Biological evolution depends on variation. Individual and team variation promotes adaptability.

7. Rely on rational analysis. The HB community places great value on rational arguments, using principles such as deductive logic and analytical methods such as Bayesian statistics. These methods are certainly powerful, but they don't apply to most of the judgments and decisions we face. They aren't suited for ambiguity and complexity (Lopes, 1991). If principles such as deductive logic and Bayesian statistics were so essential, we would expect that people who systematically violated them would pay the price. But the violators actually have greater success in life than those who are aligned with the principles of rational analysis (Berg & Gigerenzer, 2010).

8. Rely on procedures and checklists. The HB community also values procedure guides and checklists, in part because these tools impose consistency and can be empirically validated. There is no denying the utility of procedural guides and checklists. But, as I will point out in a part 5 essay, "From Chimps to Champs," some managers, influenced by the HB community, seek to substitute rational analysis, procedures, and checklists for expertise. These managers envision a workplace in which people no longer make decisions. However, very few complex tasks can be reduced to procedures or to steps in a checklist. The unrealistic dream of doing away with experts ignores the tacit knowledge needed to get most jobs done.

Each of these eight biases is valid and has merit. But when pressed too far, each becomes counterproductive. I admire the HB community for taking bold positions, for making the most extreme statements they believe they can defend. I like that stance better than a stance of trying not to make dramatic assertions or claims that might be incorrect. I appreciate what the HB community has attempted and what it has accomplished. By using a naturalistic perspective on the extreme positions the community has adopted and the biases it has embraced, the rest of us can find a more reasonable and balanced position.

—*October 10, 2016*

3.3 Positive Heuristics

Strategies for Engaging in Speculative Thinking

In the early 1970s, Danny Kahneman and Amos Tversky identified a set of heuristics that people use—availability, representativeness, anchoring, and adjustment, even drawing inferences from small samples. Previously, thought leaders like Karl Duncker, Alan Newell, and Herb Simon had discussed the importance of heuristics, but Kahneman and Tversky actually identified a set of specific types of heuristics that we commonly apply. For this, Kahneman and Tversky deserve the accolades and prizes they received.

However, the Heuristics and Biases community that sprung up from their work took an unfortunate trajectory. This community equated heuristics with biases. The term "bias" can mean preference or predisposition, but the primary understanding is that a biased judgment is not logical or justified. This conflation made some sense because the research methodology used by Kahneman and Tversky and others was to demonstrate that people use heuristics even when the heuristics yield inaccurate judgments. The studies, therefore, illustrated how heuristics can mislead us, but this demonstration is not the same as showing that we would be better off without the heuristics. Yes, under certain circumstances that researchers could design, the heuristics get in our way. In many other circumstances, however, the heuristics are invaluable.

I think that the community has been using an inappropriate yardstick: evaluating the accuracy of the heuristics in comparison to formal analytical methods such as probability theory and Bayesian statistics. Bayesian statistics only came into prominence in the 1980s. Probability theory achieved its current formulation by Laplace just over 200 years ago. Why would we expect that the common heuristics that we use would match formalisms such as Bayesian statistics and probability theory?

Consider research by Lichtenstein et al. (1978) showing that participants, typically college students, held inaccurate beliefs about the frequencies of different causes of death. The participants overestimated sensational causes, such as tornadoes, floods, homicides, and accidents—causes likely to receive media coverage—and underestimated silent killers that received little media attention such as asthma, tuberculosis, stroke, and diabetes. So, yes, the participants were inaccurate, but how were they supposed to know the actual data? Were they supposed to have pored through the archives and committed the findings to memory? What does it mean to accuse the participants of bias for lining up with the media reports? I agree with Lichtenstein et al. that inaccurate beliefs will affect public policy, resulting in an inefficient allocation of funds for low frequency but dramatic causes. My problem is that I don't see what we gain by labeling the participants as biased because they used a reasonable, although limited, judgment strategy.

The assertion that humans are inherently irrational makes little sense. The argument is based on an inappropriate standard. Certainly, we should be using more powerful analytical and statistical methods where appropriate (although the application of these methods is not always as straightforward as their adherents suggest). And we shouldn't automatically trust the judgments stemming from intuition and heuristics. Yet, there is more to decision-making and sensemaking than performing risk assessments.

Fortunately, I think there is a better yardstick for appraising heuristics: speculative thinking. People don't often have the luxury of making judgments and decisions backed by clear and copious data. We typically have to stretch, building arguments out of fragments. We have to speculate rather than analyze.

And that's where Kahneman and Tversky's heuristics come in. They are cognitive tools we employ in order to speculate. We make speculative leaps based on small samples. We rely on the availability of precedents in our memories. We use estimates of representativeness. We find an anchor and work from there. That's what I am calling positive heuristics. They are heuristics we depend on to navigate an ambiguous world. Heuristics that aren't going to give us perfect answers but can operate in spheres where we can't have perfection.

They're not biases that make us irrational. The positive heuristics are strengths that make us adaptive and successful.

We can add to this small set of positive heuristics using additional heuristics that other judgment researchers have uncovered. Illusory correlation refers to our propensity to see relationships that aren't there, but the positive side of that heuristic is that we are quick to spot connections and see patterns without waiting for comprehensive amounts of data to be collected. The simulation heuristic that Kahneman later described is a valuable means of making diagnoses and imagining consequences; it is a central part of the Recognition-Primed Decision model I have studied. The affect heuristic lets us take advantage of emotional reactions to make quick judgments of risks and benefits.

Kahneman seems ambivalent about the idea of positive heuristics. He explained to me that his work with Tversky treated heuristics as mental shortcuts and concentrated on their liabilities. Also, Kahneman and Tversky viewed heuristics as involuntary, subconscious reactions, not as tools we deliberately apply. True, earlier investigators such as Herbert Simon and George Polya had viewed heuristics as deliberate tools, but Kahneman and Tversky chose not to follow this usage. My reaction is that I don't care if positive heuristics are used subconsciously or deliberately—what matters is how they help us proceed despite confusion.

Imagine what would have happened if researchers had built upon the early discoveries of Kahneman and Tversky by taking this different trajectory—studying positive heuristics for enabling us to do speculative thinking. Researchers could be seeing heuristics as a source of strength rather than a source of bias and error and could be evaluating heuristics by how well they let us speculate rather than by how closely their use conforms to statistical analyses.

—*April 8, 2017*

3.4 The Myths of *Moneyball*

The Misleading Messages of a Bestseller

Michael Lewis's book *Moneyball* tells the story of how a Major League Baseball team, the Oakland Athletics, stopped relying so heavily on scouts to judge ballplayers' talents and turned to statistical analyses. *Moneyball* expresses one of Lewis's favorite themes: the so-called experts don't know what really matters, and, to make matters worse, they are highly confident in their own judgments. They don't know what they don't know. *Moneyball* also expresses another favorite Lewis theme: smart outsiders outwitting the so-called experts (see *The Big Short*). *Moneyball* was published in 2003 and is still a bestseller; it was turned into a movie starring Brad Pitt as Billy Beane, the general manager of the Oakland Athletics.

Lewis is a sufficiently talented writer not to let facts get in the way of entertainment. His version of events is reasonably but not entirely accurate (e.g., the 2012 essay by Will Braund, "How True Is *Moneyball*?," which unfortunately is no longer accessible. Also see Barra, 2011). These inaccuracies don't bother me very much.

My real concern is with the central message of *Moneyball*. The myths it presents appear to be taking hold, not only within the general public but within the judgment and decision-making community whose members often cite *Moneyball* to back up their professional recommendations.

This essay describes the three *Moneyball* myths that worry me the most. And I need to explain that the essay is not an attack on Michael Lewis. I have greatly enjoyed each of his books I have read, and I have read most of them. I also met him for lunch a few times and found him to be witty and charming. I am a big fan.

The *Moneyball* myths are necessary for telling the story—a more nuanced treatment wouldn't have become a bestseller.

However, when I see actual articles in professional journals that cite *Moneyball*, I feel a need to sound a warning.

Here are the three myths I want to examine more closely:

First, baseball scouts don't know which players are genuinely skilled.

Second, baseball scouts have a facade of expertise but nothing of substance.

Third, baseball scouts are allergic to statistics.

Let's examine these three claims.

Claim 1. Baseball scouts don't know which players are genuinely skilled. They rely on scouting prejudices, including absurd features. "Some of the scouts still believed they could tell by the structure of a young man's face not only his character but his future in pro ball. They had a phrase they used: 'the Good Face'" (p. 7).

Even if we accept *Moneyball*'s premise that the statistical analyses outperformed the scouts' judgment, it doesn't follow that the scouts' judgments were useless. Remember—before the wide availability of baseball data, all that teams had available was the judgment of the scouts. If that judgment were useless, it would mean that scouts were no better at identifying talented young players than fans in the stands. And no one has ever done that research.

We have anecdotes to the contrary. In 1988, a scout heard about a shortstop in Panama with no training as a pitcher who had come in as a replacement for a struggling starting pitcher and had done well. The scout watched the shortstop/pitcher throw and liked his smooth motion and athleticism. Even though he weighed only 155 pounds and threw only 85–87 miles/hour, the scout signed him to a $2,500 contract with the Yankees. His name was Mariano Rivera.

Anecdotes like these are not data, but we don't have data. To my knowledge, no one has compared the judgment of professional scouts against a control group. It wouldn't be hard—show video clips of hitters swinging at pitches, or pitchers winding up and letting go, just the motions, not the outcomes. Some of the video clips would show minor leaguers about to be released. Other video clips would show successful players. Or else get video clips from Japan, from the Nippon Professional Baseball League and its related minor league, so the participants couldn't recognize the successful players.

Would the baseball scouts do better than controls at identifying which ones are the successful major leaguers and which ones washed out at the bottom of the minor leagues? Perhaps there would be no difference. I suspect that the scouts would greatly outperform the controls.

Why haven't the decision researchers who tout *Moneyball* been skeptical about Claim 1? I think it is because Claim 1 fits their preconceptions, and they don't feel a need to test those preconceptions—which is the criticism that *Moneyball* makes of the scouts.

Claim 2. Baseball scouts have a facade of expertise but nothing of substance.

Following from Claim 1, if scouts do have expertise, then what might it consist of? One possibility is that scouts might appreciate athleticism and mechanics.

Back to the Mariano Rivera anecdote. The scout who watched Rivera admired his smooth motion. Similarly, scouts might admire a hitter's smooth swing. Statistics do not capture these kinds of subtleties. But we see it in action: baseball commentators on TV regularly comment on a pitcher's motion. Or they will use replays to show how a hitter is "stepping into the bucket," compromising his ability.

Consider other sports. During the Summer Olympics in the diving competition, experienced television commentators alerted us when a diver rotated too far to enter the water cleanly, creating a bigger splash. And, sure enough, in the slow-motion replay, we saw the problem. However, the commentator saw it as it happened. Surely that counts as expertise, gained only after countless hours watching athletes perform their craft.

Even though baseball scouts may have important skills, their ability to judge talent may still be inferior to statistical analyses. While irrelevant to the thesis of this essay, this observation should be considered, and tested, by comparing the judgments of scouts to those of the data analysts, rather than to a control group.

Presumably, the analysts would use the most advanced statistics currently available, so it makes little sense to compare these analysts to the kind of scouts lampooned in *Moneyball*. It is only fair to engage the most advanced scouts—those selected by a rigorous vetting process and then further trained through the current state-of-the-art methods for developing expertise. In *Superforecasting*, Tetlock and Gardner (2016) showed how to develop predictive expertise regarding world events—it can't be harder to develop predictive expertise in baseball scouts. Let's put *Moneyball* to the test.

Claim 3. Baseball scouts are allergic to statistics. ("Billy was forever telling Paul that when you try to explain probability theory to baseball guys, you just end up confusing them" (p. 34)).

This claim is fun to make, backed up by anecdotal evidence. But Lewis himself describes how baseball scouts were using statistics. They just weren't using very good statistics—they relied on the traditional statistics at the time. The scouts were happily studying the batting averages of hitters and the earned run averages of pitchers. The scouts weren't scared off by numbers. They depended on these misleading statistics too much, not too little.

Moneyball cites the work of Bill James, who, in the 1970s and 1980s, showed what could be done with the data that were just becoming available. Even before I read *Moneyball*, I had devoured several of the Bill James Abstract books when I started playing fantasy baseball in the early 1990s, and I became an instant convert to the power of statistical analyses in baseball. Therefore, this essay is not criticizing statistical approaches. Rather, the essay explains why we might want to reconsider the contempt heaped on baseball scouts.

Moneyball has become a poster child for why we shouldn't trust the experts. It is a prime exhibit in the War on Experts. The objective of that war is to devalue experts in a variety of fields and recommend that experts be replaced by algorithms, checklists, and analyses. That recommendation is sometimes helpful but often reckless and counterproductive.

Of course, the real issue is not scouts versus analysts but rather how to design statistical and computational tools to allow scouts and other decision-makers to be more successful. But we will have trouble pursuing that path if we buy into the myths of *Moneyball*.

—*January 8, 2017*

3.5 Getting Crunched by the Numbers

You Shouldn't Judge Performance without Understanding a Person's Intentions

---

In our age of data analytics, with all our powerful methodologies and computational power, it sometimes feels that we merely need to turn on the analytical engines and sit back and wait for the discoveries. These discoveries all boil down to number crunching. Or do they?

Often there is more to a story than portrayed by the data. The data can mislead us. Unleashing our data analytics tools to gobble up the data can set us up to get crunched by the numbers.

That's why we need to use our intuition and perspective taking to get a sense of what's behind the numbers. We need to know the intentions of the decision-makers in order to make sense of their performance.

Here are three examples:

Example 1: Baseball

In game 1 of the National League Division Series, October 3, 2019, the Los Angeles Dodgers started a 25-year-old Walker Buehler, a left-handed pitcher. He had a very good record this year, 14–4. However, his last few outings were terrible. In his previous 16 innings, he gave up eight runs and walked nine batters. For those who don't follow baseball, these are very mediocre data—not the reassuring performance you'd want in a pitcher to kick off your postseason. Several commentators questioned whether Buehler was up to the job. But the data were misleading, and Buehler did an outstanding job in that first game.

When asked about it afterward, he explained that the Dodgers had clinched their division leadership very early, and he decided to use his final appearances to tweak his pitches and try different things. He didn't particularly care about his record for the year. Instead, he wanted to hone his skills for the playoffs. So those last 16 innings didn't mean anything. If you didn't know his intentions and just tracked the data, you'd have drawn the wrong conclusion, just like the clueless commentators.

Example 2: Rowing

My younger daughter Rebecca rowed in college. During the winter, crew teams didn't compete in the open water around New York City but instead held competitions indoors on rowing machines.

In one such competition, Rebecca's team matched up against another college, and Rebecca quickly spotted the star of the other team, a young woman who was much taller than Rebecca (and height matters a lot in rowing). I described this incident in my book *Streetlights and Shadows* (2009). The gist is that Rebecca realized she'd have a tough time beating her opponent, so she altered her strategy. In a 2,000-meter race, the typical strategy is to do a final all-out kick for the last 200 meters. Rebecca expected that her taller opponent could outdo her in that final kick, so Rebecca decided to start her kick with 500 meters remaining and to preserve enough energy to pull that off.

The race started and the opponent jumped out to a large lead. Rebecca thought that if the opponent could keep that pace up for the entire race, there was little chance of catching her, and it wasn't worth trying. But Rebecca had a hunch that the opponent was going to slow down after 500 meters, and so Rebecca just kept to a comfortable pace. Sure enough, the opponent did slow down, and by the halfway point, 1,000 meters, Rebecca had closed a lot of the gap. At this point, Rebecca envisioned the rest of the race—at the pace they were rowing, she'd pull even by 1,500 meters and then start her kick, taking a commanding lead and holding it. She was pretty sure she was going to win the race.

Rebecca's teammates were oblivious to Rebecca's strategy and intentions, and at the halfway point, they were shouting encouragement to her not to give up and that she had a good chance for second place. Rebecca remembers being amused to think that she was the only person in the gym who appreciated that she had the race pretty well sewn up. No one knew her intentions to start her kick with 500 meters to go. No one knew that she had preserved her strength to carry out that plan. Therefore, without knowing Rebecca's intentions, you'd have no way to anticipate what came next—the easy win Rebecca had arranged. And, yes, Rebecca was correct that her opponent had a stronger kick than she did. If Rebecca had followed the typical strategy of waiting until the last 200 meters to kick, she'd have lost the race.

Example 3: Helicopter navigation

Many years ago, my colleagues and I did a research project on army helicopter teams and how they coordinated during a mission. We had a chance to observe a simulator training exercise. There would be ten two-person crews navigating a difficult course, maneuvering around simulated hills, and dodging simulated missiles. I was stationed in the simulator control room where I could watch the action on a set of monitors. My two colleagues embedded in the ready room so that they could interview the members of each helicopter crew as the crew prepared for its turn. I vividly remember one crew. It was composed of two women, and the men in the simulator control room had very low expectations for them. Sure enough, after the first few legs of the mission, the female crew seemed to get lost. Instead of turning west after the first set of hills, they kept going straight and only realized their mistake when they got to a second set of hills and turned west after passing these hills. The comments I heard in the simulator control room were not kind.

The observers were surprised when the female crew made up the time they lost and finished with a strong overall performance.

And then it was my turn to be surprised. I mentioned this crew to my colleagues and how it had gotten lost, and they told me, "Oh no. They never got lost. That was their plan. They looked at the map showing the simulated enemy anti-air batteries and decided that by going around the second set of hills they'd be shielded and could move really fast, rather than ducking missiles all the way."

Because I didn't know their intentions (nor did the other men in the simulator control room), it was so easy to draw the wrong conclusion.

All these examples illustrate how critical it is to understand the intentions of the decision-makers. Otherwise, just relying on the data, we can draw the wrong conclusions. We can get crunched by the numbers.

—*October 4, 2019*

3.6 The Curious Case of Confirmation Bias

The Concept of Confirmation Bias Has Passed Its Sell-By Date

Confirmation bias is the tendency to search for data that can confirm our beliefs, as opposed to looking for data that might challenge those beliefs. The bias degrades our judgments when our initial beliefs are wrong because we might fail to discover what is really happening until it is too late.

To demonstrate confirmation bias, Pines (2006) provides a hypothetical example (which I have slightly modified) of an overworked emergency department physician who sees a patient at 2:45 a.m.—a 51-year-old man who has come in several times in recent weeks complaining of an aching back. The staff suspects that the man is seeking prescriptions for pain medication. The physician, believing this is just one more such visit, does a cursory examination and confirms that all the man's vital signs are fine—consistent with what was expected. The physician does give the man a new prescription for a pain reliever and sends the man home. Because he was only looking for what he expected, the physician missed the subtle problem that required immediate surgery.

The concept of confirmation bias appears to rest on three claims:

- First, firm evidence, going back 60 years, has demonstrated that people are prone to confirmation bias.
- Second, confirmation bias is clearly a dysfunctional tendency.
- Third, methods of debiasing are needed to help us to overcome confirmation bias.

The purpose of this essay is to look closely at these claims and explain why each one of them is wrong.

Claim 1: Firm evidence has demonstrated that people are prone to confirmation bias

Confirmation bias was first described by Peter Wason (1960), who asked participants in an experiment to guess at a rule about number triples. The participants were told that the sequence 2-4-6 fit that rule. They could generate their own triples, and they would get feedback on whether their triple fit the rule. When they had collected enough evidence, they were to announce their guess about what the rule was.

Wason found that the participants tested only positive examples—triples that fit their theory of what the rule was. The actual rule was any three ascending numbers, such as 2, 3, 47. However, given the 2-4-6 starting point, many participants generated triples that were even numbers, ascending and also increasing by 2. Participants didn't try sequences that might falsify their theory (e.g., 6-4-5). They were simply trying to confirm their beliefs.

At least, that's the popular story. Reviewing the original Wason data reveals a different story. Wason's data on the number triples (e.g., 2-4-6) showed that six of the 29 participants correctly guessed the rule on the very first trial, and several of these six did use probes that falsified a belief.

Most of the other participants in that study seemed to take the task lightly because it seemed so simple. But after getting feedback that their first guess was wrong, they realized that there was only 1 right answer—only 1 correct rule—and they'd have to do more analysis. Almost half of the remaining 23 participants immediately shaped up—10 guessed correctly on the second trial, with many of these also making use of negative probes (falsifications).

Therefore, the impression found in the literature is very misleading. The impression is that in this Wason study—the paradigm case of confirmation bias—the participants showed a confirmation effect. But when you look at the data, most of the participants were *not* trapped by confirmation bias. Only 13 of the 29 participants failed to solve the problem in the first two trials. (By the fifth trial, 23 of the 29 had solved the problem.)

The takeaway should have been that most people *do* test their beliefs. However, Wason chose to headline the bad news. The abstract to his paper states, "The results show that those [13] subjects, who reached two or more incorrect solutions, were unable, or unwilling, to test their hypotheses"

(p. 129). Wason found confirmation bias in the subjects who failed, not in the majority who succeeded.

Since then, several studies have obtained results that challenge the common beliefs about confirmation bias. These studies showed that most people actually are thoughtful enough to prefer genuinely diagnostic tests when given that option (Kunda, 1999; Trope & Bassok, 1982; Devine et al., 1990).

In the cognitive interviews I have conducted, I have seen some people *trying* to falsify their beliefs. One fireground commander, responding to a fire in a four-story apartment building, saw that the fire was in a laundry chute and seemed to be just beginning. He believed that he and his crew had arrived before the fire had a chance to spread up the chute—so he ordered an immediate attempt to suppress it from above, sending his crew to the second and third floors.

But he also worried that he might be wrong, so he circled the building. When he noticed smoke coming out of the eaves above the top floor, he realized that he *was* wrong. The fire must have already reached the fourth floor, and the smoke was spreading down the hall and out the eaves. He immediately told his crew to stop trying to extinguish the fire and instead shift to search and rescue for the inhabitants. All of the residents were successfully rescued, even though the building was severely damaged.

Another difficulty with Claim 1 is that confirmation bias tends to disappear when we add context. In a second study, Wason (1968) used a four-card problem to demonstrate confirmation bias (see figure 3.1).

Four cards are shown, each of which has a number on one side and a color on the other. The visible faces show 3, 8, light gray, and black. Participants are asked, "Which two cards should you turn over to test the claim that if a card has an even number on one face, then its opposite face is light gray?" (This is a slight variant of Wason's original task; see the top part of figure 3.1.)

Most people turn over cards 2 and 3. Card 2, showing an "8," is a useful test because if the opposite face is not light gray, the claim is disproved. But turning over card 3, "light gray," is a useless test because the claim is not that *only* cards with even numbers on one side have a light gray opposite face. Selecting card 3 illustrates confirmation bias.

However, Griggs and Cox (1982) applied some context to the four-card problem—they situated the task in a tavern with a barkeeper intent on following the law about underage drinking. Now the question took the form,

Confirmation Bias

Which 2 cards should you turn over to test the claim that if a card has an even number on one face, then its opposite face is light gray?

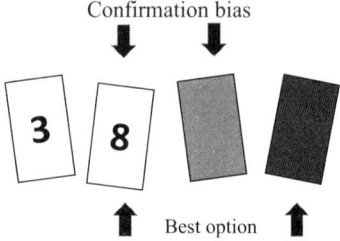

Which two cards should you turn over to test the claim that in this bar, if you are under 19 years of age, you are drinking a soft drink and not alcohol?

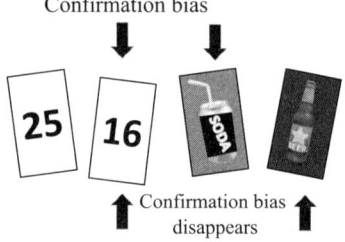

Figure 3.1
Wason 4-card task, Griggs and Cox added context.

"Which two of these cards should you turn over to test the claim that in this bar, 'If you are drinking alcohol then you must be over 19?'"* Griggs and Cox found that 73 percent of the participants now chose "16" and the beer—meaning the confirmation bias effect seen in Wason's version had mostly vanished. (See the bottom part of figure 3.1.)

Therefore, the first claim about the evidence for confirmation bias does not seem warranted.

Claim 2: Confirmation bias is clearly a dysfunctional tendency

Advocates for confirmation bias would argue that the bias can still get in the way of good decision-making. They would assert that even if the data

---

*At the time Griggs and Cox did their study in Florida, it was legal to drink at 19 years of age.

don't really support the claim that people fall prey to confirmation bias, we should still, as a safeguard, warn decision-makers against the tendency to support their preexisting beliefs.

But that ploy, to discourage decision-makers from seeking to confirm their preexisting beliefs, won't work because confirmation attempts often do make good sense. Klayman and Ha (1987) explained that under high levels of uncertainty, positive tests are more informative than negative tests (i.e., falsifications). Klayman and Ha refer to a "positive test strategy" as having clear benefits.

As a result of this work, many researchers in the judgment and decision-making community have reconsidered their view that the confirmation tendency is a bias and needs to be overcome. Confirmation bias seems to be losing its force within the scientific community, even as it gains traction in the popular press.

Think about it: of course we use our initial beliefs and frames to guide our explorations. How else would we search for information? Sometimes we can be tricked, in a cleverly designed study. Sometimes we trick ourselves when our initial belief is wrong. The use of our initial beliefs, gained through experience, isn't perfect. However, it is not clear that there are better ways of proceeding in ambiguous and uncertain settings.

We seem to have a category error here—people referring to the original Wason data on the triples and the four cards (even though these data are problematic) and then stretching the concept of confirmation bias to cover all kinds of semirelated or even unrelated problems, usually with hindsight: If someone makes a mistake, then the researchers hunt for some aspect of confirmation bias. As David Woods observed, "The focus on confirmation bias commits hindsight bias."

For all these reasons, the second claim that "the confirmation tendency is dysfunctional" doesn't seem warranted. We can make powerful use of our experience to identify a likely initial hypothesis and then use that hypothesis to guide the way we search for more data.

How would we search for data without using our experience? We wouldn't engage in a random search because that strategy seems highly inefficient. And I don't think we would always try to search for data that could disprove our initial hypothesis because that strategy won't help us make sense of confusing situations. Even scientists do not often try to falsify their hypotheses, so there's no reason to set this strategy up as an ideal for society at large.

The confirmation bias advocates seem to be ignoring the important and difficult process of hypothesis generation, particularly under ambiguous and changing conditions. These are the kinds of conditions favoring the positive test strategy that Klayman and Ha studied.

Claim 3: Methods of debiasing are needed to help us to overcome confirmation bias

For example, Lilienfeld et al. (2009) asserted that "research on combating extreme confirmation bias should be among psychological science's most pressing priorities" (p. 390). Many if not most decision researchers would still encourage us to try to debias decision-makers.

Unfortunately, that's been tried and has gotten nowhere. Attempts to reprogram people have failed. Lilienfeld et al. admitted that "psychologists have made far more progress in cataloguing cognitive biases . . . than in finding ways to correct or prevent them" (p. 391). Arkes (1981) concluded that psychoeducational methods by themselves are "absolutely worthless" (p. 326). The few successes have been small, and it is likely that many failures go unreported. One researcher whose work has been very influential in the Heuristics and Biases community has admitted to me that debiasing efforts don't work.

And let's imagine that, despite the evidence, a debiasing tactic was developed that was effective. How would we use that tactic? Would it prevent us from formulating an initial hypothesis without gathering all relevant information? Would it prevent us from speculating when faced with ambiguous situations? Would it require us to seek falsifying evidence before searching for any supporting evidence? Even the advocates acknowledge that confirmation tendencies are generally adaptive. So how would a debiasing method enable us to know when to employ a confirmation strategy and when to stifle it?

Making this a little more dramatic, using a confirmation surgery technique to cut out the imaginary brain area generating this confirmation tendency, how many decision researchers would sign up for that procedure? After all, I am not aware of any evidence that debiasing the confirmation tendency improves decision quality or makes people more successful and effective. I am not aware of data showing that a falsification strategy has any value. The confirmation surgery procedure would eliminate confirmation bias but would leave the patients forever searching for evidence to disconfirm any beliefs that might come to their minds. The result seems more like a nightmare than a cure.

One might still argue that there are situations in which we would want to identify several hypotheses, as a way of avoiding confirmation bias. For example, physicians are well-advised to do differential diagnoses, identifying the possible causes for a medical condition. However, that's just good practice. There's no need to try to debias people.

For these reasons, I suggest that the third claim about the need for debiasing methods is not warranted.

Conclusions

Where does that leave us? Fischhoff and Beyth-Marom (1983) complained about this expansion: "Confirmation bias, in particular, has proven to be a catch-all phrase incorporating biases in both information search and interpretation. Because of its excess and conflicting meanings, the term might best be retired" (p. 257).

I have mixed feelings. I agree with Fischhoff and Beyth-Marom that over the years, the concept of confirmation bias has been stretched—or expanded—beyond Wason's initial formation so that today it can refer to the following tendencies:

- *Search:* to search only for confirming evidence (Wason's original definition)
- *Preference:* to prefer evidence that supports our beliefs
- *Recall:* to best remember information in keeping with our beliefs
- *Interpretation:* to interpret evidence in a way that supports our beliefs
- *Framing:* to use mistaken beliefs to misunderstand what is happening in a situation
- *Testing:* to ignore opportunities to test our beliefs
- *Discarding:* to explain away data that don't fit with our beliefs

I see this expansion as a useful evolution, particularly the last three issues of framing, testing, and discarding. These are problems I have seen repeatedly. With this expansion, researchers will perhaps be more successful in finding ways to counter confirmation bias and improve judgments.

Nevertheless, I am skeptical. I don't think the expansion will be effective because the concept of bias is going to do much more harm than good. If you take confirmation bias seriously, you may try to prevent people from speculating at the outset, even though rapid speculation is valuable for guiding exploration. You may try to discourage people from seeking confirming evidence, even though the positive test strategy is so useful. The whole orientation of correcting a bias seems misguided. Instead of appreciating the strength of our sensemaking orientation and trying to reduce the occasional errors that might arise, the confirmation debiasing approach typically tries to eliminate errors by inhibiting our tendencies to speculate and explore.

Fortunately, there seems to be a better way to address the problems of being captured by our initial beliefs, failing to test those beliefs, and explaining away inconvenient data—the concept of *fixation*. This concept is consistent with what we know of Naturalistic Decision Making, whereas confirmation bias is not. Fixation doesn't carry the baggage of confirmation bias in terms of the three unwarranted claims discussed in this essay. Fixation directly gets at the crucial problem of failing to revise a mistaken belief.

Best of all, the concept of fixation provides a novel strategy for overcoming the problems of being captured by initial beliefs, failing to test those beliefs, and explaining away data that are inconsistent with those beliefs.

My next essay will discuss fixation and describe that strategy.

—*May 5, 2019*

3.7 Escaping from Fixation

Using Curiosity to Reduce Diagnostic Errors*

Diagnostic errors crop up in all kinds of settings, often with very serious consequences. What might cause them? The Institute of Medicine report "Improving Diagnosis in Health Care" (Balogh et al., 2015) identified some of the usual suspects: workload, time pressure, lack of expertise, fatigue, communications breakdowns.

The report also listed a cognitive problem—jumping to an initial hypothesis that is wrong and getting stuck on that diagnosis. That's the problem I want to tackle in this essay—this getting-stuck error.

Why do we sometimes get stuck on an incorrect diagnosis?

Frequently, this getting-stuck error is blamed on confirmation bias: we jump to a conclusion, and then, instead of testing it, we look for evidence to support it. However, as I explained in my last essay, the confirmation bias explanation has some serious weaknesses. (Smith (2018) raised similar concerns about confirmation bias.)

Fortunately, there's a better account of getting-stuck errors: fixation.

---

*The primary ideas in this essay emerged from a collaboration over several years with Terry Fairbanks, the vice president for Quality and Safety at MedStar Health. Terry and I designed a workshop on diagnostic errors, and in 2020, I had the opportunity to put on a modified version of that workshop in a project sponsored by the Center for Operator Performance, working with Joseph Borders and Ron Besuijen.

The concept of fixation is that we get stuck on an initial explanation. Often, that initial explanation will be accurate, but when it is wrong, with hindsight, we can see that we held on to it too long.

But fixation errors[†] aren't just holding onto our initial explanation too long. Fixation gets compounded when we dismiss any anomalous evidence that runs counter to our original diagnosis instead of taking these anomalies into account and revising our beliefs. De Keyser and Woods (1990) speculated about some ways that fixation works. Feltovich et al. (2001) called these tactics "knowledge shields" that we use to deflect contrary data.

Chinn & Brewer (1993) listed six basic ways that knowledge shields can operate, ways that we can react to anomalous data that are inconsistent with our beliefs: (1) we can ignore the data; (2) we can reject the data by finding some flaw or weakness in the way the data were collected or analyzed or even speculate that the data reflected a random occurrence; (3) we can decide that the data don't really apply to the phenomenon of interest; (4) we can set the data aside for the present in the expectation that future developments will show why the anomaly is not really a problem; (5) we can find a way to interpret the data that allows us to preserve our beliefs; (6) we can make cosmetic changes to our beliefs and fool ourselves into thinking that we have taken the data into account. Chinn and Brewer found that college students displayed each of these tactics and so did established scientists. Chinn and Brewer also listed a seventh type of reaction—we can accept the data and change or discard our initial beliefs.

The sensemaking model presented by Klein et al. (2007) describes two pathways for reacting to data that question how we have been framing a situation. First, we can try to preserve the frame we have been using, employing the six tactics described by Chinn and Brewer, or, second, we can accept the anomaly (the seventh reaction listed by Chinn and Brewer) and reframe the situation. Both reactions have value. If we overreact to anomalies, even ones that are basically noise, we can keep reframing and reframing in

---

[†]The term "fixation error" is sometimes used for situations in which a person keeps focusing attention on one display and ignoring others or focusing on one problem and ignoring others (e.g., a pilot struggling to get the landing gear in place and ignoring indications of low fuel). This essay only considers fixation during the diagnosis of problems that have arisen, as in a physician trying to determine what is causing a patient's symptoms or a panel operator in a petrochemical plant trying to understand why the temperature inside a reactor has dropped so sharply.

response to every anomaly. We might never arrive at any interpretation, a condition referred to as "vagabonding." On the other hand, if we underreact to anomalies and preserve the frame too long, we display fixation.

Some might argue that fixation is not a type of error. Rather, it is just the extreme case of preserving our initial frame.

Trying to preserve our initial frame is a useful tendency. It isn't realistic to keep rethinking everything whenever we encounter some possible anomaly. Fixation may seem like an error because in hindsight, after we know the correct diagnosis, we can determine that we went too far in preserving our initial beliefs.

But in another sense, fixation does seem like an error because we aren't trying to test our diagnosis when we encounter contrary evidence that shouldn't be ignored or dismissed. It's hard to tell when our efforts to preserve our initial frame shade over into fixation, yet I think we can generally agree that there is a point at which the anomalies are so frequent and serious that a reasonable person should no longer dismiss them.

Consider the case of Joseph Stalin in World War II. Stalin had forged a nonaggression pact with the German leader Adolf Hitler in 1939. Stalin was confident that this treaty would hold, at least in the short term, even as he kept getting all kinds of information suggesting that Hitler was planning a surprise attack on the Soviet Union. Stalin used his knowledge shields to dismiss all this evidence. He ignored most of it and dismissed other reports as false rumors designed to stir up trouble with his German ally. He even ordered the execution of some informants because he suspected they were secret agents attempting to mislead him. He kept explaining away the evidence right up to the actual German assault in 1940, Operation Barbarossa. As a result, the Soviet defenses were caught unprepared. The Germans quickly occupied territory, seized weapons, killed and captured many soldiers, and almost took Moscow. Even at the time, looking at what was knowable, we can conclude that he was fixated on a false belief.

The concept of fixation describes how we can hold on to our initial diagnosis despite strong contrary evidence. We deploy a variety of tactics to shield ourselves from having to think about the implications of the contrary evidence.

Fixation and confirmation bias seem to be explaining the same thing. What's the difference?

Defective thinkers or effective thinkers?

The concept of confirmation bias asserts that we need to change the way we think, whereas the concept of fixation claims that there's nothing wrong with our thinking, just that we sometimes preserve our beliefs too stubbornly.

The concept of confirmation bias is part of a framework that views people as defective thinkers who are riddled with all sorts of biases that interfere with rational thinking. However, attempts to debias people to eliminate confirmation bias have repeatedly failed. We can't do it, and we shouldn't do it because we don't want to lose the benefits of the heuristic of seeking confirming evidence. When we label this heuristic tendency as a bias, we discourage people from speculating at the outset—and rapid speculation is valuable for guiding our exploration, especially when we face wicked problems, under ambiguous, complex, and changing conditions involving contextual influences. The concept of correcting a bias makes it seem that the purpose of thinking is to avoid making errors, rather than encouraging us to be curious and to explore and discover. These are the reasons to avoid the "defective thinker" formulation.

In contrast, the notion of fixation is part of a framework that views people as effective thinkers who are capable of insights. Our natural tendency is to quickly speculate, and we typically get it right. Sometimes we get it wrong, or sometimes the conditions change so that the initial diagnosis becomes overtaken by events, and then we usually reconceptualize smoothly (e.g., Fugelsang et al., 2004; Klein et al., 2005). But sometimes we don't reconceptualize smoothly or quickly enough—we get stuck and then we need help getting unstuck. The fixation approach isn't trying to change the way we think. Instead, the idea is to help us escape from fixation when it occurs.

So what can we do? Let's start with some common pieces of advice that don't seem to be very helpful.

Questionable advice

Some people suggest that we should keep an open mind as a way to prevent fixation on an initial hypothesis, but I don't like that advice very much. We are not built to keep an open mind. And an open mind is essentially a passive mind, not an inquiring or speculative mind.

Another common piece of advice is to identify all the assumptions we are making in order to identify any weak or false assumptions. But in the cases I have examined, the assumptions that get us in trouble are often those we make unconsciously, and we wouldn't be likely to list these up front.

Some researchers encourage decision-makers to inhibit intuitions and speculations until they have a chance to thoroughly analyze the data, but this tactic seems like a recipe for paralysis by analysis. The idea of thinking first then acting sounds safe but misses the types of learning and discoveries that arise through action.

Each of these kinds of advice has one thing in common—they are intended to reduce the chance of making an error. I don't believe that they would actually reduce errors—I am not aware of any evidence that they work. They would likely make things worse, not better, because they would reduce the chance of gaining insights.

And now a few other pieces of advice that I do find worthwhile, but with some reservations.

One valuable tactic is to use differential diagnosis, which involves setting out alternative diagnoses. This approach is well-known in the healthcare community. For many challenging cases, it seems only natural for a diagnostician to consider various possible causes. In complex and unfolding situations, however, decision-makers may be unable to imagine the true cause of the problem, and so they won't be able to include it in the initial logical comparison set.

Another good tactic is to use generic questions that we can pose to ourselves or to others.

1. Cohen et al. (1997) suggest a crystal ball method: "I am looking in an infallible crystal ball, and I see that the diagnosis you are considering is wrong. What else can it be?" Crosskerry (2003) has suggested the same kind of exercise.
2. You could ask, "What's the worst thing this could be?"
3. This question is basically a test for fixation: "What evidence would it take for you to abandon your diagnosis?" If we can't think of any such evidence, that's a good sign that we are gripped by fixation.
4. We can use a prospective hindsight tactic: "Imagine that you got the diagnosis wrong, what cue or hint had you been ignoring?"

These kinds of questions might help people once they realize they've been fixating. Maybe these questions should be posed by team members who suspect that the prime decision-makers are fixating.

Now let's back up to consider another approach for escaping fixation and reducing diagnosis errors. We want to speculate and explore hypotheses—we just don't want to get trapped.

Harnessing the power of curiosity

This approach tries to use curiosity to overcome our commitment to our initial diagnosis.

The core of the strategy is to become more curious about anomalies—the hints we can be noticing. That doesn't mean chasing every anomaly because that's not realistic. Instead, it means trying to at least notice contrary indicators, perhaps just for a few seconds, and wonder what is causing those indicators. We want the anomalies to at least get on our radar. For instance, in taking a medical history, a physician might go through the motions of filling in all the blocks, but an actively curious physician would be asking the next question, working off minor discrepancies to tease out additional clues.

The idea of harnessing curiosity fits in with research I have done on the nature of insight. I discovered three different paths that lead to insights. One of these is the correction path in which we recover from a fixation on flawed beliefs. I investigated 120 cases of insights and 27 of them involved the correction path. Then I wondered how these 27 decision-makers escaped from their fixation. In 18 of these 27 cases, the decision-maker noticed a hint, an event or comment, or some sort of clue. Instead of dismissing this hint, explaining it away like Chinn and Brewer described, these 18 individuals wondered about the hint and took it seriously. I believe that even more of the 27 cases revolved around examining the hint/anomaly—I only counted those 18 cases for which the records were sufficiently clear. I go into a more detailed analysis of this correction path in the part 6 essay, "Getting Unstuck."

The notion of harnessing curiosity is based on the success stories of people who managed to escape from fixation and make important discoveries.

Let's take this further. Once we become more curious about anomalies, we can try to keep track of how many anomalies we are explaining away. If our initial diagnosis is wrong, we should be getting more and more signals that contradict it. There's more and more to explain away, and that's another leverage point we can use. Mark Smith, the chief innovation officer at MedStar, explained to me that he uses a two-strikes rule in examining a patient. If he feels confident in a diagnosis, he may disregard an initial anomaly but if he notices a second anomaly, that's a wake-up call to step back and reexamine what's going on.

Yet another leverage point is to notice how much work we are doing to explain away all these anomalies. Cohen et al. (1997) coined the term "snap back" to describe how the sheer effort of explaining away so many contrary data points can induce us to lose faith in our initial diagnosis and seek another one.

I see the power of curiosity as an antidote to fixation. We want to shift the mindset of diagnosticians so that they wonder about anomalies instead of dismissing them.

Diagnostic errors are just one side of the coin. The other side is diagnostic successes. Diagnostic error is a serious problem and gets a lot of attention, whereas diagnostic success is often taken for granted. We need to consider both sides of this coin. Otherwise, we may take steps to reduce diagnostic errors that also cut our chances for diagnostic success, leaving us worse off. Framing the problem as one of fixation, encouraging us to do some re-conceptualizing, seems like a better approach than framing it as a bias, requiring us to change the way we think.

—*June 11, 2019*

3.8 The Substitution Trap

Some Surprising Examples of a Decision Bias

The Heuristics and Biases literature claims that the substitution bias occurs when we replace a difficult judgment task with an easier one. According to Kahneman and Frederick (2002), we don't even notice when our intuitive System 1 mode of thinking makes this shift, which underlies many biases and illusions. According to leaders in the Heuristics and Biases community, to reduce this bias, we need to energize our reflective and analytical System 2 mode of thinking; where feasible, we should rely on algorithms and artificial intelligence (AI) systems rather than on our heuristics and intuitions.

One example of the substitution bias is the bat-and-ball problem: "A bat and ball together cost $1.10. The bat costs $1.00 more than the ball. How much does the bat cost?" Our immediate impulse is that the bat costs $1.00. But our intuition has betrayed us. (The bat costs $1.05.)

I am not enthusiastic about judgment biases, but recently I noticed some clear examples of substitution bias.

However, the examples aren't about how ordinary people fall prey to substitution bias. Rather, the examples show how the *analytical community* falls into this substitution trap.

Example 1: The gamble metaphor for choices. Many academic decision researchers assume that decisions that are made in the face of uncertainty can be seen as gambles. Beach (2019) disagrees. Gamblers (e.g., roulette bettors) passively await the results of their choices, but the rest of us work hard to make our choices succeed. "If a gambler worked to win his bet, he or she would be cheating. If a business person did not do it, he or she would be fired" (pp. 102–103).

Therefore, the analytical decision researchers have replaced a difficult topic—how we make choices—with an easier and less interesting one for which they have analytical methods for conducting experiments: gambles in well-structured conditions. They are exhibiting the substitution bias.

Example 2: The computational metaphor for decision-making. Decision analysts have suggested structured methods for choosing between options, such as multiattribute utility analysis. These methods allow us to compute our preferences. However, there's no evidence that using these methods actually helps people.

The methods treat choices as consisting of attributes that can be predefined and contrasted, but the methods don't take context and expertise into account. The proponents take a very difficult issue—how people make decisions—and substitute a much easier one: How can people take a variety of features into account? An example would be cost-quality trade-offs, like pondering whether to pay for a sunroof on a new car. This easier task can be readily calculated, studied, and systematized.

Example 3: Detecting anomalies. In a part 5 essay, "Anomaly Detection," I will show that the analytical community treats anomalies as outliers and offers up various statistical methods and artificial intelligence (AI) approaches for highlighting these outliers. However, anomalies are not simply outliers. They are violations of our expectancies. We need expertise to generate expectancies within a context. The analytical community has substituted "statistical outliers" (which can be computed) for "cases of violated expectancies," which is a much messier issue.

Example 4: Using Bayesian statistics to identify situations. Bayesian statistics let us update our beliefs based on the evidence while also considering how likely the base rate of different outcomes are. Bayesian statistics let us make judgments about what is going on as we receive new information. However, our assessment of a situation is more than updating beliefs. My view is that we build stories about how things came about and how they are likely to transform and that we judge the plausibility of the transitions from one story-state to another using our mental models. (To be fair, Bayesian models can be used to represent stories, just as stories can be represented using language, semantic networks, and other structures.) From this perspective, using Bayesian statistics is a

The Substitution Trap

substitution for story-building and understanding other less formal ways people make plausibility judgments.

These examples show why I am claiming that the substitution bias is a real problem, not for individual decision-makers but for the analytical community. I see this community as ignoring, devaluing, and distorting cognitive phenomena and substituting formulations that are easier to calculate, the classical dodge of the substitution bias.

I am not claiming that the analytical researchers are making the substitutions intentionally. I think they are gripped by rationalist fever dreams, so the use of algorithms and calculative methods seems reasonable to them.

The prime takeaways from this essay are (a) to be alert for the substitution bias on the part of modelers and analysts and AI developers, (b) to scrutinize their work to see if they are distorting the cognitive phenomena they claim to be addressing, and (c) to use that scrutiny to gain a deeper understanding of these phenomena.

—*October 31, 2020*

3.9 Costly Mistakes?

The Problem with Error-Phobia

Last night on Monday Night Football (October 15, 2018), the Green Bay Packers beat the San Francisco 49ers with a field goal in the closing seconds, after the San Francisco quarterback C. J. Beathard threw a costly interception with 1 minute 13 seconds left in the game and the score tied 30–30.

At least, that's one of the big stories from this game. That's one of the headlines. That's a major issue in the post-game remarks by the San Francisco head coach—"Our quarterback has to learn from this." It was a tough loss. The head coach was glum and obviously disappointed by the way his quarterback had cost his team a victory.

And it is a truly stupid analysis.

Here is the situation: There is 1 minute 55 seconds to go in the game. The score is tied 30–30. San Francisco receives a kickoff and gets to its 47-yard line, 1st and 10. This is their chance to win. They just have to march downfield and get in range to kick a field goal.

Beathard completes a 7-yard pass. His next pass is incomplete. Now it is 3rd down and 3 yards to go on the Green Bay 46 yard line. There is 1 minute and 16 seconds left in the game.

That's when Beathard, the San Francisco quarterback, throws his "costly" interception. Green Bay had mounted a strong pass rush, threatening to sack Beathard. He could have thrown the ball away for another incompletion. But instead, he gambles and tries a long pass, 35 yards. That pass is intercepted by a Green Bay defender at the Green Bay 10 yard line with just over a minute left. Thereupon the Green Bay quarterback, Aaron Rodgers, drives his team into field goal range and Green Bay wins with seconds to spare.

But imagine that the San Francisco 3rd down pass was incomplete, as was likely. Imagine that Beathard plays it safe and throws the ball away. San Francisco would almost certainly have punted the ball. San Francisco would have hoped to pin Green Bay down around its own 10-yard line, right? And that's exactly what the interception accomplished. The interception was in no way a "costly" mistake. In fact, the Green Bay defender might have been better off dropping the ball, forcing San Francisco to punt.

Why am I making such a big deal about this?

I am frustrated by analyses like these because they jump on mistakes, any mistakes, costly or inconsequential, creating a mindset that the way to win is to not make mistakes. I see that attitude pervading other parts of our society. I described this mindset in my book on insights (Klein, 2013). The diagram shown in the next essay shows two ways to improve performance: reducing errors and increasing insights, and I believe that most organizations over-emphasize the reducing-errors portion.

The Monday Night Football game demonstrates this error-phobic mindset. The San Francisco quarterback, who had played extremely well all game, threw an interception, which is statistically counted as an error, and he gets castigated as the scapegoat, the player who cost his team the game, even though the interception had no consequence on the outcome.

This is error-phobia in action. This is error-phobia on display to infect leaders with a misguided approach to managing people.

—*October 16, 2018*

3.10 Playing to Win

Don't Let the Fears of Decision Biases and Errors Paralyze You

To be successful—and this is true of organizations as well as individuals—we need to do two things. We need to cut down on our mistakes. We also need to increase our insights. I have diagrammed these activities as two arrows (see figure 3.2).

The down arrow shows the reduction in mistakes. And we know several methods to cut down on errors. We can use procedures to list all the steps so that we won't forget any and so that we can monitor other people to make sure they're doing the task correctly. We can provide checklists. We can describe clear standards for accomplishing the entire task and standards for each step. We can call for critical thinking activities to identify assumptions, flag areas of uncertainty, and establish criteria for drawing logical inferences and conclusions.

Most organizations place their heaviest emphasis on the down arrow, reducing mistakes because managers can readily apply the methods that are already available. Besides, mistakes are visible, which makes it easier to manage them and also makes it easier to blame the managers if mistakes persist. Some organizations have adopted highly rigorous methods such as Six Sigma to improve quality and keep mistakes at a minimum.

Leading social science researchers have encouraged us to pursue the down arrow. They have described decision biases that are lurking everywhere unless we kick in our critical thinking to spot blunders.

No one can argue with the importance of reducing mistakes. But we can argue with the amount of energy and scrutiny that goes into the down arrow because when hunting down mistakes dominates an individual or

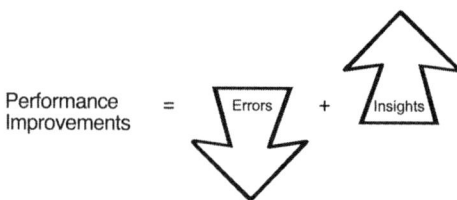

Figure 3.2
Two arrows to improve performance.

an organization, there is little room left for gaining insights. The effort to reduce mistakes can distract us, getting in the way of spotting new patterns and making new connections. It can make us passive, viewing our goal as avoiding errors; we come to believe that our job is to follow the procedures and steps carefully.

This perspective doesn't seem very satisfying. Not many of us would want to come home and explain to family and friends that it had been a great day at work because we hadn't made any mistakes. I think we would want something more, such as describing what we achieved, what obstacles we overcame, what discoveries we had made. And that's where the up arrow comes in.

The down arrow, the fixation on reducing mistakes, is a defensive strategy. It is playing not to lose.

The up arrow is playing to win.

The up arrow is about gaining insights, making discoveries, seizing opportunities, reaching for achievements and improvements and successes, and making things happen. The up arrow is about excitement.

Managers don't have the same tools for fostering the up arrow as the down arrow. They don't know how to increase insights. And besides, if workers fail to gain insights, no one will notice, whereas errors are public and invite blame. It is no wonder that organizations put their energy into the down arrow. It is no wonder that many individuals do the same, trying to adhere to rules and fearing the risks of innovation.

Both arrows are important. We can't tolerate high levels of error, but I don't think we want to define and evaluate ourselves by our skill at avoiding mistakes. Once I was invited to give a keynote talk at a healthcare conference. The group that invited me was intent on reducing erroneous medical diagnoses by cutting down on judgment and decision biases. I told them they were imbalanced. In addition to reducing erroneous diagnoses, they needed to foster diagnostic successes. If they only worried about mistaken diagnoses, they might adopt practices that cut down on the insights of the talented practitioners, leaving patients worse off.

And that reminds me of Winston Churchill during World War II, growing increasingly frustrated with his admirals who refused to take any action that might expose their ships to enemy attack. "Why have a navy if the ships will only venture into safe waters?" Churchill fumed. Individually, each captain and commander didn't want to take any chances that might get his ship sunk. But collectively, their timidity was losing initiative and jeopardizing the United Kingdom.

On the optimistic side, I have been having some productive conversations with corporate leaders who do appreciate the need to properly balance the arrows, the trade-offs of errors and insights. They are enthusiastic about trying to change the culture of their organizations so that they can indeed play to win.

—*March 18, 2015*

3.11 Stealth Decisions

A Dirty Secret about the Way We Make Decisions
___

Most of us like to believe we are rational. We try to make decisions based on realities, not fantasies. If we are analytical types, we may try to identify all the important goals and priorities and rank the competing options to see which comes out ahead. If we are intuitive types, we may rely on the patterns we have built up through experience. Either way, we are trying to make decisions that will accomplish our objectives. At least that's what we think.

Most of our decisions are so obvious, we don't give them much thought. One of the options stands out so clearly that we run with it. We don't even have the experience of deciding.

The cases that do capture our attention don't have an obvious way forward. We wrestle with the alternatives. However, many years ago, Marvin Minsky (*The Society of Mind*, 1988)—the artificial intelligence researcher—described a paradox that had been identified earlier. It was called Fredkin's paradox. Minsky explained that we don't need help with easy decisions, as between a wonderful option versus a terrible one. We only struggle when the options move closer together. The more the strengths and weaknesses of the options become balanced, the tougher the choice. And the toughest choices are when the strengths and weaknesses are perfectly aligned, and we have no basis for selecting one option over another. Those are the decisions that drive us crazy, muttering to ourselves on the street. Those are the decisions that chew up committee meeting time, week after week.

However, Minsky pointed out that if the strengths and weaknesses are perfectly in balance, then it doesn't matter which option we choose. We are suffering for nothing. We might as well flip a coin. Thus, we don't need analytical methods for the easy decisions because they're so obvious, and the analytical methods won't help for the difficult decisions because there is nothing to be gained. Decision researchers refer to a "flat maxima" to describe a zone where the options are essentially equivalent in value. I prefer to describe this situation as the Zone of Indifference because it doesn't matter what we choose (see figure 3.3).

The gentleman in this graphic is firmly within the Zone of Indifference. A choice that should take only 5–10 seconds has paralyzed him for too many minutes.

But that's not the dirty secret.

We do agonize over the tough choices. We are not happy with coin-flipping. And so, in my observation, in many cases, we go sideways! We stop trying to calculate which option will best achieve our stated goals. Instead, we look for constraints and consequences. We look for showstoppers that would rule out one of the options. These showstoppers don't have anything to do with our original goals, but they govern our decisions, and that's the dirty secret.

Figure 3.3
The Zone of Indifference.
Source: www.CartoonStock.com, licensed use.

Here's a trivial example. I was invited to give a talk at a military academy, and my sponsor and I were trying to select the best date to fit in with the schedule of topics being covered that semester. When we didn't get anywhere, we quickly shifted to an assessment of the possible dates to see which might create conflicts or problems. "Better not select that Friday," my sponsor said, "because it's right before a three-day weekend, everyone will be heading out of town in the early afternoon and it will take you forever to get to the airport." Getting me to the airport wasn't part of our original goal set. I wasn't interested in giving the talk in order to make a safe departure. Yet once the sponsor pointed out the issue, I vetoed that date.

What's happening here? We are supposed to be rationally making choices to accomplish important goals, and that's not happening. When we get stuck in the Zone of Indifference, we shift gears and look for consequences and constraints that could disqualify some of the options. We look for showstoppers. Sometimes we might look for collateral advantages, but these don't carry the same weight as showstoppers. We use our experience to rule out candidates so that we can break out of the Zone of Indifference.

—*January 22, 2015*

3.12 Reflections

We are swimming against the tide here, and this part is aimed at countering that current. The skeptical stance, as exemplified by the Heuristics and Biases (HB) movement, is extremely dominant, with its message of all the ways our thinking and judgments and decision-making are flawed.

Part 3 is not out to disprove the HB approach. Naturalistic Decision Making (NDM) is not a criticism of HB. However, the Judgment and Decision Making and the HB mindsets are so pervasive that it is going to be difficult for some readers to enter into a sources of power mindset, even fleetingly, to explore it.

The most important takeaway from part 3 is to appreciate a balance between flagging the flaws in thinking and appreciating the strengths. Without a balanced view, you run the risk of being captured by rationalist fever dreams, the belief that rational analysis is sufficient to handle complex and confusing conditions. Part 3 should have given you the building blocks for this more balanced perspective.

Putting the conventional judgment and decision researchers into perspective. Part 3 suggested some of the tendencies, or biases, that conventional decision researchers exhibit such as over-reacting to errors and heuristics, and distrusting experts. The Judgment and Decision/HB community puts a great deal of faith in rational analysis, and it may be that this bias for rational analysis is overdone. In some cases, analytical decision researchers claim they are studying everyday phenomena but instead substitute simpler paradigms that give a misleading impression. In this part, you have seen a few examples—using a gambling metaphor for choices, using a computational metaphor for decision-making, treating anomaly detection as spotting outliers, and using Bayesian statistics to identify situations.

Putting heuristics into perspective. Some of the common heuristics that we are cautioned against may be quite valuable cognitive tools—the use of small samples, the reliance on representative cases and available cases, the ability to work from anchors. We would be worse off without these heuristics.

Putting data analysis into perspective. You've seen why we might be careful about relying too heavily on data and you have read a few examples—a baseball pitcher whose recent outings went poorly, a rower who knew she was going to win a race despite being far behind, a helicopter crew who appeared to be lost in mountainous terrain.

Putting biases into perspective. You might have some skepticism about one of the most-cited biases, confirmation bias, and you might agree that there is less there than its proponents believe. The original data don't provide the support that is claimed. And the tendency to seek confirming information is not necessarily dysfunctional. Fortunately attempts to stamp out this so-called bias have been unsuccessful. It may be better to talk about fixation errors instead of confirmation bias. You should be able to appreciate why we might do well to avoid the concept of biases with all of its baggage about how people are defective thinkers and its unrealistic and unhelpful advice to keep an open mind, to identify questionable assumptions, and to inhibit speculations.*

Putting error-phobia into perspective. Reducing errors is a good thing, but going overboard about it is perhaps not such a good thing. Part 3 should have helped you question whether the analytical decision research community has adopted an unbalanced view of errors, and error tendencies, such as inconsistency, without considering the larger implications for increasing insights and speculations and accurate diagnoses. Part 3 should have helped you understand that not all mistakes are costly—by making people afraid of mistakes we may be compromising their efforts to win achievements. I have seen this error-phobia occur in different contexts—military

---

*We should be careful when using the term "bias" because a judgment bias is different from racial biases. I suspect some readers may be making this connection, especially given all of the effort to set up programs to overcome racial biases. The problem here is that the word "bias" is ambiguous. "Bias" can mean a prejudice, but the essay on confirmation bias used "bias" to mean a dysfunctional cognitive heuristic, with no consideration of prejudice, racial or otherwise.

exercises and hospital emergency department operations. Skilled decision-makers can become paralyzed when they don't have sufficient information to act and are afraid to speculate because they might be wrong. Figure 3.2, the two arrows for improving performance, portrays the balance that part 3 is advocating and shows what we may miss if we over-emphasize the reduction of errors.

Putting analytical decision-making into perspective. We would like to think that we make decisions by pursuing our most important goals, but part 3 has suggested something else: when faced with tough choices, we may rely on fairly inconsequential factors to break a deadlock.

Putting rationalist fever dreams into perspective. Part 3 may have led you to a viewpoint that our standards for decision-making that work well in context-free laboratory conditions might not be so appropriate for naturalistic settings. And that is one of the discoveries of NDM research. You may still be uncomfortable with that viewpoint, but hopefully, you can now entertain it more seriously.

But if we start to question rationalist fever dreams, how does that affect our confidence in information technologies and artificial intelligence systems that are predicated on these rationalist dreams? And if we start to give up our faith in rationalist fever dreams, what kinds of intelligent machines should we be designing?

4 Smarter Machines or Machines That Make Us Smarter?— Information Technology versus Expertise

Overview

The rationalist fever dream mentality is now finding expression in technology. That mentality is guiding the professionals who design the automation and artificial intelligence (AI) systems that are becoming more prominent in our lives.

I have the sense that many computer science developers adhere to the worrisome tendencies we captured in part 3: emphasizing errors and consistency over insights, achievements, and adaptability, discouraging the use of heuristics and intuitions, promoting reliance on procedures and analytical tools over judgment and experience.

In addition to being disinterested in the skills and expertise of the people using the systems they develop, the designers sometimes appear to be in a competition to formulate the most elegant programs and algorithms, and to bolster their reputation by their technological prowess. That's fine, I suppose, except that when you ignore the people who will be operating these systems or disregard their needs, you increase the potential for accidents and failures.

I recall one panel on which I served, for sponsors seeking to inject more AI into their workplaces. I kept reminding the other panelists about the importance of expertise and their reaction, again and again, was to agree that expertise mattered, and they planned to capture it algorithmically. Clearly, we were talking past each other, and I was getting frustrated until I realized that for these AI specialists, expertise consisted of nothing more than facts and rules, and of course, these could be captured by algorithms. The AI panelists were oblivious to the cognitive dimension. Possibly they were incapable of grasping it.

The panelists' complete confidence in the eventual triumph of AI in all settings stands in sharp contrast to the record so far. True, AI systems do marvelously well in stable environments. However, we don't live in stable environments, and AI systems can turn out to be extremely brittle when faced with ambiguity. For an explanation of why this is so, see Gigerenzer (2022).

What's to be done? My friend Ben Shneiderman once told me that instead of investing so heavily in building smarter machines, we should be investing in machines, technology, and strategies for making us smarter. That advice seems more important each day.

This part starts off with "Playing to Our Strengths" (4.1) an essay that Ben Shneiderman and I wrote to describe critical human abilities that should be recognized and supported by computer scientists building sophisticated systems: the ability to engage in frontier thinking (which I also describe as speculative thinking in other essays), the ability to make use of social relationships, and the acceptance of responsibility for actions taken.

The second essay (4.2) in this part, "Failure of Imagination," describes several examples of what can go wrong when system developers assume they know how to constrain the decisions of the operators and fail to anticipate situations in which those constraints can prove deadly.

Essay 4.3, "Derailing Yourself," presents a fatal accident, the 2015 derailing of an Amtrak passenger train, killing eight people and sending 185 to the hospital. The engineer didn't have any display showing that he was approaching a sharp curve. He thought he had passed that curve and increased the speed at just the wrong time. Amtrak's response is sadly predictable—it installed automatic braking systems as a safeguard. But Amtrak showed no interest in something as simple as providing the engineers with GPS location displays. The mentality here is to automate the problem away rather than help the operator do a better job.

The next essay (4.4), "Data versus Insights," examines the increasing popularity of Big Data and the use of AI to manage the enormous flood of data to be processed. I claim that organizations need to gain insights about situations, not to process more and more data. A preoccupation with Big Data may not be as helpful as the proponents advertise.

In essay 4.5, "The Second Singularity," I observe that while many articles and books on artificial intelligence have speculated about the singularity—the mythical point at which machine intelligence overtakes human expertise—we should perhaps be more worried about a singularity that is more plausible and closer at hand, resulting from the erosion of human expertise. Too many organizations want to invest in AI to replace the decision-making of their employees and are failing to invest in or safeguard that expertise.

At this point, part 4 changes course to look at approaches for designing machines that can make us smarter. It's not hard. Think about Wikipedia and Google search, as well as the GPS devices in our cell phones. All these technologies help us to make better judgments and decisions and to do better work. The more technologies like these that we have, the better off we'll be.

Essay 4.6, "The Invention of Hyperlinks," recounts a technology even simpler than Wikipedia, Google Search, or GPS systems. It is a technology that has become so ubiquitous that we all now take it for granted. The essay shows how Ben Shneiderman came up with the idea, almost by accident.

Essay 4.7, "Small Data," follows on from essay 4.4. As a complement to the huge data streams marking Big Data, we should be alert to ways for using minimal data and finding single indicators that dramatically shift our interpretation of events. In contrast to the rush to collect and process the huge data streams, let's see if there are ways to identify the smoking guns.

"Improv Chess," essay 4.8, argues that there are simple ways to rejigger games like chess and Go so that they aren't just about massive amounts of search. By tweaking the rules, we can make success depend on adaptability, improvisation, and expertise —areas where our speculative thinking capabilities come into play.

Essay 4.9, "AIQ: Artificial Intelligence Quotient," describes a set of tools to help people become more intelligent about the AI systems they operate. The field of Explainable AI (XAI) seeks to help system operators better understand how their AI systems are thinking, but many of the XAI techniques themselves involve AI. In contrast, none of the AIQ tools depends on AI, and most of them don't require any technology at all. They don't try to provide explanations to the users. Instead, the AIQ tools support self-explaining—helping the users take control of their own inquiries and discoveries. And that is the essence of making people smarter instead of building smarter systems.

4.1 Playing to Our Strengths

Supporting Frontier Thinking, Social Engagement, and Responsibility*

Captain Sullenberger (Sully) is rightfully celebrated for his amazing skill as an expert pilot. When bird strikes shut down both engines, he managed to land his airliner safely in the Hudson River. Sullenberger's remarkable performance was due to his long experience as a pilot, quick assessment of the possibilities, and skillful handling of the controls.

Every day expert nurses, firefighters, and parents also solve real problems that save lives and bring comfort to those they serve. Similarly, doctors, teachers, and plumbers use their experience to help others in meaningful ways. These experts act in difficult situations in which information may be incorrect and incomplete and in which existing guidance may be inadequate. Still, they press on by blending their experience in many situations with what they know about the current problem, recognizing familiar patterns, and identifying anomalies quickly enough to make decisions and take action. Experts also make mistakes, sometimes serious ones, but careful study of these mistakes can refine existing practices, improve training or checklists, and lead to better tools.

---

*Ben Shneiderman wrote this essay; I am the second author. This essay reflects a series of conversations Ben and I enjoyed over the years. Ben is a distinguished professor of computer science at the University of Maryland and a member of the US National Academy of Engineering. His most recent book is *Human-Centered AI* (2022). Contact him at ben@cs.umd.edu.

Experts are adept at using sophisticated tools, such as 3D fetal sonograms or air-traffic control systems, which increase their comprehension of what is happening and preserve their control. These tools can have high levels of automation, as long as the expert users can comprehend, predict, and control the actions of the tools. And for that to happen, designers need to keep in mind that their technologies and practices are aimed at supporting and strengthening skilled and expert users; otherwise, the automation they introduce runs the risk of interfering with expertise and actually degrading performance, as has happened in some aircraft and medical device designs.

Unfortunately, too many designers seem oblivious to the skills and needs of the experts who will be using their creations. Our purpose in this essay is to offer some guidelines for constructing tools and automated aids that improve expert decision-making rather than degrading it.

The expert programmers who created and then improved features of Google's Translate deserve recognition for their contributions. They clearly understood that "artificial intelligence is not about building a mind; it's about the improvement of tools to solve problems."

Although they were clear that they were building tools, many journalists mislabeled their work as another demonstration that humans could be replaced. From the 1947 stories of "giant electronic brains," these misleading reports about the role of technology have undermined the trust in human experts. Even the recent artificial intelligence (AI)-100 report from Stanford claimed, "The difference between an arithmetic calculator and a human brain is not one of kind, but of scale, speed, degree of autonomy, and generality." We disagree with this central statement. Human thinking is not calculation or reckoning. Human creativity is different from what neural networks and genetic algorithms produce. Even artificial intelligence experts reject the idea that their conference papers should be reviewed by machine learning programs. Ironically, these human experts who are devoted to creating "smart" and "intelligent" machines know that human experts are better at appreciating discoveries and innovations.

We believe that experts excel in at least three admirable human traits:

1. *Frontier thinking:* Humans can deal with frontiers of knowledge, where incomplete and incorrect information cause confusion and where goal-setting is a key skill. Even in these challenging environments, experts can formulate and solve problems to create something new. Human experts often make astonishing breakthroughs, opening fresh paths to

surprising research destinations. They do more than optimize performance or recognize statistical patterns—they create wholly new products and services, discern distinctive categories, and see new kinds of relationships. Skill at the frontiers of knowledge and the capacity to push past the frontier is what humans have always demonstrated. They produce unexpected patentable inventions, engage in debates to promote compelling causes, and form companies to deliver revolutionary products and services.

2. *Social engagement:* Humans are inherently social, a skill which they use to learn, build trust, help others, and ask for favors. Human discourse is different from asking Siri, Google, or Alexa for information. Human exchanges inform each participant, clarify issues, and build agreements. Human collaboration has been a key to its astonishing successes throughout the existence of our species, from the complex collaborations around hunting, foraging, and community building to the modern teams who run companies and develop Wikipedia. Human leadership to inspire participation requires a combination of skills that run large companies, transform cities, and shape national governments. This leadership can also be malicious, corrupt, and warlike, but that is the dark side of being human. The bright side of human expertise shows meaningful respect, seeks genuine compromise, and nurtures trust. Humans are very skilled at building and using common ground to permit efficient communication and then noticing when common ground has eroded and needs to be repaired.

3. *Responsibility for their actions:* Humans are responsible parties who deserve honors when they bring benefits and who should be accountable when their decisions lead to harm. Honest reporting and trusted investigation of errors promote improvements that provide greater protections. Exceptional performances, such as Sullenberger's, advance understanding, improve training, and push experts to perform at ever-higher levels of achievement. Responsibility clarifies product design since it encourages designers to give users control and provides investigators sufficient data to understand what happened. We accept responsibility, which permits others to trust us. We also engage in other trust-building activities: we try to be predictable; we warn others when our behavior may surprise them, we take unnecessary steps to assist others, and so forth.

As designers come to recognize these human traits, their designs will improve, leading to safer, more effective, and more successful technologies. The sooner journalists understand that excellence in technology design emerges when these human traits are supported rather than supplanted, the sooner their writings will celebrate the ways remarkable human skills can be enhanced by advanced systems.

We see a future in which the appreciation for human experts grows, even as designers create more powerful tools. The best of these tools will boost the performance of human experts using more of their creative capabilities. And for that to happen, the designers will need to find ways for letting all of us, not just the experts, comprehend, predict, and control the actions of our tools.

—*March 6, 2017*

4.2 Failure of Imagination

Sometimes Designers Can Be Too Clever

I have run across several examples of systems that were carefully designed to get a job done but didn't consider some of the environments and contexts in which the system would have to operate. I am not faulting the designers for not doing a careful analysis because you can't consider every possible context. However, I am faulting the designers for deciding they could cut corners to make things simpler—these were corners that shouldn't have been cut. As a result, the designers imposed constraints on the people operating the systems and distorted their understanding of what was going on.

The designers were so intent on building smart systems that they gave low priority for whether the systems would make their operators smarter—with unfortunate results.

The first example is the Air France 447 accident in 2009. The airplane took off from Rio de Janeiro in Brazil, headed to Paris, carrying 228 passengers and crew members. We will never be certain what went wrong, but here is the most plausible account I have found. (There are, of course, additional theories.) Three hours after it took off, ice crystals formed on the airspeed sensors, preventing the airplane from determining its speed. As a result, the autopilot turned off.

The airplane was an Airbus 330, using the latest available intelligent technology. The manufacturers had led aircrews to believe that it was impossible to stall the plane. The airplane was just too smart and would not allow pilots to engage in unsafe actions that might result in a stall. And that was true as long as the sensors were working.

However, with the autopilot disengaged, all bets were off. Now the airplane could enter into a stall. Unfortunately, the pilot flying probably did not know this (or had never been told it, or forgot it if he was told). So he continued to climb steeply, feeling a false sense of invulnerability. The plane was in fact climbing so steeply, and its airspeed was so reduced, that it was on a trajectory to stall.

At some point, the airspeed sensors seem to have unfrozen, even though the autopilot didn't come back on. Now the airplane did sense the airspeed and did identify the near-stall condition. As a result, a stall warning came on. This auditory warning confused the pilot flying who thought the airplane was unstallable. He continued climbing.

And then the stall warning went off!! Why did it go off? One possibility is that the airplane's speed was too slow. No one expected a jetliner to be flying so slowly. The only time the speed would be so slow would be when the plane was taxiing on the ground. You don't want stall warnings going off when the airplane is on the ground. One line of speculation is that the designers had imposed a minimum—if the speed was below this minimum, the stall warnings would be inhibited. And that's what may have happened to Air France 447. The stall warning ceased due to the slow speed. The pilot flying must have felt relieved that the stall warning went off and took this as a good sign instead of a very ominous sign.

Then a more experienced pilot realized the flight configuration was extremely dangerous. He seemed to have taken over the controls, and he put the airplane's nose down to increase the speed. As a result—the stall warnings came back on! This happened because the airspeed had increased over the minimum. Now the pilots were thoroughly befuddled. Putting the nose down (to escape the stall conditions) was getting them yelled at by the system, but continuing to climb was absurd. As they tried to sort out what was happening, the airplane did stall, and it dropped into the ocean. It was several years before the airplane was located and the flight data recorder could be recovered.

No one had imagined that a jetliner could be flying so slowly. As a result, the stall warning, intended to help the pilots avert danger, actually helped to kill them. And a system designed to be unstallable became a death trap.

The second example comes from the Doug Stanton (2009) book *Horse Soldiers*, about US Special Forces in Afghanistan shortly after the 9/11 attacks. The soldiers had to be flown into position from Uzbekistan to link up with Afghan tribal warriors fighting the Taliban. The helicopter pilots faced several problems in performing this mission. One was the terrain, the mountains steeply rising to 20,000 feet. The US pilots were used to flying at 3,000 feet—to them, 10,000 feet felt like a maximum but in Afghanistan, 10,000 feet was a low altitude for some of the hills/mountains they had to contend with. A second problem was that the flights had to be conducted at night, for purposes of security; the pilots actually preferred to fly blacked out (no lights on inside or outside the aircraft) rather than becoming a target for antiaircraft weapons. A third problem was the weather—sometimes they couldn't seem to punch through the bottom of the cloud layer, which was some sort of mass of sand and snow, hovering in mid-air. A fourth problem was that the thinness of the air at that altitude (which made helicopter operations difficult) resulted in hypoxia—oxygen debt. The helicopter had an onboard breathing system, with masks fed by oxygen bottles, but unfortunately, there was a break in that system. During the first flight, the lead pilot discovered the problem as he observed his co-pilot and others acting irrationally. So he shut off the air to everyone on board except himself. He managed to land safely (with everyone else semiconscious), but the complicated layout of the helicopter prevented the maintenance crew from fixing the leak, so it became part of the challenge.

For this essay, the most relevant challenge was flying nap-of-the-earth, to evade detection—sometimes 20 feet above the ground, moving at 160 mph, at an altitude that sometimes reached 12,000 feet. At night. Fortunately, the helicopter had a multimode radar (MMR) giving a lookahead capability that showed whether the aircraft could clear any rock outcroppings that might be in its path. The MMR showed the pilot if there was enough power, lift, and speed to make it over the next hill. Thank goodness for the MMR.

Except the MMR system was designed to shut down above 5,000 feet! The theory was that it would be clear sailing at altitudes higher than 5,000. So why keep it running, draining power? The designers had not been thinking of flying nap-of-the-earth in northern Afghanistan.

As the pilots passed over each ridge, the MMR would be turning on and off, with error messages about BAD DATA. To make matters worse, once the MMR turned off, it took a few minutes to reboot it. Talk about flying blind.

Thus, we have here a second example of a failure of imagination. Why keep the MMR system running above 5,000 feet? No reason, if you are flying out of an airbase in Georgia (the US state, not the country). Lots of reasons if you are crossing from Uzbekistan into northern Afghanistan at night.

A third example, much less dramatic, is the effort by display designers for weather forecasting systems to "smooth" the data and show trend lines instead of all the noise of different readings. Novice forecasters appreciate these smoothed displays that help them see the overall trends. However, experienced weather forecasters dislike the smoothing. They want to see all the noise, the turbulence, the unsettled conditions. That's where the weather is happening. The experienced forecasters know to keep an eye on the unsettled, noisy areas to pick up how weather systems are starting to form.

These three examples illustrate design decisions that must have seemed reasonable in meeting the official specifications and requirements, decisions that now seem regrettable. As stated previously, I don't advocate for trying to identify every type of contingency that might be faced. There are too many potential complications and contextual complexities.

Instead, I think we should be more cautious about reducing the capabilities of the decision-makers to adapt to unexpected and unimagined challenges. That means that we don't shut down warning signals for slow airspeeds—instead, we find another way to inhibit the annoying warning while the airplane is on the ground. It means that we don't shut down essential radar systems above some nominal "safe" altitude. It means we don't eliminate an important cue such as noisiness of data just because it makes the display look so messy. It means that we try to give the system operators, the decision-makers, more capabilities and clarity instead of foreclosing options. Making the job easier in normal operations can make it impossible under abnormal conditions.

—July 1, 2018

4.3 Derailing Yourself

Lessons from the Amtrak 188 Tragedy*

On May 12, 2015, Amtrak passenger train 188 derailed just north of Philadelphia at 9:21 p.m. A 98-ton locomotive and seven 50-ton cars went off the tracks at the Frankford Junction, one of the sharpest curves on Amtrak's Northeast Corridor. Of the 258 people on board, eight died and 185 were taken to hospitals. It was one of Amtrak's most serious train accidents.

The speed limit for the Frankford Junction curve was 50 mph. Amtrak 188 had reached a speed of 106 mph when it entered that curve (see figure 4.1).

How could this have happened? It makes no sense. This essay is an exercise in explanation to move the reader from an initial state of disbelief to an eventual realization that this could happen to any of us. To move you from a view that this was a bizarre event to a view that it was all too plausible.

Some people assume that the train engineer had become irrational—that he knew the curve was coming up and yet accelerated rather than slowing down.

According to the 2016 National Transportation and Safety Board (NTSB) report, that assumption is wrong. The 32-year-old engineer, Brandon Bostian, showed no trace of alcohol or drugs in his system when he was tested following the accident. He was not texting or using his cell phone. He was not deranged or suicidal.

The NTSB report concludes that Bostian had gotten confused about where he was: He thought he had already passed the Frankford Junction

---

*This essay is based on an article by Matthew Shaer (2016) and on the 2016 NTSB report.

Figure 4.1
Amtrak derailed.
Source: National Transportation Safety Board (2016).

curve and needed to accelerate to keep on schedule. That's why he opened up the throttle, only to make the horrifying discovery that he was just entering the curve.

And now I must add a story, a 4-part story, to describe how this loss of situation awareness occurred.

The first part of the story is that Bostian's attention was diverted because he had heard a radio report that another train, near the Frankford Junction, had been "rocked"—that someone on an overpass had dropped a rock on the locomotive, hitting the windscreen and sending glass into the face of the engineer. The engineer had issued a warning about dangerous activity in the area, something for Bostian to worry about. Bostian was also aware that a train crew might be on the tracks inspecting potential damage on the train that had been rocked, and so these crew members might be at risk when Amtrak 188 passed by.

The second part of the story is that Amtrak 188 had just passed a smaller right-hand curve, and there was a similar small right-hand curve after the Frankford Junction, so it was possible that Bostian, distracted by the rocking incident, confused that first curve with the second small right-hand curve right after the Frankford Junction curve. Bostian might well have believed he was past the Frankford Junction curve, had just come around that second curve, and was free to increase his speed to 110 mph.

But why would Bostian make that confusion—why couldn't he see where he was?

The third part of the story is that the accident occurred in the evening, at 9:21 p.m., so Bostian couldn't readily observe any landmarks.

But why didn't he just glance down at his display to see where he was on the track? And here we come to one of the most interesting parts of the story, the fourth part: *there wasn't any display.*

That's right: Amtrak doesn't provide its engineers with a display showing their current location and the upcoming stretch of track, and the Federal Railroad Administration does not require such displays. As automobile drivers, we have GPS devices showing roads and landmarks. You would think that with a train on an unmoving track, it would be child's play to design a GPS-based display. But Amtrak seems to have determined that such a display is not necessary because engineers have memorized the routes they are taking. True enough, except that it doesn't allow for engineers to become confused, to momentarily forget where they are.

I don't know the reasoning and analyses that went into the decision not to provide engineers with real-time displays of their current and upcoming situations, but I speculate that it involves the "job as envisioned" mindset—reviewing how one expects the job to be done and not getting sidetracked with additional considerations.

In contrast, many human performance professionals have trained themselves to try to take the cognitive perspective. They try to take the mindset of the "job as performed," rather than the job as it is officially envisioned. They try to imagine what can go wrong, how people can become distracted, and what resources they might need to recover and adapt. Some designers get stuck on the concept of how a device is supposed to work, whereas others immediately begin imagining how it might malfunction.

This "job as performed" mindset relies on experience to draw on previous kinds of breakdowns and use them as analogs. This mindset also gets activated when designers are oriented toward speculation as opposed to calculation. It's a mindset that might have gotten a location display installed in Amtrak 188 so that it didn't accelerate to 106 mph going into the Frankford Junction.

One of the primary recommendations emerging from this tragedy is that Amtrak recommended that automatic braking systems be installed in its locomotives to use automation as a safeguard against future incidents. The recommendation does make sense except that it illustrates the automation/technology mentality: building smarter systems rather than investing in ways to make the operators smarter. Installing automatic brakes but not location displays for the engineers. Reducing the scope of activity for the human operators and not bothering with technology to make the human operators more effective.

And now that we are done with the story, are you convinced that this was a plausible explanation and that if you had been controlling Amtrak 188 it might have happened to you? Think about the times you are driving home at night, on a familiar road, and get distracted by a news item on the radio or by another driver making a risky left-hand turn in front of you, and for an instant you wonder, "Where am I?" as you search for cues to reestablish your sense of location, cues to alleviate your momentary dislocation. You don't need to spend more hours memorizing your route. Instead, you need markers to help you reorient. And Brandon Bostian didn't have those markers.

—March 5, 2019

4.4 Data versus Insights

Big Data May Not Be the Ideal Way to Generate Insights

In the quest to learn more about consumers—their behaviors and decisions—an exciting development is the availability of massive amounts of data. These data sets come from mobile devices, cameras, microphones, wireless sensors, software logs, and many other sources. In addition, companies have the analytical tools for sorting through the data to spot trends and detect statistical relationships. The result has been a revolutionary opportunity to learn about consumer activities and preferences.

But every strategy has boundary conditions, even Big Data. Data analysis is not an end in itself. The point is to learn about consumers, and not to get the most out of the data. Various commentators have weighed in with opinions about the strengths and limitations of Big Data. I want to examine a single issue: the potential of Big Data for helping decision-makers gain insights.

I am not interested in small insights, such as details about consumer habits. My concern is about deep insights—significant shifts in decision-makers' beliefs, such as Netflix anticipating that customers were going to flock to mail-based DVDs and streaming video years before Blockbuster was ready to expand on its VCR-format, store-based business model. Organizations seeking deep insights may want to reflect on the strategies they are using to make discoveries.

The nature of deep insights

My research on the nature of insights (Klein, 2013) found that deep insights often require people to abandon some strongly held beliefs, either because of contradictory evidence or because people were trapped by flawed beliefs that prevented them from solving important problems. Our natural tendency when encountering evidence that doesn't match our mental models of how things work is to discount the evidence and explain it away. And most of the time that tendency makes sense because the evidence isn't accurate. However, there are times when the anomalous evidence needs to be considered, and by dismissing it, we remain fixated on our flawed beliefs, as I discussed in the part 3 essay, "Escaping from Fixation."

Consider the insight of Joe Wilson and his colleagues at Xerox. They were trying to make a business out of a xerography process for making copies, but their machine was very large and expensive, and they weren't able to sell it. Then a marketing representative commented that consumers at trial sites were getting addicted to Xerox copiers and had little idea of the number of copies they were making.

Xerox shifted its business model from making money from the machines by selling or leasing them, to a different model—making money from the copies. Even at a nickel a copy, Xerox could cash in because the average office was soon making 10,000 copies a month. To arrive at this insight, the Xerox executives had to abandon their original concept and take advantage of an unexpected observation from a marketing representative who stayed in touch with the clerks in the offices where he placed trial versions of the Xerox 914 copier.

Big Data isn't designed to capture deep insights

Can Big Data deliver deep insights such as this one? One reason for doubt is that the strategy of picking up trends and extrapolating them into the future assumes that the conditions won't change; when conditions do change, the past trends no longer predict the future.

Another reason for doubt is that the format for data analysis is usually designed for making reasonable assumptions about how things work, but deep insights emerge when we overthrow some of those assumptions. The way we design databases cannot accommodate deep insights that will render those databases obsolete. The way data are analyzed and coded reflects the current beliefs and assumptions of the researchers based on what has happened in the past.

One example that comes to mind is that prior to the 9/11 attacks, US security organizations were not coding for people who were taking flying lessons and not wanting to learn how to land. Therefore, the analysis and coding will be insensitive to subtle anomalies if the anomalies aren't being coded. That's not to say that the anomalies weren't noticed. An FBI agent in Phoenix did pick up on the strange pattern and tried, unsuccessfully, to alert his supervisors. But it seems unlikely that an intelligent search system would have noticed the anomaly, any more than it would pick up the significance of a Xerox marketing representative's comment that office managers don't appreciate how many copies they are making.

Without the intelligence to notice the importance of anomalies, databases and coding methods cannot evolve to capture deep insights. Data analyses are usually designed to increase speed and power—the more data crunched per second, the better—not to uncover deep insights.

Perhaps Big Data approaches will be able to crunch their way to deep insights using exhaustive computational power. However, this process is likely to produce lots of false alarms. True insights aren't accompanied by lots of useless and irrelevant conclusions. Decision-makers don't have to wade through tons of garbage in the hope of finding a hidden gem. Big Data may eventually gain the necessary intelligence to avoid all the false alarms, but it isn't clear how many years that is going to take. Companies need deep insights now.

Cognitive analyses and deep insights

There aren't any methods for consistently generating deep insights. However, we might be able to increase the odds by the approach we take. To understand how consumers think about products and make decisions about purchases, we can probe them more carefully using methods such as cognitive analysis.

But even more important than the method is the stance we take, seizing on hesitations and equivocations (e.g., "it depends") and inarticulateness ("I can't put it in words," and "it was just a feeling I had"). Rather than being discouraged by these kinds of deflections, we can take them as challenges and as opportunities to make discoveries that have resisted description. We can push past the words people use to examine the things that confuse consumers, dilemmas they face, flaws in their own mental models. We won't always be successful, but if we give up at the slightest sign of resistance, we will never succeed.

Here is an example from a project I helped to lead. The sponsor, Procter & Gamble (P&G), wanted to gain deep insights into the way homemakers thought about laundry stain removers. My small research team visited homes to conduct cognitive interviews. In one of the first interviews I led on this project, I asked the homemaker what her mental model was regarding a stain removal product she used. She gave me a quizzical look, turned to my assistants, and said, "Is he for real?" Not a happy moment, except for my assistants who laughed all the way back to our office. I vowed never to use the jargon "mental model" in interviews again, but even with more neutral language, we found that none of the homemakers could offer a coherent account of how the product was working.

So we switched gears. We had a graphic artist draw a few alternative cartoon representations of different ways the product might be getting rid of stains (we got hints of these from a few of the homemakers; see figure 4.2). Then we presented the cartoons and asked which was closest to what the homemaker thought was actually happening. Now the dynamic changed. The homemakers had no trouble identifying the cartoon that came closest, usually adding some additional details that they thought the cartoon got wrong. In that way, we captured their mental models.

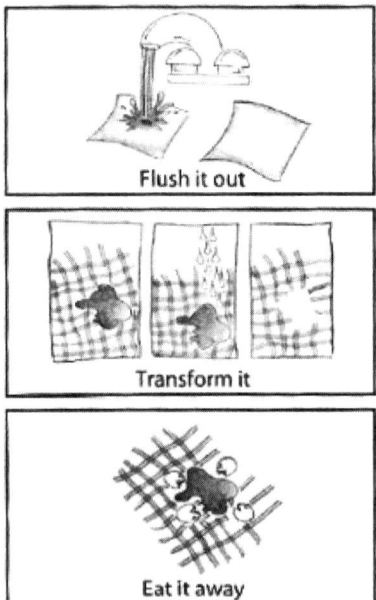

Figure 4.2
Stain removal graphics.

Because mental models are a type of tacit knowledge, it is not surprising that the homemakers couldn't articulate their beliefs. Instead of giving up, we just needed to find the right route into their thinking. Our sponsors gained an important understanding of how to present a clearer and more effective message to their customers about how the product worked and to visualize why the higher quality made a difference.

A second example, also with laundry products, further illustrates the use of qualitative methods to gain deep insights. The sponsor, P&G again, wanted to market a low-cost detergent to homemakers who were very motivated to minimize supermarket expenditures. After three years of research using surveys and focus groups, the research team had collected large amounts of data. The team believed it understood the decision strategy of these "economical housewives": purchase the least expensive detergents. Nevertheless, they gave my colleagues and me a chance to do our own investigation. We again used cognitive interviews. This time, we relied on photographs of the laundry aisle of a supermarket. The different brands of detergent were clearly visible but not the price details at the bottom of the shelves. During the interview, we pretended to walk the homemakers down the imaginary aisle to see which products the homemakers considered and when they asked for price information.

We learned that these economical housewives did not just buy the cheapest product because if the clothes came out feeling scratchy, their families were unhappy. Their strategy was to pre-identify 3–4 detergents that were acceptable to their families—their detergent set. Then the housewives clipped coupons and inspected in-store specials on their shopping day. They bought whichever of their detergent set was the cheapest that day.

If their detergent set was smaller than 3, the odds of getting a bargain were too small. If the detergent set was larger than 4, the computational work was too great. These economical housewives were just as picky as the others. What set them apart was their strategy for buying an acceptable product at an affordable price. The P&G research team had no idea that the economical housewives were using such a sophisticated strategy. Our discovery changed their approach to marketing their new product and resulted in a highly successful product roll-out.

Both projects generated deep insights that had resisted other methods. A Big Data approach was unlikely to have obtained insights about mental models and purchasing decision strategy.

Qualitative, small-scale cognitive interviewing methods have limitations, just as a Big Data strategy has limits. Each is suited for certain types of research questions but not others. A Big Data strategy is invaluable for capturing all kinds of subtle trends revealed in a variety of different kinds of data; it is not well-suited for capturing deep insights that require corporate decision-makers and data analysts to jettison core beliefs. We don't know when Big Data approaches fail to unearth deep insights because we can never determine what discoveries haven't been made. Nevertheless, if the goal is to attain deep insights, then we may not want to rely exclusively on Big Data.

—*September 13, 2014*

4.5 The Second Singularity

Human Expertise and the Rise of AI

The popular media loves stories about "the singularity"—the point at which computers get smarter than people, achieve consciousness, and take over.

The use of the term "singularity" in this way was coined by Vernor Vinge (1993), who asserted that "within 30 years, we will have the technological means to create superhuman intelligence. Shortly after, the human era will be ended." This idea was popularized by Ray Kurzweil in his 2005 book *The Singularity Is Near*. Kurzweil explained how computers, especially using artificial intelligence (AI), combined with discoveries in genetics, nanotechnology, and robotics, will create a condition in which machine intelligence overtakes human intelligence. Kurzweil was not writing science fiction. He described the singularity as not only a real possibility but an inevitable one.

Many researchers and philosophers have criticized Kurzweil and argued that the singularity is not near. They don't think the singularity requires our urgent attention. I am in this skeptical camp. I don't deny the progress in machine intelligence, but I see evidence that the current rage for AI is oversold. Projects such as IBM's Watson that were going to sweep the field are now getting downplayed. Funders are tired of all the overpromising. Leading AI researchers are writing opinion pieces about how the field of deep learning is hitting a wall.

We have a better sense of the strengths and the limitations of AI than we did when Kurzweil's book appeared almost 15 years ago. The notion of a singularity seems a bit less frightening these days.

What does worry me is a "second singularity."

What I am calling "the second singularity" is not just about computers getting more powerful, which they are, but the simultaneous reduction in expertise that we are seeing in many quarters. As organizations outsource decision-making authority to machines, workers will have fewer opportunities to get smarter, which just encourages more outsourcing.

I fear that the second singularity is actually much closer to us in time than Kurzweil's original notion of a singularity. I am calling it a second singularity in deference to Kurzweil's analysis, rather than for chronological reasons.

Now, the reduction of expertise isn't happening across the board. There is also a growing set of skills for which more people become experts, such as programmers, network administrators, and cybersecurity watchdogs. The number of physicians in the United States has risen from 813,000 in 2000 to 1,085,000 in 2015.

The Congressional Research Service reports that scientists and engineers grew from 6,187,760 in 2012 to 6,934,800 in 2016, and the American Bar Association reports that the number of practicing lawyers has increased by 15 percent over the past ten years, even as online legal services have grown.

Therefore, in a number of ways, expertise is increasing—different types of expertise are needed these days, in domains that didn't exist 50 years ago.

Nevertheless, there are several areas in which valuable expertise is getting lost, such as many manufacturing specialties and in healthcare, and in aviation, both for flying and for maintenance. In many petrochemical plants, managers are looking for ways to automate operations. Similarly, directors of child protective services agencies are exploring tactics to automate the work of intake specialists and caseworkers.

Expertise is not a permanent quality. It can erode within any organization or sector within a few generations, where "generations" is measured in 5- to 10-year chunks. Worker turnover, reduced recruitment standards, cuts in training budgets, and dangerous retreats to so-called just-in-time training all can take a toll. And then you have a ratcheting effect as the reduced expertise just leads to greater reliance on mechanical decision-making, which discourages any more investment in promoting workers' intuitive capabilities. It can quickly go downhill from there.

We may only discover the value of expertise after it has been lost.

For practical reasons, organizations want to reduce their reliance on experts. It takes time and funding to develop experts, so it is cheaper to rely on algorithms or machines.

Or at least it seems cheaper if you don't factor in all the effort of building the algorithms or designing the AI system and don't worry about the effort of modifying these to meet changing conditions. And if you don't worry about brittle systems that break down when stressed by unexpected conditions sensor failures or things like that. (Think of the Boeing 737 MAX crashes.) In the past, we have relied on experienced operators to detect when the machines aren't appropriately aligned and to intervene. We lose that safeguard if we do away with the experienced operators. And if we don't worry about malicious actors eager to exploit vulnerabilities in the AI systems. Even if the algorithms and AI systems don't quite perform as well as humans, at least they are more reliable (as long as conditions are stable), and in our Lean Six Sigma culture, reliability is highly prized.

Making matters worse is an attempt to de-value expertise, which I will elaborate upon in more detail in the part 5 essay "The War on Expertise." My colleagues Ben Shneiderman and Robert Hoffman helped me with this essay, and together we described how this war on expertise (Klein et al., 2017) is being waged by five different communities that are all claiming that expertise is overstated, or unreliable, or even nonexistent. The message from these communities is that we can't rely on experts and that we should rely on other means for making decisions—algorithms or checklists or AI or codified best practices.

My colleagues and I explained the fallacies that are driving this war on expertise. We showed how none of the arguments stand up to scrutiny. The daily miracles of surgeons, teachers, pilots, control room specialists, and even programmers should serve as a sufficient rebuttal to this war on expertise.

Nevertheless, the take-home message from these five communities is just what corporations and other large organizations want to hear—it provides them with an excuse to replace human expertise with machine expertise.

Therefore, in selected domains, we are seeing organizations actively reducing their stock of expertise in favor of automated or checklisted decision-making. That's the second singularity. Once the second singularity is approached, it will be very difficult to go back. The expertise may be permanently lost. The tacit knowledge, the perceptual skills, the mental models, may be gone forever.

Figure 4.3 shows the two singularities. The top curve, (a) shows a normal rate of increase of human expertise. Curve (b) shows the reduction in expertise that we should be worried about. And curve (c) shows the rise in machine intelligence. Kurzweil's singularity is the intersection of curves

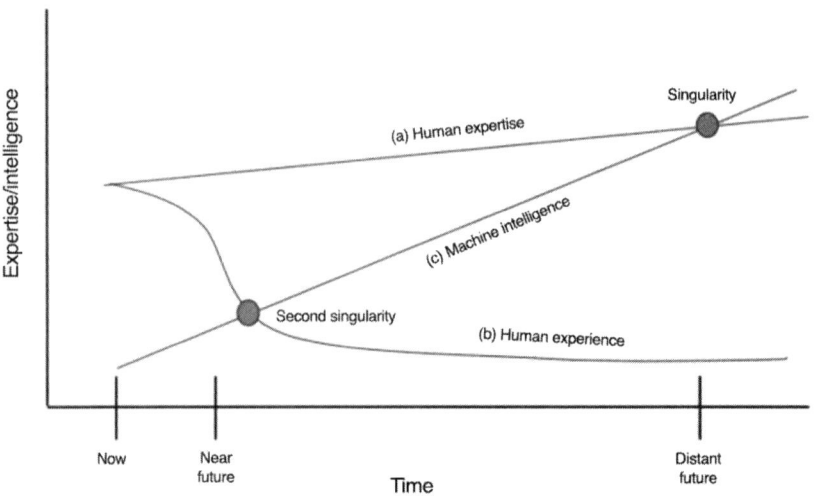

Figure 4.3
The second singularity.

(a) and (c) in the distant future, reflecting the faster gains in machine intelligence than human expertise. But in areas where human expertise is allowed to wither away, we see the second singularity not much past the near future. That's where curves (b) and (c) intersect. In some cases, the second singularity has already occurred.

I am not worried about domains in which it does make sense to build machines that can reliably conduct some of the tasks that people currently perform. If I contemplate a future in which my self-driving car can reliably parallel park itself without my intervention and my parallel parking skills erode, I'm for it. In fact, we seem to be already there for a growing number of automobile models. Therefore, we shouldn't worry about preserving expertise merely out of nostalgia. No one except a few archaeologists knows how to chip rocks to make flint knives anymore, and our society is none the worse.

What we should worry about is the set of domains where the expertise being eroded is valuable and essential. We should worry about domains in which surprising events can occur, domains in which the machine will be brittle and where skilled operators will be necessary to align the machine's model of the world with the actual world (see Woods & Sarter, 2000). We should worry about domains that are trading long-term security for short-term convenience and economics. I think for these domains, for these organizations, the second singularity is already too close and getting closer.

What can we do?

First, we can try to raise awareness of the second singularity and the risks it poses.

Second, we can try to promote a greater appreciation for expertise and the strengths it provides.

Third, we can advocate for governments and corporations to reduce their support for building smarter machines and instead to support ways to build machines that make us smarter.

Fourth, we can encourage a practical science of expertise, out of the laboratory and into the workplace. This activity would treat expertise as an essential and fragile commodity and would construct tactics to strengthen it.

The second singularity is not inevitable. It would be the product of our own making. We don't have to let it happen.

—*December 3, 2019*

4.6 The Invention of Hyperlinks

We Take Hyperlinks for Granted, so Let's Imagine That They Were Never Invented

It's the early 1980s, primitive days in the development of computers. Ben Shneiderman, a computer scientist at the University of Maryland, is hard at work with graduate student Dan Ostroff preparing a videodisk exhibit for a museum. He has set up a computer screen with a menu of numbered choices a user can make to view videodisk photos on a television screen.

The computer screen shows the photo captions and then lists the numbered choices to allow exploration in this virtual tour. This capability is all very new and exciting. The users don't have to go through all the material in order, like reading a story. Instead, the users can identify what photos they want to inspect next and jump there by simply typing the menu item number. Such wonderful freedom.

Shneiderman highlights a photo that interests him, types the number into the text box, and hits "enter" to view that photo and read the caption. As Shneiderman plays around with the menu, he gets frustrated by the effort of shifting his attention from the caption to the numbered menu items and then to the keyboard to enter the numbers.

Then it hits him: "The caption has all the information I need—why not just click on the text in the caption to display the next photo? I don't have to read the numbered items in the menu. I don't have to enter the numbers on the keyboard anymore."

He has invented the hyperlink.

At first, he calls his discovery an "embedded menu," but that term is quickly replaced by "hyperlink." Tim Berners-Lee cited Shneiderman's hyperlink work in his spring 1989 manifesto for what would become the World Wide Web.

We now take hyperlinks for granted, so let's imagine that Shneiderman never invented them, and no one else did. We are going to subtract hyperlinks from our user experience.

Think about how you would navigate around your computer or your smartphone. How would you take advantage of touch screens? How would you perform drag and drop operations? You'd be working through menus. Even if we toss Siri into the mix, imagine telling Siri how to sort through your photographs or select a size and color of a sweatshirt to order.

Hyperlinks are so natural that they've become invisible unless we make a special effort like this as a way to appreciate them. Hyperlinks were one application of Shneiderman's theory of direct manipulation, which also led to the tiny touch-screen keyboards on mobile devices, tagging family photos, gestural interaction, and other visual interfaces. All these discoveries earned Shneiderman election to the National Academy of Engineering. Shneiderman and his community not only conjured up these ideas, but they also wrote the guidelines and specifications so that these capabilities operate on all the devices we use, whether powered by Apple, Microsoft, or any other vendors. The guidelines have become international standards.

These features are invisible and natural. They are so natural that a 3-year-old can navigate our devices. Even a 3-year-old who has never previously had a chance to play with a smartphone. Next time you have the chance, take a few pictures of a 3-year-old (with their parents' permission, of course), and show the child the results. Hand the phone to the child, who should have little trouble scrolling through the photographs, swiping forward and backward. And if you close the file and turn your back, don't be surprised if the 3-year-old sneaks over and opens the file back up. And then starts opening other apps. Or navigates hierarchies, getting at files of family members or recent trips. If you're not careful, the 3-year-old will wander over to your laptop and try to click on words and images, perhaps hoping to get to music or videos.

In addition to hypertext and direct manipulation, human-computer interaction researchers have brought us several other innovations, such as 1-click faceted menus (a staple of e-commerce), bulletin boards that evolved into blogs and wikis, search interfaces, and so forth.

The Invention of Hyperlinks 129

When we consider our smartphones and laptops, it's natural to think about the technologies crammed into these devices. We may also think about the screen designs that make it possible to get what we want. Most people ignore the invisible part—all the work that's gone into evolving and standardizing the user experience that is now second nature to us.

Hyperlinks don't have embedded artificial intelligence—they are a very good example of how to design machines in a way that makes us smarter.

(You can read more about the early history of hyperlinks: http://www.cs.umd.edu/hcil/hyperties and about direct manipulation: https://en.wikipedia.org/wiki/Direct_manipulation_interface by following these two URL links—but you already knew that.)

—*January 4, 2018*

4.7 Small Data

Let's Reverse Our Strategy for Data Collection

Currently, the Big Data bandwagon continues to pick up momentum, as described in essay 4.4. The Big Data approach is exciting, as it lets us take massive amounts of information into account. The Big Data approach is also unsettling as we face our insignificance and admit that the algorithms and smart machines know so much more than we ever can.

The earlier essay described some reasons to be uneasy about Big Data, the way the Big Data analytics will follow existing trends but miss subtle yet important changes in the situation that render these trends obsolete. In addition, there is the issue of missing data. People sometimes notice that something did NOT happen, and the absence of an event helps us make sense of a situation. Big Data typically covers events that did happen and ignores events that did not occur, even though these nonoccurrences can be significant.

This essay, however, is not about limitations in Big Data.

Instead, I want to suggest that we move in the opposite direction: trying to collect as little data as possible, ideally just a single data point—but a data point that swings a decision. Rather than getting drowned in data overload, there are times when the right observation will put ambiguous cues into focus.

Here are some examples.

1. (This example comes from Trevor Hadley, a former US government analyst.) In 2015, the CIA was trying to decide whether Russia and China were going to hold joint naval exercises in the Mediterranean Sea. There

were no official statements. The trends were unclear; the evidence was inconclusive. Then an outside analyst wondered what it would take to re-supply a Chinese flotilla and began hunting through online purchase orders from ship chandlers in Cyprus. He found new orders, huge orders, for rice and noodles where none had existed previously. Just to be safe, he also investigated the local coast guard notices to mariners and uncovered corroborating evidence. But it was the rice and noodles that did the trick. Case closed.

2. (This example also comes from Trevor Hadley.) In 2011, the US intelligence community wanted to know if the French intended to intervene in the civil war in Libya. The French denied that they were even considering such an intervention, but the intelligence community had learned not to take such denials too seriously. There were reasons to expect the French to intervene. Attempts to make a forecast failed. A prediction market wasn't helpful.

   Then an intelligence analyst spotted an obscure statement in a French civil service directive, a memorandum proposing modifications to life insurance regulations for members of the French military. The memo listed countries where the French military was currently active—including Libya! The memo was pulled from the website in a few days and replaced with a version that omitted Libya, but it was too late. The US analysts had the information they needed. (Several months later, the presence of French forces fighting in Libya was confirmed.) Case closed.

3. The US government wanted to forecast how the United Kingdom would vote on Brexit. (So did many, many other countries.) The analysts poured over the polls, searching for some information that would tip the balance, but the signs just were not sufficiently clear. Then one observer noted that the European Union (EU) standards would require British housewives to use a different method for making tea. The current teapots for boiling the water were simply too energy inefficient, unnecessarily raising the carbon footprint. The EU required a more efficient device for boiling the water, but that would take five times as long! What effect was that going to have on inviting a neighbor over for a quick cuppa? Not entirely convincing evidence but certainly influential as a tipping point. Case closed.

4. In 1990, the US intelligence community was trying to forecast whether Saddam Hussein actually intended to invade Kuwait. Some felt that he was getting ready to attack. Others doubted that he would be so

foolhardy. They saw his movement of 30,000 troops on the Iraq/Kuwait border as a bullying tactic intended to intimidate Kuwait into making concessions. The usual types of evidence didn't result in any conclusive judgment. The Egyptians believed that there would be a peaceful resolution of the complaints Saddam Hussein leveled against Kuwait. So did the US ambassador to Iraq. And so did the Kuwaitis—even after Iraq had placed all those troops on its border, Therefore, Kuwait didn't mobilize its 18,000-soldier army and allowed many to go on leave.

What was Saddam Hussein going to do? One US intelligence analyst, working in the Department of Energy, noted that the Iraqi military had commandeered over 10,000 civilian trucks. The removal of all of these trucks was bound to have crippling effects on the Iraqi economy, disrupting all kinds of commercial activities. And this truck commandeering had been kept secret—it had not been publicly announced. It could not intimidate the Kuwaitis because they had no idea that it had been done. Why would Saddam Hussein do such a thing unless he suddenly decided he needed the trucks for a military action? Case closed.

5. The Toyota runaway acceleration problem. This problem caused Toyotas to accelerate uncontrollably, despite the driver's frantic efforts to press on the brake and slow the car down. The case received national attention. Some thought the problem stemmed from thick floor mats that trapped the accelerator pedal, but the primary malfunction seemed to be a glitch in the software. Toyotas contain more than a hundred million lines of code, so some software bugs seem inevitable. Hundreds of cases of runaway acceleration were called in. Toyota was forced to pay billions of dollars in fines and settlements.

However, the human factors community had a different diagnosis: the drivers were mistakenly pressing the accelerator pedal thinking it was the brake pedal. When the car speeded up rather than slowing down, the drivers perceived that the brakes had failed and that the acceleration was unintended and uncontrollable. The drivers naturally pressed the pedal harder and harder, believing it was the brake, only to see the acceleration get worse.

There is no easy way to prove this explanation, with lots of back-and-forth debates about the data. But it turns out that there are two killer arguments. One is that by examining the black boxes in the automobiles, investigators found that the brake pedal had not been depressed in the cases of runaway acceleration. The second killer argument comes from a Malcolm Gladwell podcast in season one of his *Revisionist History* series. Gladwell arranged for the magazine *Car & Driver* to put a Toyota Camry through its paces on a test track. The trained drivers mashed the accelerator pedal all the way down to the floor and then, with the accelerator pedal still mashed to the floor, hit the brakes. The car stopped. Trial after trial, the car stopped. No problem, no screeching, no smoke. The brakes easily overpowered the accelerator. No need to review the statistics. No need to review the hundreds of millions of lines of code. Case closed.

These examples suggest that less is more. That the quality of information matters more than the quantity.

The term "Small Data" is used in several different ways these days. There is even a marketing research book by Martin Lindstrom (2016), *Small Data: The Tiny Clues That Uncover Huge Trends*. And a Wikipedia entry. Here are a few attributes that I have identified regarding Small Data.

First, most of the references contrast Small Data to Big Data by asserting that Small Data is about a personal connection to a limited amount of information, whereas Big Data is about the need for smart machines to sort out the ever-expanding volume of available signals.

Second, the personal connection fostered by Small Data depends on engaging a person's expertise and experience.

Third, Big Data is primarily about correlations, whereas Small Data is about causal relationships.

Fourth, the Small Data approach is intended to foster insights (see Klein, 2013) and to transform mindsets. Bonde (2013) makes this point explicitly, that Small Data is intended to help us gain insights that we can put into practice.

Fifth, just about everyone agrees that Big Data and Small Data are not mutually exclusive or in competition. We can use both approaches.

Sixth, there is a divergence about how to search for meaningful items of Small Data. Some suggest that we should start with Big Data and then reduce the output, creating logs and other artifacts. I am not enthusiastic about that strategy. Instead, I think the power of Small Data comes when we use our mental models to notice or find the critical pieces of information, the smoking guns. The five examples in this essay all illustrate the skillful discovery of critical data, rather than condensing the output of a Big Data exercise.

Seventh, there are times when we can support the decision-makers by selecting a few representative cases from a much larger population and then give details about these cases. For example, if a politician is pondering how an increase in the price of gasoline will affect low-income people, it might be useful to define three specific individuals, say an elderly man on a fixed income who uses public transportation, a single mother shuttling between two or three jobs, and a retiree volunteering with a church group to drive congregants to various social, medical, and welfare-related events.

Eighth, it takes expertise to notice the critical data points once we come across them. It takes reasonably sophisticated mental models to appreciate how the data point can be put into action—to see what it affords us.

One risk of the Small Data approach is that it can be misused to cherry-pick examples and anecdotes that convey a misleading impression. Therefore, the Small Data approach should be used in the context of existing evidence. The Small Data approach does not eliminate the analysts' obligation to survey the relevant variables. I wrote "case closed" at the end of each of the five examples but in actuality, the investigators appropriately sought additional data to confirm or to disconfirm their speculations. The Small Data approach, however, can curtail the tendency toward accumulating more and more data merely to satisfy compulsive needs for completeness. The Small Data approach values the meaningfulness of data over its accumulation.

The examples in this essay suggest that we should reshape our efforts to gather information. Instead of vacuuming up every available tidbit, we might do well to direct our information gathering toward sensemaking and discovery. We might search for truly diagnostic cues, for anomalies, and for missing data—expected events that didn't happen. We can be on the lookout for "differences that make a difference."

—*July 22, 2018*

4.8 Improv Chess

A Way to Promote Speculative Thinking

"Improv Chess" is an idea for game tournaments that would encourage participants to rely on speculative thinking. Instead of relying on memorized sequences or carefully worked out weights and preanalyses, this format requires you to stretch your knowledge and your ideas and to discover implications and affordances.

The way it works at a chess tournament (or you could substitute Go, or backgammon, or checkers, or any other type of game) is that you show up ready to play chess but with one small variation.

The tournament organizers meet in advance and select a tweak. They identify a small change in the rules, but they don't announce that change until the tournament is about to start.

What kind of change? It could be that pawns no longer can start by jumping two spaces—they can only jump one space. Or extra rooks would replace the knights. Or the king disappears, leaving an empty square, and the queen is now even more central—you win by capturing the opponent's queen. Or there is a square in the middle, say D4, that no piece is allowed to occupy.

That's it. A last-minute rule change. And suddenly, the millions of games that the machine learning systems play against themselves become irrelevant. What matters is an immediate appreciation of the limitations, opportunities, and new strategies. The format favors adaptation and discovery over the compilation of prior cases.

Actually, Bobby Fischer developed his own innovative chess game, Fischer Random Chess, which achieves pretty much the same outcome

I am aiming at. Fischer's scheme is designed to eliminate the requirement to memorize lots and lots of chess openings.

Fischer Random Chess leaves the pawns where they usually are. The remaining white pieces are still on the first rank, but they are randomly placed, with a few constraints: the bishops are still on opposite-colored squares. The white king must go somewhere between the two white rooks. The black pieces mirror the white pieces.

Fischer Random Chess achieves the same kind of scrambling as Improv Chess and is much easier to implement. However, Fischer Random Chess primarily pertains to the openings, whereas Improv Chess can resonate throughout the entire game if, for example, the D4 square can never be occupied, or the king is taken out of play.

Another advantage of the Improv format is that it can be used with other games, including games like Go and backgammon that don't have an initial position.

Ben Shneiderman has suggested some formats to render board games more ambiguous by unexpectedly shifting the piece's identity or location mid-game. For example, you could randomly change a single piece to some other piece. I like this idea, using an impartial computer to make piece substitutions at random points in the game. The piece substitutions would have to be legal, of course. They would also be symmetrical—the same point-level substitution would be made simultaneously for both players. Such a procedure would turn a game into a real scramble, favoring the quick-witted who could best adapt throughout the game.

Shneiderman also suggested having a quarter of the board obscured for each player so the other player (or the chess computer) would have incomplete knowledge. That procedure would inject uncertainty into the game. It resembles the game *Kriegspiel*, which is a variant of chess. In Kriegspiel, I play an adversary but neither of us sees where the other person has moved. We each have a chessboard in front of us, and we move our own pieces. A referee watches both of us and enters each move on a master board; the referee informs the players if they have made an illegal move or have made a capture. The game continues until someone wins by checkmate. The game was somewhat popular at the RAND Corporation a few decades ago. Some people were frustrated and said it was just random. Others said there were actual strategies—they were the ones who typically won their matches.

Improv Chess

During Improv tournaments, laptops may be banned. Or else the players would be prohibited from linking their laptops to supercomputers that can rapidly play themselves a million times to learn the new, tweaked rules; the laptops themselves would be prohibited from engaging in this type of machine learning.

The reason for this stipulation is that I want the Improv format to emphasize conceptual understanding and causal reasoning instead of the correlational reasoning the machine learning currently deploys.

Some of the most powerful machine learning approaches rely on statistical techniques for classifying patterns using neural networks with multiple layers—commonly described as deep learning. These are the approaches responsible for dramatic advances in speech recognition, image recognition, language translation, and game playing for Go and other activities. There's no denying their accomplishments. But as Marcus (2018) points out, "deep" refers to the large number of layers, not to greater abstraction. Marcus uses the example of the Atari game *Breakout*, which is solved by a system in about four hours of training—the system learns to dig a tunnel through a wall of bricks. However, the system has no idea what a tunnel is or what a wall is. And when AI researchers make a slight perturbation, such as moving the height of the paddle or inserting a wall mid-screen, the AI systems fail. They are not adaptive. The current state of the art doesn't seem capable of handling Improv Chess.

Perhaps the use of Improv formats will give humans an advantage; perhaps it will encourage computer scientists to press further in their quest to add commonsense reasoning and conceptual diagnoses to their systems. Regardless, I envision the Improv format as a means of celebrating and strengthening intelligent capabilities such as speculative thinking.

—*January 1, 2019*

4.9 AIQ: Artificial Intelligence Quotient

Helping People Get Smarter about Smart Machines

Are you ready to work with software tools that have artificial intelligence (AI) capabilities embedded in them? Are you ready to become perpetually confused about how these tools are working and whether to take their recommendations seriously?

Apparently, many people aren't.

Even the computer scientists developing machine learning and deep neural nets don't fully understand how their creations think. The reason is that once the algorithms take over, massaging enormous data sets, correlating and back-propagating like crazy, even the people who designed and developed the systems no longer fully understand how they arrive at their answers. The developers can guess, but it is just a guess. And most of the people using their systems don't even know how to guess.

For the past few years I have been working with Robert Hoffman and Shane Mueller to address this problem. We have been part of a large program called XAI, which stands for explainable artificial intelligence. This program is sponsored by DARPA, the Defense Advanced Research Projects Agency. Most of the teams working on XAI are building impressive systems to use AI to make their own AI systems more readily understood.

In contrast, Robert, Shane, and I have been trying to develop straightforward tools to increase explainability. We call our set of tools AIQ, Artificial Intelligence Quotient, and our goal is to help the people using AI systems get smarter about how their own systems work. We want to raise their IQ about the AI systems they're wrestling with.

We want them to have better mental models about their AI systems (see Borders, Klein, & Besuijen, 2019). Having a better mental model isn't just about understanding how a system works. Better mental models are also about appreciating how a system doesn't work—how it fails and what are its limitations. Better mental models are about diagnosing why these failures and limitations occur. Finally, better mental models depend on learning workarounds for the failures and limitations.

So far we've assembled nine different tools, but I expect that we'll keep expanding the tool kit. Here are just three of the tools in the kit.

Cognitive Tutorial. One of the tools is an up-front tutorial to provide users with a better mental model (how the system works, how it fails, why it fails, and how to adapt). Shane and I had created an earlier version of this Cognitive Tutorial almost a decade ago (Mueller & Klein, 2011) and conducted some successful trial applications for complex logic systems. We've updated that version to handle AI systems.

Explainability Scales. We have developed and validated several measurement scales: trust in an AI system, explanation goodness, explanation satisfaction, and mental model adequacy, along with methods for analyzing user mental models of the AI (Hoffman et al., 2018).

Self-Explaining Scorecard. This scorecard is a scale for gauging the power and sophistication of AI techniques to improve explainability—not to offer explanations but to make it easier for the people using a system to figure it out for themselves. We have applied it to several ongoing XAI efforts (Klein, Hoffman, & Mueller, 2020).

We continue to apply, evaluate, and further extend the AIQ tool kit. One of the other AIQ tools, the Discovery Platform, is described in a later essay in this collection.

In the past, efforts to make AI systems more explainable were carried out by—no surprise—AI specialists, and the tools and techniques they developed relied on—no surprise again—AI capabilities. These tools were often impressive and powerful but they had the drawback that the everyday operators, without AI experience, had to understand the explanation tool as well as the AI system being explained.

In contrast, the AIQ tools don't require any AI; most of them don't even depend on computer support. We aren't building smarter machines. We

# Artificial Intelligence Quotient

want the AIQ tools to make people smarter, to increase their intelligence, their IQ if you will, about the specific AI systems they have to work with.

Acknowledgment and Disclaimer: This material is approved for public release. Distribution is unlimited. This material is based on research sponsored by the Air Force Research Lab (AFRL) under agreement FA8650-17-2-7711. The views and conclusions contained herein are those of the authors and should not be interpreted as necessarily representing the official policies or endorsement, either expressed or implied, of AFRL or the US government.

—July 1, 2020

4.10 Reflections

The bottom line for part 4 is simple and is contained in the title: let's put more energy into building machines that make us smarter, instead of machines that are themselves smarter.

I have seen many instances in which technology developers resonated with the challenge of designing impressive systems and were less interested in how these systems would be put into play and deployed by flawed humans. Sometimes the results have been impressive.

Sometimes the results have been tragic, as discussed in part 4—the Airbus 330 that was billed as unstallable, until it stalled. The military helicopter with advanced lookahead radar that automatically shut off above 5,000 feet so that it wouldn't drain power, which is not the system you'd want flying at night in the mountains of Afghanistan with lights off. The Amtrak locomotive engine that didn't have any displays to show the engineers where they were on their route. These examples illustrate systems that made their users dumber, rather than smarter.

If technology leaders continue to make users dumber, they may hasten the arrival of what I am calling the second singularity—a crossover point at which the intelligent technology outstrips the humans. Part 4 showed how this can happen, not through the advancement of intelligent technology, but the de-skilling of the humans. Part 4 didn't mount a criticism of artificial intelligence. There are other books that wade into those waters (e.g., Gigerenzer, 2022). Rather, my concern is about identifying and supporting human sources of power and not compromising these through technology.

One theme in part 4 is for designers to be more aware of the capabilities of the people who will be using their systems—the sources of power described back in part 2. In this context, several strengths emerge most vividly: (1) frontier thinking and speculative thinking, (2) social engagement and adaptive teamwork, and (3) acceptance of personal responsibility.

In an era of Big Data, individuals and organizations have access to an enormous amount of information, and the only way to sort through this information is by using intelligent technology. Sorting through data, however, is not the same as gaining insights. Part 4 described the way people achieve insight, not by searching through more and more data but by pouncing on individual data points that offer opportunities to make discoveries. Examples such as the Xerox insight into how to market its revolutionary copier show the power of a small number of significant data points. Another example is the tilt alarm that went off in the heads of a few people prior to the 9/11 attacks when they heard about people from the Middle East who were taking flying lessons but weren't interested in practicing takeoffs and landings.

It's not easy to gather promising data points, and this is another source of power—to find ways to elicit tacit knowledge, such as mental models. That's what happened when my research team and I found a way to use rough graphics to enable housewives to describe how they thought stain removal products worked.

A second theme is that there are compelling examples of advanced technology that does make us smarter. Wikipedia, the Google search engine, and smartphones all have made our lives easier and richer and more productive. The more technologies like these, the better. Another example is hyperlinks—a technology so ubiquitous that we completely take it for granted. A technology that makes us smarter.

Part 4 helped you to view the use of Small Data as a source of power, showing how people in the intelligence community used minimal data to make bold assessments such as a Russia/China joint exercise in the Mediterranean, or the French intention to intervene in the civil war in Libya, or whether Saddam Hussein intended to invade Kuwait. Other examples such as the Toyota runaway acceleration problem show how the right data can resolve a thorny issue better than the collection of large amounts of semi-random data.

The Small Data approach emphasizes causal reasoning instead of correlations. These examples suggest that technology designers can do a better job of making people smarter by making it easier to find tell-tale data points, rather than drowning people in data overload.

Reflections

We can also make people smarter through games—games that promote insight and flexible thinking. Even a game such as chess can be redesigned, using technology to foster adaptive thinking.

Part 4 concluded with a description of a non-algorithmic tactic to make people smarter about the smart machines they operate. The Artificial Intelligence Quotient (AIQ) toolkit consists of a set of methods such as a cognitive tutorial and a collaborative approach to XAI in order to achieve that.

These are the two major themes in part 4: making designers more aware of the sources of power people employ and encouraging designers to develop tools and tactics that use technology to make people smarter. By pursuing these objectives, we can increase expertise instead of diminishing it.

And that raises the question of what we mean by expertise.

5 Seeing the Invisible—Expertise

Overview

The topic of expertise is an important theme for this book, for the Naturalistic Decision Making movement, and for society at large. This topic is important and surprisingly contentious. Many people—too many people in my opinion—are skeptical of expertise and eager to debunk it when given the chance. The essays in this part offer examples of expertise but also describe some of the critics and their perspectives.

The topic of expertise has taken on new urgency these days. I am writing this overview, April 6, 2021, a little more than a year into the COVID-19 pandemic. We can see the havoc, confusion, and angry debate that arises when expertise is lacking on critical issues. At the beginning of the pandemic, we didn't know very much about what caused it, how it was transmitted, how to be safeguarded against it. We weren't even sure how to tell if someone had the disease. Physicians were treating patients who later turned out to be sick and infectious with COVID-19. Hospital staff members were frantically trying to keep up with the latest bulletins and even the latest rumors, sometimes reporting on what they had heard on the radio as they drove to work. ("We need to ask patients if they've lost their sense of taste and smell. Really. I just heard it on NPR.")

In the past, many of the leaders in our healthcare establishment have taken comfort in Evidence-Based Medicine and best practices, offering these tools as a substitute for expertise. Too many experienced physicians were recommending useless treatments that they believed would work but turned out to have little value. The antidote to "anecdotal medicine" was to conduct carefully controlled double-blind studies—the cornerstone of the evidence-based medicine movement. In this way, science and data would prevail over unreliable so-called expertise. At least, that is the claim. In practice, things aren't so simple. D. E. Klein et al. (2016) explained six of the cognitive challenges of carrying out Evidence-Based Medicine. You must accurately identify the patient's problem to start with. Then, if you want to apply the evidence, you must gauge how much confidence you have in the data. And if your judgment, based on your experience, conflicts with the evidence, you have to decide what to do next. Further, Evidence-Based Medicine relies on studies of a single disease to see if a treatment works or not, but many patients show up with more than one illness, and a treatment that might be effective against one of the illnesses might make one of the others worse. And what if you apply the Evidence-Based Medicine treatment and it doesn't seem to be working—how do you judge whether to stick with it or not? Finally, what do you do about remedies that seem plausible but haven't been tested yet?

This last challenge was a particular problem with COVID-19 because there just wasn't time to do the proper testing of different types of remedies. Healthcare providers desperately swapped stories of approaches that seemed to work elsewhere. Emergency departments in Italy were reporting a technique of proning. Instead of placing patients on their backs, it seemed as if you could dramatically cut the need for ventilators by shifting patients to their sides or their stomachs. Who knew? But it was worth trying, especially because ventilators were so scarce.

The importance of expertise became more visible when we had to scramble without it.

And we also got to see the controversies and political sniping about who was an expert. Every time the experts changed their recommendations, they'd get attacked. "They were telling us one thing about masks a few weeks ago, now they're telling us the opposite. We can't trust anything they tell us." This attitude shows a popular belief that real experts are infallible, so any time so-called experts changed their minds, they lost credibility.

The world was desperate for expertise and at the same time cynical about experts. In my view, the cynicism was overdone. The professionals with the most experience were rapidly trying to gain expertise but were caught up in a public learning curve and given very little sympathy.

COVID-19 illustrated the assaults on expertise, but these assaults had begun many decades earlier in scientific and intellectual circles.

Part 5 begins with a set of essays describing these attacks. Essay 5.1, "The Flea," sets up the context for discrediting experts. Next comes essay 5.2, "From Chimps to Champs," offering more detail about the efforts to discredit experts. Essay 5.3, "The War on Expertise," details the five scientific communities that have, in parallel, urged us to give little credence to expertise.

At this point, part 5 shifts away from the detractors. The next set of essays describe different aspects of expertise. These are aspects that all of us share, to some extent, and aspire to achieve in greater measure. Essay 5.4, "Anomaly Detection," explains how important it is for us to notice anomalies and how much this detection depends on experience. Essay 5.5, "Anticipation," explores different aspects of our ability to generate expectancies. Essay 5.6, "Missing Pieces," showcases a critical but often overlooked aspect of expertise—the ability to notice events that did not occur. Essay 5.7, "Leverage," provides an example of how expertise let a British scientist find leverage points for solving an existential problem during World War II—Hitler's imminent plan to bombard London with V-1 rockets and force a British surrender.

Essay 5.8, "The Skill Portfolio Account of Expertise," throws in a complication, or maybe it is an enrichment. Perhaps we can move beyond a unitary concept of expertise in which we think of people as falling on a continuum from low to high. Instead, we can envision a repertoire of skills that experts might possess; we might not expect experts to possess all of these skills. The result is a more fluid and flexible concept of expertise and hopefully one that is more useful.

With these illustrations of different facets of expertise, part 5 grapples with the question of what criteria we can use to judge who really is an expert. Essay 5.9, "How Can We Identify the Experts," lists no fewer than ten different criteria and explains why none of them is foolproof. However, used in conjunction with each other, they can hopefully allow us to form better judgments about whom to trust.

Essay 5.10, the last one in this part, is "The Art of Being Stupid." Few of us qualify as experts. Instead of pretending to know more than we do, we can sometimes do better by accepting our limitations instead of hiding them. We can use our ignorance to learn from the experts we encounter. Experts are often unable to explain what makes them so good, and that leaves it to others to find ways to help them articulate their tacit knowledge.

5.1 The Flea

How to Make Experts Stupid

There is an old joke about a scientist and a flea. The scientist put a flea on the table and then smacked his hand heavily on the table and the flea jumped. The scientist next tore off two of the flea's legs and smacked again, and again the flea jumped. The scientist tore off two more legs, repeated the procedure, and again the flea jumped.

The scientist tore off the last two legs, smacked his hand on the table, and—no jumping. He tried again, smacked his hand heavily on the table, but the flea still didn't jump.

The scientist wrote down his observation: "When a flea loses all its legs, it becomes deaf."

Similarly, if you take experts and put them in a situation where they have to perform an unfamiliar task (two legs off), and remove any meaningful context (two more legs off), and apply an inappropriate evaluation criterion (last two legs off), you might conclude that experts aren't very capable, but that is clearly a mistake.

I was reminded of this joke when I read some accounts of how advanced artificial intelligence (AI) systems were outperforming experts. For example, in healthcare, a diagnostician treating a patient might look at an X-ray for signs of pneumonia, but AI systems can detect pneumonia in X-rays more accurately. Or the physician might study the results of a battery of blood tests, but AI systems can detect problems from electronic health records more accurately than physicians.

What's missing from this picture is that the physician also has a chance to meet patients and observe them—how they are moving, especially compared to the last office visit. How they are breathing, and so forth. The AI systems don't have a way to take these observations into account, and so the comparative studies screen out any observation and require the physicians to base their judgments entirely on the objective records. That's two legs off. The physicians aren't allowed to consider any personal history with the patients—another two legs off. The physicians can't consult with family members—a final two legs off. And so the researchers conclude that the physicians aren't very skillful—not as accurate as the AI.

I think what we need is a way for the AI developers to enhance the physicians' judgments, not replace them. Here is an example, a study by Wang et al. (2016). The pathologists' error rate was 3.5 percent, whereas the AI model error rate was only 2.9 percent. A clear win for the AI model it would seem. However, the combined error rate, adding the pathologist to the AI, was 0.5 percent (see figure 5.1).

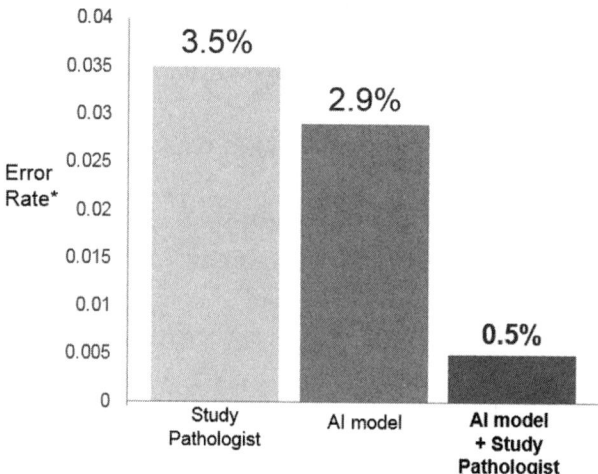

Figure 5.1

AI + pathologist performance. *Notes:* *Error rate defined as 1 – Area under the Receiver Operator Curve; ** A study pathologist, blinded to the ground truth diagnoses, independently scored all evaluation slides.

Source: T. Kontzer, "Deep Learning Drops Error Rate for Breast Cancer Diagnoses by 85%," 2016. Retrieved from Nvidia blog: https://blogs.nvidia.com/blog/2016/09/19/deeplearning-breast-cancer-diagnosis.

Another study (Rosenberg et al., 2018) describes how an AI-powered mechanism used "swarm intelligence" among a group of expert radiologists reviewing chest X-rays for the presence of pneumonia. The swarm beat the standard radiologist performance by 33 percent, but it also beat Stanford's state-of-the-art deep learning system by 22 percent.

Siddiqui (2018) has described another example of human/AI partnering. At a children's hospital in Philadelphia, about 1 in 1,000 feverish children turn out to have a deadly infection, as opposed to a simple cold. Experienced physicians can identify that anomalous infection about three-quarters of the time. To increase the accuracy of detection and reduce the number of children being missed, some hospitals are now using quantitative algorithms from their electronic health records to choose which fevers were dangerous. The algorithms are relying entirely on the data and are more accurate than the physicians, catching the serious infections nine times out of ten. However, the algorithms had ten times the false alarms. One hospital in Philadelphia took the computer-based list of worrisome fevers as a starting point but then had their best doctors and nurses look over the children before declaring the infection was deadly and bringing them into the hospital for intravenous medications. Their teams weeded out the algorithm's false alarms with high accuracy. In addition, the physicians and nurses found cases the computer missed, bringing their detection rate of deadly infections from 86.2 percent by the algorithm alone to 99.4 percent by the algorithm in combination with human perception.*

It is easy to make experts stupid. But it is more exciting and fulfilling to put their abilities to work.

—*December 5, 2018*

---

*I thank Lorenzo Barberis Canonico for bringing these studies to my attention.

5.2 From Chimps to Champs

What's behind the Campaign to Discredit Experts?

I am troubled by the way some professionals take a dismissive, even contemptuous, stance regarding experts.

Experts have skills that go far beyond anything the rest of us can do. They see things that are invisible to others. They make connections and inferences we'd never think of. They spot problems we'd miss until it was too late.

Certainly, experts in a field are never perfect. They can be overconfident. They can be mistaken. So it is reasonable to take a skeptical view of experts, especially when the experts are self-proclaimed, like pundits on television news shows. A healthy skepticism invites inquiry into how good an expert is and what it takes to become an expert.

What disturbs me is an attitude that goes beyond healthy skepticism into knee-jerk contempt—that the experts in a field, any field, shouldn't be taken seriously.

I first encountered signs of this contemptuous attitude when I attended conferences on judgment and decision-making. Researchers in the Heuristics and Biases (HB) tradition gleefully described experiments showing that even the experts fell prey to the biases. In 1971, Tversky and Kahneman reported that expert statisticians made poor choices when they followed their intuition about generalizing from small samples. McNeil et al. (1982) showed that experienced physicians were just as susceptible to framing effects about how to treat lung cancer as graduate students and ambulatory patients. Even the experts were inherently biased in their judgments. The lesson was: you can't trust experts.

The Judgment and Decision Making field places special importance on the work of Paul Meehl (1954), who conducted a number of studies showing that linear statistical models exceeded or matched the clinical judgments of experts, suggesting that we'd be better off replacing the judgments of the experts with those of the statistical models. What doesn't get much attention is that the factors loaded into the linear statistical models came from the experts themselves; the primary benefit of the statistics was to increase consistency.

An article by Kahneman & Klein (2009) put the matter bluntly: "The basic stance of Heuristics and Biases researchers, as they consider experts, is one of skepticism. They are trained to look for opportunities to compare expert performance with performance by formal models or rules and to expect that experts will do poorly in such comparisons" (p. 518).

I have been noticing this contemptuous attitude about experts for many years, but then a few months ago something happened that truly alarmed me.

A colleague of mine, Joseph Borders, was approached by a manager in a very large petrochemical company about setting up a cognitive skills training program for the panel operators who control massive units within a manufacturing plant. These panel operators work under tremendous stress. If they unnecessarily shut down a plant, the costs of missed production can run into millions of dollars. But if they fail to shut down a malfunctioning plant, they can trigger an explosion that has even greater consequences in terms of dollars and lives. Joseph and I could see why the plant manager would want to build expertise in the panel operators.

However, the project never came off. Months later, the manager sheepishly explained to us that the plan to build the expertise of panel operators had been blocked. A higher-up had explained that the plant didn't need its panel operators to make better decisions because the operators were hopelessly biased. Instead, he intended to take the decision-making out of their hands and rely on some sort of artificial intelligence (AI) instead.

Obviously, I was stunned by this explanation. Not only was the executive's faith in AI misplaced (the tacit knowledge needed to spot subtle cues can take years to develop), but the executive's distrust of the panel operators seemed like a very dangerous attitude. And if petrochemical plant executives are now acting on their fears of biases in their panel operators, that suggests how far the campaign to discredit experts has come.

Where does this fear of experts come from? Largely from the HB community and the studies showing that experts demonstrate the same kinds of biases as novices. These findings damage the reputation of experts.

Of course, the situation may not be as grim as the skeptics proclaim. First, the effect of judgment biases may be overstated, for reasons I have presented in previous parts of this book. Several studies have found that the judgment and decision biases become weaker or disappear when people are given naturalistic tasks rather than artificial ones. Second, the biases stem from our use of heuristics, and heuristics are very useful. The HB community has performed little or no research on the benefits of using heuristics; these benefits must far outweigh the drawbacks. Third, people who are most prone to use heuristics and commit biases, and who violate the precepts of Bayesian statistics, do very well in life. Berg & Gigerenzer (2010) reported that they earned more money and held more accurate beliefs compared to people who lined up with the rational choice strategies.

Where does this leave us? There are several compelling reasons why people want to dismiss expertise. I don't think these reasons stand up well to scrutiny, but that doesn't matter if they aren't scrutinized. It doesn't matter if the only message that comes through is that we must take decisions out of the hands of experts.

Therefore, I think we need to be more energetic in conveying a different message, that expertise matters. We need to conduct more research and collect more evidence demonstrating what experts can accomplish. An example is the work of Jim Staszewski (2004), a professor at Carnegie Mellon University. The US Army had spent $38 million in developing improved minesweepers, but when they were tested, they provided no advantage over the previous model of equipment. Both had about a 20 percent detection rate. Staszewski and his colleagues (Higgins et al., 2008) located a few army engineers who had mastered the new equipment. When tested, these experts achieved dramatic results, over 90 percent detection rates. The research team then used cognitive interviews and other methods to identify what the experts were seeing and applied these findings to construct a course to teach new army engineers how to use the new type of minesweeper effectively. That's what experts can buy you.

Kahneman & Klein (2009) identified the conditions needed for people to gain intuitive expertise: a reasonably well-structured as opposed to chaotic environment and the opportunity for rapid and meaningful feedback on judgments and decisions. We concluded that "a psychology of professional judgment that ignores intuitive skills is seriously blinkered" (p. 525).

Phil Tetlock illustrates the type of transition that can turn the tide. Tetlock (2005) reported the results of a study of the forecasting accuracy of leading experts and pundits, given clear prediction targets (e.g., "Should we expect in the next ten years defense spending as a percentage of government expenditure to rise, fall, or stay the same?"). The results were dismal—not much better than would be achieved by a chimp throwing darts. Tetlock concluded that "humanity barely bests the chimp" (p. 51). Naturally, the expertise skeptics were delighted.

However, ten years later, Tetlock was part of a research team led by Barbara Mellers that attempted to develop forecasting expertise. And they succeeded, as described in Tetlock & Gardner's (2016) book *Superforecasting*. Tetlock showed that amateurs, not part of any government agency, were able to outperform the professional forecasters and win a forecasting championship. These superforecasters weren't just lucky. They sustained their high levels of forecasting accuracy over several years. Sure, 30 percent of the superforecasters dropped out of the top ranks in the sample, but 70 percent stayed at the top. Their performance stemmed from research, analysis, self-criticism, and gathering the perspectives of others. They worked hard to develop and maintain their level of expertise, and they succeeded magnificently.

In the first Tetlock project, experts weren't much better than chimps. In the second project, they were champs. Tetlock's appreciation of experts changed as he worked with them and watched them in action. His transition should inspire others to shake loose of their biases about experts and take expertise more seriously.

—September 10, 2016

5.3 The War on Expertise

Five Professional Communities Are Trying to Discredit Expertise

There is an intentional effort to reduce our confidence in experts and to cast doubt on expertise itself. This effort, in many ways, feels like a war waged for intellectual turf, scientific credibility, political and even economic gain.

My view is that most of the claims of these expertise-deniers are misleading and that the arguments tend to be overstatements. But these claims and arguments cannot simply be ignored because they are having some effect. Therefore, I want to rebut the misleading claims and the overstated arguments. My colleagues and I have prepared several rebuttals: a chapter that is titled "The War on Expertise" (Klein et al., 2018) and a short article (Klein et al., 2017) based on that chapter.

In this essay, I want to briefly summarize the major themes of the war on expertise.

The five communities engaged in this war on expertise are Decision Research, Heuristics and Biases (HB), Sociology, Evidence-Based Practices, and Computer Science (see figure 5.2).

Decision Research. The primary studies conducted by this community have shown that statistical models outperform experts. Yet what is often forgotten is that the variables in the formulas were originally derived from the advice of experts. The primary advantage of the formulas is that they are consistent. However, the formulas tend to be brittle—when they fail, they fail miserably. And the experiments tend to be carefully controlled, avoiding the messy conditions that experts must contend with such as ill-defined goals, shifting conditions, high stakes, ambiguity about the nature

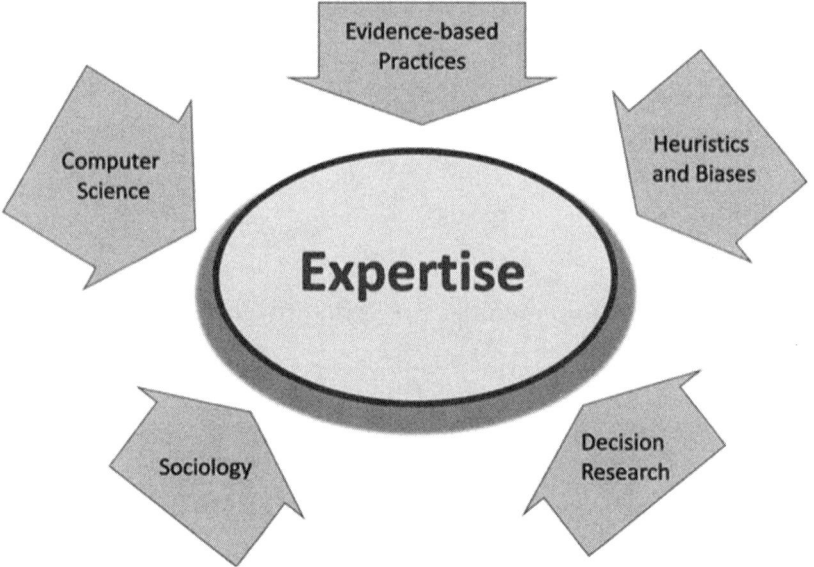

Figure 5.2
The attack on expertise.
Source: Ben Shneiderman, used with permission.

and reliability of the data. Further, the research usually focuses on single measures and ignores aspects of performance that are ambiguous and difficult to quantify. Finally, the advantages of the statistical methods tend to be found in situations in which the outputs are not very accurate, even when they are somewhat better than the expert judgments.

Heuristics and Biases. Kahneman and Tversky (Tversky & Kahneman, 1974; Kahneman, 2011) showed that people, even experts, fall victim to judgment biases. However, most of the HB research is with college students performing artificial, unfamiliar tasks, with no context to guide them. When researchers use a meaningful context, the judgment biases usually diminish. And besides, the heuristics are usually helpful, as Kahneman and Tversky themselves pointed out.

Sociology. Members of this community assert that expertise is a function of the community and the artifacts surrounding the task, referring to "situated cognition" and "distributed cognition." The expertise-deniers argue that expert cognition is socially constructed and is not a function of individual knowledge. Clearly, team and situational factors play a role in expert performance, but this extreme position seems untenable—if we replace the experts on a team with people whose skills are mediocre, we can watch how the overall performance suffers.

Evidence-Based Practice. The idea here is that professionals, such as physicians, should base their diagnoses and remedies on scientific evidence instead of relying on their own judgments. Obviously, too many quack treatments and unjustified superstitions achieved popularity, and controlled experiments have helped weed these out. However, scientifically validated best practices aren't a replacement for skilled judgment, which is needed for gauging confidence in the evidence, revising plans that don't seem to be working, and adapting simple rules to complex situations. In medicine, patients often present several conditions at the same time, whereas the evidence usually pertains to a single condition.

Computer Science. Information technology, artificial intelligence (AI), automation, and Big Data have each claimed to be able to replace experts. However, each of these claims is unwarranted. Let's start with AI. AI successes have been in games like chess, Go, and *Jeopardy!*—games that are well-structured, with unambiguous referents and definitive correct solutions. But decision-makers face wicked problems with unclear goals in ambiguous and dynamic situations, conditions that are beyond AI systems. Next, look at automation, which is supposed to save money by reducing jobs. However, case studies show that automation typically depends on having many experts design the systems and to keep them updated and running. Further, automation is often poorly designed and creates new kinds of cognitive work for operators. Last, Big Data approaches can search through far more records and sensor inputs than any human, but these algorithms are susceptible to seeing patterns where none really exist. Google's Flu Trends project was publicized as a success story but subsequently failed so badly that it was removed from use. Big Data algorithms follow historical trends but may miss departures from these trends. Further, experts can use their expectancies to spot missing events that may be very important, but Big Data approaches are unaware of the *absence* of data and events.

Therefore, none of these communities poses a legitimate threat to expertise. Left unchallenged, the overstatements and confusions that lie behind these claims can lead to a downward spiral in which experts are ignored and denied credibility. Of course, we need to learn from the critiques of each of these communities. We need to appreciate their contributions and capabilities in order to move beyond the adversarial stance taken by each community. Ideally, we will be able to foster a spirit of collaboration in which their positive findings and techniques can be used to strengthen the work of experts.

—*September 6, 2017*

5.4 Anomaly Detection: The Art of Noticing the Unexpected

What the Analytical Tradition Is Missing

Pattern matching is about spotting connections and relationships, but when we detect anomalies, we are seeing *dis*connections—things that do not fit together. Although anomalies get much less attention than pattern matching, the ability to spot anomalies is extremely important, enabling us to escape fixation and question the way we are making sense of a situation (Klein et al., 2006, 2007).

For example, in my 2013 book, *Seeing What Others Don't*, I tell the story of a young police officer, waiting for traffic to move, who notices that in the new BMW just ahead of him, the driver has taken a deep drag on his cigarette and then flicked the ashes. That surprises him—what owner of a new BMW would do that? He investigates further, pulling the driver over and discovers that it was a stolen car.

Anomaly detection helps us to spot inconsistencies in our diagnosis of a problem, and therefore to escape from fixation. It lets us notice that a preexisting plan might not work in our current environment. It helps us adapt to changing conditions, perhaps triggering our "Spidey sense" that something doesn't feel right.

What is an anomaly? There are two different perspectives: a statistical perspective and a cognitive perspective.

The *statistical perspective* treats an anomaly as an outlier. Wikipedia offers this definition: "the identification of rare items, events or observations which raise suspicions by differing significantly from the majority of the data. . . . Anomalies are also referred to as outliers, novelties, noise, deviations and exceptions."

The statistical perspective includes all kinds of methods to spot these outliers, such as visual analytic tools to make the outliers stand out.

The *cognitive perspective* is that an anomaly is a violation of our expectancies. Something happens that we didn't expect. For example, a pattern is disrupted or a surprising event occurs (back to the BMW example).

This essay is about the cognitive perspective. The cognitive perspective does not include the powerful methods found in the statistical perspective. However, it captures something that is missing from the statistical perspective: our ability to form expectancies. The cognitive perspective includes the way we can notice missing data—events that were expected but failed to occur—which typically don't show up in the statistical methods that analyze events that have occurred. The cognitive perspective captures mental models and the causal factors that allow us to appreciate the significance of a particular deviation.

Most deviations and outliers are uninteresting. At the cognitive level, anomalies matter primarily when they have the potential to alter the way we understand a situation. And that type of sensemaking is very different from the flagging of outliers found in statistical methods.

Now we can amend the cognitive definition of anomaly offered earlier. An anomaly is a violation of our expectancies that enables us to revise the way we understand a situation. Therefore, anomaly detection aligns closely with problem detection (see Klein et al., 2005).

Anomaly detection depends on a regular environment. If the environment is completely random there's no way to spot an anomaly. Anomaly detection also depends on curiosity—the cues and discrepancies that catch our attention. And anomaly detection depends heavily on our experience.

Expertise. We use our expertise, our pattern repertoire, to form expectations. More experience will result in better anomaly detection because our expectations are sharper, making anomalies easier to see. Experience also provides us with tacit knowledge, such as recognizing stimuli as familiar. The recognition of familiarity lets us detect anomalies that are departures from familiarity.

Expertise also provides us with richer mental models—richer sets of causes to take into account when assessing a potential anomaly.

Barriers to anomaly detection. One of the strongest barriers is our mindset. A mindset to be curious about inconsistencies is different from a mindset to dismiss or explain away any inconsistencies, what Perrow (1984) has called *de minimus* explanations. This dismissive mindset leads us to preserve a frame in the face of anomalies and contrary evidence, resulting in fixation errors.

Conclusion. The notion of an anomaly as an outlier is simple enough—and too simple. It ignores the cognitive dimension, that an anomaly is a violation of an expectancy. And it ignores the way we use sensemaking tactics to judge whether the violation of expectancies has the potential to change our story about what is going on. Algorithmic, statistical methods aren't sensitive to these aspects of anomaly detection. Tools based on analytical methods may have some value but because of their insensitivity to the cognitive dimension, they may flag irrelevant outliers and miss the important ones.

—*October 21, 2020*

5.5 Anticipation

How Do We Prepare Ourselves for the Unexpected?

This essay explores the way we do anticipatory thinking: imagining how unexpected events may affect our plans. Anticipatory thinking (AT) lets us recognize and prepare for difficult challenges. It's different from making predictions because we don't necessarily expect events to play out the way we imagine—complex situations are too hard to predict. Instead, we are getting ourselves ready, bracing ourselves, preparing ourselves. We particularly need AT to flag low-probability events that pose severe threats.

AT is not trying to guess the future; it is trying to adapt to possible futures. It's about readying ourselves. And it's about guiding our attention—gambling with our attention based on what we are preparing ourselves to handle.

Three topics, in particular, seem important for making progress on the nature of AT: how does AT work, the role of expertise in AT, and dysfunctional tendencies that interfere with AT.

How does AT work? It must engage our ability to generate expectancies and to draw on our mental models. For me, the causal factors we learn to appreciate are the core of our mental models, allowing us to perform the mental simulations that transform our understanding of what is happening right now into what may happen in the future.

I have identified three pathways for gaining insights (Klein, 2013): a connection path, a contradiction path, and a correction path. These pathways may describe different means of achieving AT. (See essay 6.3 for a description of each path.)

The role of expertise in AT. Expertise allows us to appreciate more causal factors and build more sophisticated mental models. Expertise also helps us navigate the cognitive challenges to AT: managing ambiguity and uncertainty, making diagnoses, gathering information, determining whether to trust data, spotting leverage points, and appreciating the normal range of variation so that we can detect the anomalies that spark AT.

In addition, we can imagine how AT could be overdone—people paralyzed and indecisive as they consider all kinds of consequences. Therefore, there must be a metaskill governing when and how thoroughly to perform AT.

What gets in our way when we need to do AT? Here are some dysfunctional tendencies.

1. *Complacency.* We may stop monitoring a situation once we make a critical decision, failing to notice subsequent events that might alter the conditions and throw off our AT.
2. *Overconfidence.* We may be overconfident in our abilities. In his book *Fundamental Surprises*, Zvi Lanir has argued that much of the Israel Defense Forces' failures at the beginning of the 1973 Yom Kippur War stemmed from an unrealistic confidence in their capability to withstand an Egyptian attack. In other words, the real surprise was not what the Egyptians could do but what the Israelis could no longer do.
3. *Fixation.* We fail to revise our assumptions when the data do not fit. In my discussions with physicians, I have learned that a common reason for diagnostic failures in medicine is when the attending physician makes an initial determination based on the salient cues that are available but then locks into this determination rather than reconsidering it as new data are received. The physician then fails to perform the necessary AT.
4. *Knowledge shields.* Feltovich et al. (2001) have described the range of strategies we use to hold on to our initial beliefs by explaining away inconvenient counter-indicators.
5. *Oversimplification.* In a separate work, Feltovich et al. (2004) have described the ways we oversimplify situations—what they call the reductive tendency. Of course, some simplification is necessary in order to manage complex situations. Our challenge is to simplify skillfully and in ways that do not excessively distort the dynamics of a situation.

6. *Mindsets.* Mindsets themselves aren't the problem. Some mindsets can support AT, but other mindsets get in the way. Here are several mindset shifts that affect AT:

    - *Shifting from a procedural mindset to a problem-solving mindset*—the dysfunction is to remain locked into a mindset that a job consists of following procedures, rather than being alert to anomalies.
    - *Shifting from a reactive mindset to an anticipatory mindset.* This mindset shift is obviously tied to effective AT. Novices, in particular, seem to be content in reacting to events rather than trying to get ahead of the curve, and that's understandable because they don't have the experience base to form expectations. But it is probably important that they keep trying rather than settling into an incurious and reactive mindset. Even people with years of experience sometimes retain this passive reactive mindset.
    - *Shifting from a mindless stance to an active and curious stance*—in my research on insight, I found that the people who gained insights were actively curious and speculating, whereas those who had the same information but missed the insight were passive and had stopped speculating.
    - *Need for closure*—a mindset that tries to tie everything down as quickly as possible is likely to be insensitive to unexpected events that should trigger AT.

In addition, designers need to shift from a *mindset of how devices work to a mindset of how devices might fail*—it is too easy to fall into the rut of imagining how a device, or a plan, can succeed rather than engaging in AT to imagine the things that might go wrong. (The Pre-mortem method I describe in part 9 might help here.)

—*February 8, 2017*

5.6 Missing Pieces

The Skill of Noticing Events That Didn't Happen

We react to cues and information that we sense—usually things we see or hear.

But with experience, we also gain the ability to react to events that don't happen. This important skill doesn't always get the attention it deserves.

Imagine that you are working on a complex puzzle, and you can't look at the box to identify the picture you are making. You just sort the pieces, perhaps by color, and try to find matches. You look at each piece and scan for neighbors it might nest beside—a passive strategy. After you make enough progress, you get a sense of what the puzzle is about, and so you can detect pieces that you need to find in the pile of unsorted fragments.

Now you are actively searching. You are searching for pieces you don't have, pieces you expect to have. Pieces that are missing. You can use what you have learned thus far to form expectancies about what these pieces look like so that you don't need to search randomly anymore.

That's how we use our experience to spot the gaps.

One of the most famous examples of noticing an event that didn't happen comes from the well-known Sherlock Holmes story, "Silver Blaze," about the kidnapping of a horse (Silver Blaze) shortly before an important race.

The local inspector asks Holmes, "Is there any point to which you would wish to draw my attention?"

Holmes: "To the curious incident of the dog in the night-time."

Inspector: "The dog did nothing in the night-time."

Holmes: "That was the curious incident."

Later, we learn that the dog was one of the guardians of Silver Blaze's stable, but when the horse was removed, the dog failed to bark or grow agitated. And this behavior suggested that the horse was removed, not by a stranger, but by someone the dog knew well. So the curious incident was what did not happen.

Spotting these kinds of omissions is not just important in works of fiction. Once I interviewed a navy officer who described an incident in which he was in command of a small patrol boat. He and his crew were participating in a large-scale exercise. They had gotten off to a late start because of mechanical difficulties and were rushing to catch up to the rest of the flotilla, racing across a busy shipping channel. The weather was terrible—driving rain hammering them from the port (left) side. My informant, the commander, assigned two crew members to keep watch for approaching ships on each side of their boat as they sped across the channel, and he had his head down studying navigational charts. All of a sudden, he realized that he was getting frequent announcements from the lookout on the starboard side but hadn't heard anything from the port lookout for several minutes. And the port lookout needed to be facing directly into the wind, into the downpour. The commander leaped to his feet and scanned the situation on the left of the vessel. He was horrified to see a large tanker bearing directly toward them. He issued a panicky order to turn hard to starboard and narrowly avoided getting cut in half by the tanker. In retrospect, he imagined how the port lookout must have scrunched his eyes into slits and maybe swiveled his head to the right, little by little, without thinking about it, flinching at the sheets of rain. That's why the commander hadn't been hearing any reports from the port lookout. It was what he wasn't hearing that caught the commander's attention.

Parents know to become worried when the sounds of young children playing in the next room subside and it gets too quiet. Military intelligence analysts start to get concerned when the adversary shifts to "radio silence"—often the precursor to an attack.

An interview with a child protective services caseworker surfaced an incident in which a 2-month-old boy suffered a concussion. The culprit was his 7-year-old brother who tried to pick him up from a bed and dropped him onto the corner of a nightstand. The caseworker interviewed the mother who explained that she had gone to the bathroom for just a minute and wasn't in the bedroom when the accident occurred. The caseworker was willing to accept the mother's story but was bothered by what didn't happen: the mother expressed no guilt or self-recrimination. That's what worried the caseworker and made her probe more deeply into the mother's fitness to safeguard her children. (The caseworker discovered a history of drug use that the mother had tried to cover up—possibly why she was in the bathroom for so long.)

We draw on our expectancies and our expertise to detect missing pieces, words that aren't said, events that are supposed to happen but don't. Our expectancies let us anticipate the things that are supposed to occur so that we can be surprised by their absence.

Surprise stems from the violation of expectancies. What is unique about missing pieces is that we are surprised by what didn't happen, rather than by what did.

Information display designers might keep an eye out for missing pieces. Once my colleagues and I consulted on a project to build a decision support system for an organization that had to rapidly respond to crises such as oil spills. The sponsor had lined up a network of service providers (different types of equipment, logistics for volunteer workers, communications to government agencies and to the media, etc.). In the event of an emergency, each of the service providers was to be notified and then would confirm its readiness to assist. The system design team prepared a display showing all the service providers that had logged in. But I argued that the watchstanders really needed to see which service providers had *not yet logged in*—they were going to be the bottlenecks. They were going to require workarounds. In the original design, they were going to be invisible. I explained why they had to take center stage.

You can easily see what's in front of your nose. It's much harder, it takes experience, to see what's not there.

—*July 1, 2016*

5.7 Leverage

How We Spot Opportunities

Soon after World War II began, the British cities, particularly London, were getting clobbered by Nazi bombers. Against all expectations, Winston Churchill kept his country from giving up and suing for peace. The British sent their battered fighter pilots up again and again to try to counter the German attacks.

And then came an ominous turn. Adolf Hitler boasted about a new weapon that was going to make things even more desperate for the United Kingdom. The British intelligence service tried to anticipate what Hitler had in store for them so that they could try to find ways to counter it.

British intelligence had some evidence that the Germans were developing a pilotless bomb that could fly across the English Channel with a ton of explosives, aimed right at London. We now know that this was the V-1 weapon, a flying bomb. The British scientists wanted to understand its accuracy, speed, range, and payload. British intelligence had previously cracked the German Enigma code, so they got some tidbits that way. They determined that the new weapon was being housed in Peenemünde, in Germany, and they sent airplanes to take photographs. But scattered messages and photographs weren't enough. They wanted to know how it flew.

Then one of the chief scientists in British intelligence, R. V. Jones, had an idea. (Jones describes this incident in his wonderful 1978 book, *The Wizard War*.) If the Germans were getting ready to use this new flying bomb, they were going to have to test it first. Because the new weapon was being housed in Peenemünde, the Germans would be running their flight tests from that location. They weren't going to test the weapon to the west, where it could be observed. They only had one obvious flight path for their tests, up the Baltic coast to the east-northeast of Peenemünde. Also, the Germans would want to track the flying bomb during its flight tests, almost certainly using radar.

However, Jones knew that the Germans hadn't developed very sophisticated radar systems and hadn't really developed a highly skilled set of radar operators. The German Army radar was used to detect slow-moving British bombers. But tracking the V-1 was going to be hard because from every indication, it was going to fly about 10 times faster than airplanes.

The Germans did have two units of radar operators that stood out from the rest, the 14th and 15th Companies of their Air Signals Experimental Regiment. Therefore in April 1943, Jones went to Bletchley Park, the British intelligence station where the Enigma decoding was going on, and made a request. He asked them to please let him know if either of these German radar companies, the 14th or the 15th, got reassigned to the area east-northeast of Peenemünde, where the flight tests were likely to occur.

Months later, in June 1943, this shot-in-the-dark paid off. Bletchley Park contacted Jones and told him that the 14th Company was moving to the supposed flight test area. In the autumn of 1943, the British had a ringside seat to the German tests. The German 14th Radar Company transmitted the V-1 test results via the Enigma system, and the British, who had broken that code, simply listened in, learning the V-1 characteristics and finding ways to neutralize it.

Jones had spotted several leverage points. First, the Germans were going to have to test their new system, and the British could take advantage of these tests. Second, Jones didn't have to track the V-1. He could simply listen in on the recordings from the German trackers. Third, the Germans would likely use one of their best radar companies, so by locating those companies, the British could determine when the tests were going to start and could read the reports transmitted by that company.

I wrote about leverage points in *Sources of Power* (1998), viewing their importance for problem-solving. I argued that leverage points, and affordances, cannot be identified by analyzing features of a situation because the leverage points depend on our abilities, as well as on the situation. I used the example of a "hold" in rock climbing. What counts as a hold depends on the surface of the rock but also on our abilities and strength. In the V-1 example, Jones spotted leverage points because of what he knew about the German weapons development process but also because of what he knew about his own system—about Bletchley Park's success with the Enigma code. Spotting leverage points depends on insights about how we can use our own resources.

—June 27, 2014

5.8 The Skill Portfolio Account of Expertise

Time to Move Past a Simplistic Unitary Model

I suggest that we abandon our current unitary concept of experts. Too often, when we think of experts we think of an undifferentiated quality—someone is an expert or isn't. Or we postulate stages of moving from novice to expert. That's not good enough.

In contrast to a unitary concept of experts, a Skill Portfolio account identifies separate skills that experts possess. Experts blend these skills as needed, but the skills themselves are fairly independent—a portfolio of skills. Not all experts will have each of these skills, or need them. The skills describe what experts can do and what they know, as opposed to the outcomes of applying the skills.

Kahneman and Klein (2009) discussed the concept of fractionated expertise, drawing on previous work by James Shanteau (1992). Shanteau also commented that "auditors who have expertise in 'hard' data such as accounts receivable may do much less well with 'soft' data such as indications of fraud (personal communication, February 12, 2009)." In this essay, I am expanding on this idea of fractionated expertise.

We can distinguish five general types of skills that experts may have: Perceptual-motor skills, conceptual skills, management skills, communication skills, and adaptation skills. These are not components of expertise. Some skills may be relevant in one domain but not another. And they are reasonably independent.

1. *Perceptual-motor skills.* Some aspects of perceptual-motor skill constitute tacit knowledge: pattern recognition, perceptual discrimination, motor

skills, and the use of tools. Think of the way dentists use mirrors to repair cavities. A dentist can drill skillfully because the perceptual motor skills of mirror handling have been highly automated.

2. *Conceptual skills*. These include our mental models. For example, the dentist has a conceptual model of how the various materials in a tooth (enamel, dentine, prior filling materials, nerve roots) behave during the drilling process, along with a mental model of how teeth must be configured to be successfully filled with the epoxy or other materials. Our mental models enable us to see the big picture in a situation, to diagnose the causes of problems, and to anticipate future states. Experts also have mastered the Standard Operating Procedures and Best Practices, but their mental models are rich enough to indicate when the SOPs and Best Practices need to be modified or abandoned. Borders, Klein, & Besuijen (2019) have described a Mental Model Matrix that goes beyond a representation of how things work and includes limitations and flaws, as well as workarounds.

3. *Management skills*. Continuing the dental example, the dentist knows how to manage the assistant and the patient during the process, including knowing how the assistant's training will shape his or her behavior. Each patient will behave differently, as will different assistants, but the dentist has the management expertise to make the situation graceful regardless of emergent issues like patient anxiety, training gaps in the assistant, and so on.

4. *Communication skills*. Dentists and their assistants have developed carefully choreographed routines for managing routine procedures and can adapt these routines when they encounter new situations. Communication skills are really tested when the routines break down, like encountering a novel configuration during a root canal. The team members have to explain things to each other and direct each other efficiently and unambiguously.

5. *Adaptation skills*. Ward et al. (2018) have asserted that the essence of expertise is the ability to adapt. This concept of Adaptive Expertise is that experts are faster to adapt to changing conditions (such as COVID-19) than non-experts. Ward et al. provide evidence that adaptation can be improved by training and offer recommendations for such training. The concept of Adaptive Expertise shows why expertise does not become obsolete—in

fact, just the opposite: it becomes the basis for improvising and making discoveries.

These five general skills are identified on several criteria: First, they are acquired through experience and feedback, as opposed to being natural talents. Second, they are relevant to the tasks people perform, and therefore the set of skills will vary by task and domain. Third, superior performance on these skills should differentiate experts from average workers.

The skills will vary for different domains and tasks. Our focus should be on the most important subskills for that domain. Otherwise, it is too easy to have an ever-expanding set of skills to contend with. In some domains, one or more of these general skills may not apply at all. And, as Kahneman & Klein (2009) and Shanteau (1992) note, people may be experts in some aspects of a task but not others. For a fuller discussion of the Skill Portfolio account, using COVID-19 as an example, see: https://medium.com/about-work/business-as-unusual-how-to-train-when-expertise-becomes-outdated-ae4ff924aa29.

There will undoubtedly be disagreements about which skills to include in a Skill Portfolio account, and what level to use in describing a skill, and how distinct some of the skills are from others. We are not dealing with a Table of Elements in chemistry. I expect that these debates will be informative.

The Skill Portfolio account illustrates how shallow it is to claim that new developments will make expertise obsolete. Such claims rely on the unitary model of experts instead of a differentiated model.

—*January 4, 2022*

5.9 How Can We Identify the Experts?

Ten Criteria for Deciding Who Is Really Credible

We want pragmatic guidelines for deciding which if any purported experts to listen to when making a difficult and important decision. How can we know who is really credible?

Bottom line: We cannot know for sure. There are no iron-clad criteria.

However, there are soft criteria, indicators we can pay attention to. I have identified ten so far, drawing on papers such as Crispen & Hoffman (2016) and Shanteau (2015), and on suggestions by Danny Kahneman, Robert Hoffman, and Devorah Klein. Even though none of these criteria are foolproof, all of them seem useful and relevant:

a. *Successful performance*. A measurable track record of making good decisions in the past. (But with a large enough sample, some people will do very well just by luck, such as stock-pickers who have called the market direction accurately in the past 10 years, and will get an undeserved reputation for skill.)

b. *Peer respect*. (But peer ratings can be contaminated by a person's confident bearing or fluent articulation of reasons for choices.)

c. *Longevity*. Number of years performing the task. (But some 10-year veterans have 1 year of experience repeated 10 times and, even worse, some vocations do not provide any opportunity for meaningful feedback.)

d. *Quality of tacit knowledge* such as mental models. (But some experts may not get enough credit because they are less articulate—tacit knowledge is by definition hard to articulate.)

e. *Reliability.* (Reliability is necessary but not sufficient. A watch that is consistently 1 hour slow will be highly reliable but completely inaccurate).
f. *Credentials.* Licensing or certification of achieving professional standards. (But credentials just signify a minimal level of competence, not the achievement of expertise.)
g. *Regret.* When I ask, "What was the last mistake you made?" most credible experts immediately describe a recent blunder that has been eating at them. In contrast to experts, journeymen posing as experts typically say they can't think of any mistakes and can't imagine being wrong. (But some experts, upon being asked about recent mistakes, may choose not to share any of these, even ones they have been ruminating about, especially if they don't fully trust the questioner. Therefore, this criterion of regret and candor is not any more foolproof than the others.)
h. *Falsification.* We can ask purported experts to imagine that they were mistaken—what data might prove them wrong? This counterfactual question is designed to illustrate the cognitive flexibility of the experts and to gauge if they are susceptible to fixation errors. (This kind of flexible thinking certainly seems important for experts, but it only captures one aspect of their ability. It may be necessary, but I don't think it is sufficient.)
i. *Improvisation.* People who are proficient at their work seem to get very frustrated when the procedures fall apart. Experts, however, often seem delighted—they are going to have to improvise instead of just following procedures. This criterion is not just about the ability to improvise but perhaps even more about the enthusiasm for improvising. Ward et al. (2018) have identified the ability to adapt as a primary feature of experts. (But this enthusiasm for improvising may relate to personality style rather than expertise.)
j. *Originality.* Danny Kahneman (personal communication, ca. 2016) has suggested this one: Saying original things that aren't silly. Put another way, saying things that are new and useful. Experts reveal themselves through their comments and observations. (But here we are confounding expertise and creativity.)

Even though none of these ten criteria are foolproof, we can still make judgments about who to consider an expert. Look at criterion (d) above. Tacit knowledge includes perceptual skills. Consider the commentators at

Olympic events like diving. They see things we don't see until they show us in slow motion. I would call them experts. Pattern recognition is another aspect of tacit knowledge. The firefighters I study use pattern recognition to size up situations that seem bewildering to me—and subsequent events confirm their judgments. I consider them experts. Anticipation is another aspect of tacit knowledge. At a fire, I am looking at the size and intensity of the flames and speculating about what additional equipment will be needed. But the experienced commanders are thinking about where to stage this equipment—where to place each truck so that it won't get in the way of other trucks or run over hoses. They are way ahead of me. I consider them experts. Mental models are another type of tacit knowledge. Petrochemical plant operators I have studied can describe the units in the plant and the ways they are connected and how they work but also how they don't work, how they are likely to break down, how a subtle event (e.g., the failure of a sensor) will affect performance, how it can be detected, and how you can work around it. They are aware of causes and causal interactions I cannot even guess at. I consider them experts.

Let's go back to anticipatory thinking. During the Cuban Missile Crisis in 1962, some members of John F. Kennedy's team wanted to launch a surprise attack against Cuba. Others, the real experts, pointed out the likelihood that the USSR might retaliate with a strike against West Berlin, which would probably trigger a nuclear war. They weren't offering predictions. Instead, they were using their mental models to illustrate geopolitical implications. I consider this second group to be experts. They saw things, saw implications, that others did not.

Therefore, criterion (d) offers us a great deal of leverage in assessing who is an expert. It offers us a transitive measure—seeing things that others do not. That's what experts do, and it is what marks them as experts. Klein & Hoffman (1992) provide additional discussion of how experts can see the invisible—the tacit knowledge forming the core of strategy (d).

Are there experts in every field of human enterprise? I don't think so. Some fields are very proceduralized. People are considered experts if they know which page of the procedural manual to turn to. I don't consider them experts.

What about astrologers? In prescientific eras, astrologers developed tacit knowledge, were highly articulate, and were regarded as experts. In a prescientific world, people wouldn't consider most of the criteria I listed at the beginning of this essay. We rule out (a) successful performance, (d) quality of tacit knowledge, (e) measurement of reliability, and (f) professional certification. That leaves (b) peer respect and (c) longevity. So, yes, in a prescientific world, a highly articulate astrologer passes muster. Same as a stock selector or TV political pundit does even today.

Finally, let's examine criterion (e) reliability. This criterion is necessary but not sufficient. It is necessary because expert credibility depends on generating the same recommendations given the same inputs.

Some people would expand the notion of reliability to cover reliability between experts, but Jim Shanteau (2015), one of the leading experts on expertise, has pointed out that there is value in having different experts express varying perspectives. We often use experts not as prognosticators but as consultants, and we can benefit from their divergent viewpoints.

Therefore, we are really looking for within-expert reliability. Shanteau has shown that within-expert reliability varies by domain. For weather forecasters making short-term forecasts, within-expert reliability is .98. For other domains, it is still sizable, although greatly reduced, yet I believe still much higher than for novices (e.g., the correlation is .62 for grain inspectors and .40 for clinical psychologists, where 1.0 is perfect within-expert reliability).

Also, we need to be careful not to encourage people to strive for reliability that is too high—which would lead to rigidity rather than the continuing exploration that is central to becoming an expert.

Now we have ten criteria. To be considered an expert, a person should meet at least one of these criteria, maybe even two or three of them. We shouldn't try to tick off the number of criteria met because quality also matters, especially with criterion (d) the quality of a person's tacit knowledge. And we should also be on guard against criteria that might fool us, such as the person's confident bearing.

We might try to become more skillful at identifying experts, making judgments about which experts to rely on, getting feedback, and reflecting on what we should have been noticing and what we should have been discounting. In that way, perhaps we can develop expertise at identifying experts.

—*September 1, 2018*

5.10 The Art of Being Stupid

Sometimes Being Ignorant Can Pay Off

We are continually encouraged to become smarter—to gain IQ points, to work smarter, to raise more intelligent children. Various mental workout regimens and medications are advertised to improve our memories and ward off the cognitive decline of old age. We are promised a future in which genetic engineering will make us brilliant.

But there is a place for the opposite—for making ourselves stupid.

I discovered the advantage of stupidity while my colleagues and I were conducting cognitive interviews at a petrochemical plant. Our sponsor wanted us to investigate the cognitive skills of panel operators who controlled complex chemical processes at high temperatures and pressures in specially built reactors.

During an interview with a highly experienced panel operator, one of my colleagues, who was leading the interview, explored a challenging incident that had occurred a few years earlier. A valve had gotten clogged, leading to high pressure in the reactor. The panel operator noticed the problem, correctly diagnosed it, and then took actions to clear the plug that was blocking the valve.

Toward the end of the interview, my colleague asked one of our standard questions, "How might a novice have mishandled this event?" The panel operator was puzzled. It seemed obvious what to do. We pressed him and got nowhere.

However, before we moved on to another question, I tried a different tack. I pretended to be a novice. "So, in this situation, I see that the reactor pressure is getting too high. That's the only indication I have—there aren't any sensors telling me the valve is plugged. My temptation would be to close off the feed line to the reactor in order to bring the pressure down. I'm not even thinking about the valve."

He looked at me with some condescension. He admitted that junior operators might do just that, but it was a bad idea. He explained why it was the wrong action to take; his explanation provided useful information about the plant dynamics and the consequences of mistakes. My colleague then used the same strategy to imagine other errors an inexperienced panel operator might make. The expert admitted that these were also possibilities and seemed to warm up to this notion of imagining how a novice might think. He said, with some enthusiasm, that he would explore the issues we had raised with a group of new operators he'd be training the next week.

Afterward, as I reflected on this interview, I was struck by the expert's initial inability to imagine how a novice might get confused. Admittedly, my colleague and I had an advantage because we were novices. (Actually, we were less than novices because we hadn't received any training at all.) That is why it was easy for us to take a novice's perspective. Still, the expert was responsible for training novices. How effective could he be if he couldn't take a trainee's perspective?

And that's when I began to think about the advantages of being stupid—being able to strip away experience and knowledge and see the world through the eyes of a beginner or of anyone making stupid mistakes.

It takes special skill to dial back expertise and intelligence. Experts notoriously have trouble taking a novice's perspective. Experts often assume everyone knows what they do, that everyone sees what they can see.

I think trainers can benefit from making themselves stupid—taking on the perspective of someone who is struggling and confused. Teachers can benefit too. So can designers, wondering about how customers can misinterpret directions and misuse products. We can all benefit from dialing back on experience when we give someone driving directions and anticipate mistakes the person might be tempted to make.

Parents might benefit as well. I see lots of parents getting angry and impatient with young children without considering the child's perspective. But I also see positive examples, parents able to see the world through their child's eyes. One mother used to have a problem with her 3-year-old daughter who would melt down when told it was time to leave a playground.

These fights were so frustrating that the mother cut down on playground excursions. Then she imagined how aggravating it must feel to be told, "OK, it's time to leave. Now!" Accordingly, she switched her strategy and gave her daughter an advance notice, "We need to leave in two minutes, so let's go to your favorite toys for a last slide or climb." This new ritual did the trick. No more playground tantrums.

I recently heard about a case of a 7-year-old girl who was struggling in school. The teacher told the parents that their daughter seemed to be learning disabled regarding arithmetic and needed to be tested. Before scheduling the test, the mother decided to watch her daughter try to add up a column of numbers. The girl failed, but her mother noticed that her daughter's handwriting was poor and the columns she wrote were uneven. The mother tried adding up the numbers her daughter had written down and kept making mistakes. Then the mother had her daughter perform the addition task again, this time using a grid to keep the numbers organized. Now her daughter had no trouble getting the correct answer. The following year, the mother got another note that her daughter was now showing signs of a reading learning disability and needed to be tested. Again, the mother observed her daughter and saw that when she wrote something down, she often failed to leave spaces between the words. The girl had trouble reading her own writing, and so did the mother. The mother had her daughter write a passage on a computer, and now the girl had no trouble reading what she had written. The learning disability had disappeared. Shortly after this second incident, the mother transferred her daughter to a different school.

A very experienced petrochemical trainer once told me that when he first started working with novices, he would wait for them to make a mistake and then slam them. That was how he had been taught. But after a few years, he switched his strategy. Now when he sees a mistake, he becomes curious. He wonders why the trainee made the error and how he can use this information to help him/her out. He has learned the advantage of making himself stupid.

—*January 1, 2016*

5.11 Reflections

The sources of power diagrammed in part 2 depend on expertise. Effective mental models rely on expertise. The Recognition-Primed Decision model runs on expertise. The ShadowBox approach is designed to boost expertise. Information technology should ideally support and enhance our expertise. Seeing cognition is often a matter of appreciating expertise and the tacit knowledge that underlies it.

Therefore, the topic of expertise is central to the themes of this book.

Part 5 should have alarmed you by describing the attempts to dismiss and disqualify experts—the war on expertise. You have seen how five communities, each with its own agenda, have chosen to assault the concept of expertise: The Heuristics and Biases community, the decision research community, the Evidence-Based Performance community, the intelligent technology community, and the social psychology community. You should appreciate the flaws in their arguments and hopefully be on guard when you encounter expert-bashing in the media.

Expertise skeptics sometimes offer a killer observation: every time an algorithm or an intelligent technology is systematically contrasted to an expert, the algorithm or intelligent technology leaves the experts in the dust. Case closed.

Except that when we look more carefully, the case isn't closed at all. Imagine that you are an attending physician, with lots of experience, working in an emergency department. One of your tasks is to diagnose what is wrong with new patients. Perhaps it turns out that an AI system can come up with more accurate diagnoses. So if you look at the numerical data on a patient's vital signs, the AI system looking at the same data can outperform you.

But you might want to conduct a physical, hands-on examination of the patient. That is not allowed—because the AI system can't do that, and we need to be rigorous, right? So then you say you want to talk with the patient and maybe ask some questions. Again, not allowed. You want to watch the patient walk down the hall—not allowed. You want to look at the patient's X-rays. Not allowed. You want to talk with the patient's family. Not allowed.

Thus, the attempt to run a rigorous study has necessarily denied you so many of the ways that you apply your expertise. You are restricted to the numerical data on the patient's intake form. This type of study appears rigorous whereas, in fact, it is deceptive and invalid. To conclude from the results that the intelligent system outperforms experts is deeply misleading. Yet, this type of claim is getting made again and again.

Part 5 started with a joke about a scientist and a flea to make this point. The essay showed how, in the guise of rigor, researchers screen out the tacit knowledge that underlies expertise. Tacit knowledge is not something that intelligent technology can readily handle.

The work of Phil Tetlock (essay 5.2) is illustrative here. Tetlock was originally skeptical that people could have expertise in sociopolitical forecasting. When Tetlock shifted gears and tried to foster forecasting accuracy, he surprised himself—his team of superforecasters wiped out the competition in a forecasting tournament set up by the intelligence community.

Part 5 described several different facets of expertise. Experts are better than the rest of us at detecting anomalies—however, anomalies are events that violate our expectancies, whereas too many researchers treat anomalies as statistical outliers. Experts are better at anticipating events, in part because they have shifted from a procedural mindset to a problem-solving mindset and shifted from a mindless stance to an active, alert, and curious stance. Experts are better at noticing events that were expected but did not occur. And experts are better than the rest of us at identifying leverage points—part 5 used the World War II example of how R. V. Jones crafted a sophisticated strategy to ferret out some of the secrets of the German V-1 missiles. There are many more facets of expertise, but these should give readers a good idea of the ways that expertise is expressed.

Essay 5.8 offers a different take on experts—the portfolio of skills that experts possess, as opposed to thinking of expertise as a unitary dimension. Different experts, in different domains, may show some of these skills more than others.

But—who is an expert? Do we have any solid criteria for distinguishing experts from also-rans? Unfortunately, we don't. Essay 5.9 offered up ten criteria for identifying experts but none of them are foolproof. Each of the criteria, successful past performance, time on the job, reliability, credentials, and the rest, has some inherent flaw. Still, by using several criteria, we might be able to do a reasonable job of spotting the real experts. Despite the lack of a gold standard for who is an expert, part 5 should have strengthened your understanding of experts and your admiration for what they can achieve.

6 Making Discoveries—Speculative Thinking

Overview

One of the enjoyable aspects of working in the field of Naturalistic Decision Making, and continually exploring the cognitive dimension, is the chance to learn about discoveries and insights. It's very inspiring to encounter these stories about the people who make these discoveries and not feel required to belittle or debunk the achievements.

I remember one project with panel operators controlling a distillation tower in a petrochemical plant. Think of a gigantic still, but instead of making whiskey, this plant was making ethylene, a useful plastic compound. My team and I set up some very demanding scenarios in a high-fidelity training simulator for that unit. Most people think of petrochemical plants as places where various products are produced, such as fuels and different types of plastics. Having spent some time in these plants, I have a different view. I see them as potential bombs. Tremendous heat is applied under high pressures to highly volatile chemical compounds. The plant design cuts down on the risk but it doesn't eliminate it. Sometimes, rarely, there is a disaster, perhaps an explosion, perhaps a fire, or a leak of a deadly substance. Therefore, the panel operators controlling the operation have to be very skilled and prepared to adapt to different kinds of problems.

In one of the training scenarios we designed, in a distillation tower designed to transform ethane into ethylene, we injected a malfunction so that there wasn't enough heat to cook the ethane, which slowed down the conversion to ethylene. The malfunction was very subtle—we created a fault in a small override device so that it overreacted and kept a critical valve from opening fully, and that prevented most of the heat from the boiler from getting into the unit. The panel display showed how much that valve was open. But the panel didn't show the status of the override device—that device didn't even appear on the schematics.

We ran eight panel operators, some with less than a year of experience and others with more than 12 years at the unit. All of them quickly spotted the lack of heat as throwing off the production of ethylene.

But what was causing the lack of heat? Most of the operators zeroed in on the critical valve from the boiler. They immediately diagnosed the problem as a sticky valve that had frozen. From their panel controls, they tried again and again to open the valve wider, but that didn't work because of the fault in the override device. Therefore, they gave the orders to send someone to go out into the plant and try to repair the valve.

One experienced panel operator, however, decided to test the diagnosis of a frozen valve. He reasoned that if the valve was really stuck, he shouldn't be able to budge it from his location in the control room. So instead of trying to get it to *open*, he tried to get it to *close*! And he succeeded.

Now he realized the valve wasn't frozen at all, and then he remembered the override device and correctly diagnosed that device as the culprit. His insight was to find a way to test his speculation, even if it meant trying to close a valve that he wanted to open wider. None of the other operators had this insight.

Here's another incident, one that I heard from Shawna Perry, who is an emergency department (ED) attending physician with over 25 years of experience. One night, as Shawna was getting ready to leave the ED and go home, she noticed a young resident finishing out a case. The patient was very, very obese but had no obvious danger signs. The patient had some cognitive impairment and wasn't capable of communicating very well. She was supposed to be going home after a long and tiring day, but Shawna felt that the patient "seemed pale" and looked unwell, at least in her experience. The resident didn't have the experience to make that kind of judgment. Shawna came over and reviewed the patient's vital signs. Pretty low blood pressure, around 90/60. The patient also had low hemoglobin—it was 5, but it should have been in the range of 12–17. The low hemoglobin had been the problem that caused the patient to be sent to the ED.

To Shawna, the low blood pressure and low hemoglobin count usually resulted from a loss of blood. The resident didn't see any real problem, just a few small deviations from normal. Therefore, the resident was closing out the case and getting ready to send the patient home.

Shawna asked him, "Where did the blood go?"

The resident was puzzled by this question. "What's the issue?" he asked. There were no signs of bleeding anywhere.

But to his annoyance, Shawna kept asking, "Where did the blood go?"

Reluctantly, the resident ordered a scan, and they waited for the results. The scan showed that the patient had a cancerous tumor in his leg, plus the leg was broken. Blood had been seeping into that leg, but it wasn't noticed because the patient was so obese.

Shawna's experience told her something was seriously wrong, even though she couldn't diagnose it directly. But she could test it, just as the panel operator in the petrochemical plant could test his assumption. Sometimes insights let us discover what is happening, and at other times, our insight is that the obvious story isn't making sense and needs to be assessed.

That's the cognitive dimension at work. That's the ability to engage in speculative thinking when we are thrust into a confusing situation. That's the ability to sort out a complex and chaotic situation we haven't encountered before, haven't previously imagined. It moves past previous experiences and practices and lets us adapt to unfamiliar situations.

Speculative thinking seems to be a uniquely human capability. Will advanced artificial intelligence (AI) systems ever gain this capability? Maybe someday. Maybe never. Maybe in my lifetime. Maybe not in the lifetime of my grandchildren.

This debate doesn't interest me very much. Instead, I am grateful that I have the chance to celebrate the discoveries and insights that are part of the cognitive dimension.

To "see cognition," we need to be on the lookout for examples, such as the override system in the petrochemical unit and the cancerous tumor in the obese patient. We can study examples like this, large and small, and try to learn more about them: how they happen, what can interfere with them, and how to overcome barriers.

That's the topic of part 6. Speculative thinking. Look back at part 4 and the essay titled "Improv Chess." The gist of that essay was to find ways to encourage speculative thinking, adaptations, and discoveries. The "Improv

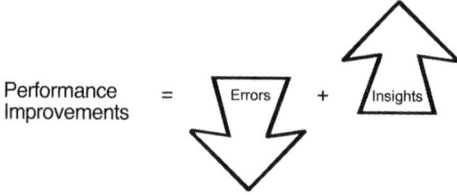

Figure 6.1
Two arrows to improve performance.

Chess" essay shows how we can give people the opportunities to succeed by inventiveness rather than by calculations.

Essay 3.10 included the simple diagram shown again in figure 6.1.

I formulated that diagram in 2005 and included it in presentations I gave. The diagram was just a minor observation about improving performance plus my speculation that most organizations emphasized the down arrow, reducing errors, and gave little thought to the up arrow, what you want to increase, namely insights and expertise. Gratifyingly, most of my audience members agreed. Some agreed very enthusiastically. I would hear again and again, "My company is all about the down arrow." But less gratifyingly, I would also get asked what I could tell people about the up arrow and, specifically, about increasing insights. And I would have to admit that I hadn't studied insights and had nothing to say about the topic.

Finally, I had had enough. I had given a talk in Singapore, using the two-arrow diagram, and gotten the usual agreement plus the usual challenge to provide some information about insights, and I had a 17-hour airplane trip back to the United States. Seventeen hours to stew. Seventeen hours to decide that I needed to study insights so that I could have something to offer. That's how I came to conduct a study of naturalistic insights, looking at the cognitive issues involved in making discoveries. This research became the basis for a journal article (Klein & Jarosz, 2011) and a book, *Seeing What Others Don't* (Klein, 2013). The topic of insights and the remarkable ways we gain them are a counterpoint to the down arrow and the different communities that can only think about ways to reduce mistakes.

The first section of part 6 consists of a set of essays describing different aspects of insight. We start with essay 6.1, "The Insight Test," to make sure we are all calibrated in our understanding of insight. Essay 6.2, "The Second Wave of Critical Thinking," puts insights and discoveries in the context of critical thinking, contrasting them to the first wave, which emphasizes the down arrow of reducing errors. In essay 6.3, "The Different Forms of Insight," I present the results of my research on naturalistic insight.

Essay 6.4, "Scientific Insights," provides some observations that might surprise you about where insights get made within the scientific method.

Essay 6.5 is titled "Cognitive Roadblocks," and it identifies some of the ways that insights can get stymied. We need to diagnose these problems if we are to help people gain insights more readily.

Part 6 then changes direction and examines a variety of ideas for strengthening the up arrow and increasing our chances to make discoveries. Essay 6.6, "Popular Advice for Achieving Insights," covers several of the common recommendations. Essay 6.7, "Dreamy Insights," considers the value of one of these recommendations—to take some time off to let our minds wander and allow the problem we are facing to incubate. Essay 6.8 is "Different Tactics for Making Discoveries," followed by essay 6.9, "The Insight Stance," both of which offer some newer recommendations for making discoveries—suggestions that I think are more helpful.

Essay 6.10, "Getting Unstuck," continues in this vein, showing how the Insight Stance might help when we are feeling trapped. This essay emerged from my investigation of insights and builds on what I learned from people who were able to travel the correction path and break free of assumptions that had been trapping them.

Finally, in essay 6.11, "The Discovery Platform," I describe a method that Shane Mueller and I developed (mostly Shane) for helping people gain insights into AI systems, such as those using machine learning—but I think this method can be applied more generally.

Note: I have done more editing to the essays in this part than in previous parts. I altered essay 6.3 to reflect changes I had made to my model of insight generation subsequent to the posting of that essay on my *Psychology Today* blog. And I renamed essays 6.6 and 6.7 in ways that more effectively convey their content.

6.1 The Insight Test

How Much Do You Know about the Way We Make Discoveries?

Our ability to create insights is critical for innovation and adaptation. Otherwise, we would remain stuck in mental ruts formed over our lifetime. Insights let us see things in new ways. Many people, however, have the wrong ideas about insights. Here is a short test, only 12 items, to assess your knowledge of insights. For each item, circle the number at the left if you agree with the statement and think it has been sufficiently established.

1. Brainstorming is an effective method for groups to generate insights.
2. Insights depend on having fresh eyes, which is why graybeards—the so-called experts—tend to be trapped by their previous experience.
3. Organizations desire insights and encourage their workers to come up with out-of-the-box ideas.
4. The way insights emerge is that we run into an impasse, struggle for a while, and then let our minds wander until suddenly there is a flash of illumination.
5. Correlation doesn't imply causality, so we shouldn't get sidetracked by coincidences.
6. A major barrier to insights arises when we have flawed beliefs and assumptions.
7. To correct flawed assumptions, we should use critical thinking methods, such as listing all the important assumptions we are making to see which might be wrong.
8. Scientists generate insights by running controlled experiments to test their hypotheses.

9. Good scientists work carefully so that they won't make erroneous claims.
10. To handle a challenging project, we should start by pinning down the goals so that we can systematically achieve success.
11. Good ideas often come about by accident, so we should expose ourselves to lots of different fields and different types of specialists.
12. A well-designed computer workstation, tailored to the way we work so that it filters out irrelevant data and highlights the important cues, can boost our chances of having insights.

Let's see how you did. Review your responses, changing any that don't seem quite right. And here is the answer key: zero. None of these items has been clearly established. Some are just wrong, contradicted by the data. Others seem unlikely and have not been supported by evidence. I go into greater detail in *Seeing What Others Don't: The Remarkable Ways We Gain Insights*, but here are some brief explanations.

1. Brainstorming. A popular technique, but the overwhelming weight of evidence shows that groups using it get fewer ideas and less creative ones.
2. Experience doesn't get us into a rut unless the task is so repetitive and mindless that we tune out. A study of insights that I conducted found that experience was essential in two-thirds of the incidents.
3. Organizations resist insights because they are disorganizing and disruptive and get in the way of smooth management. Most managers view novel ideas as impractical and unreliable.
4. This impasse strategy sometimes holds, but it is only one of several different ways that insights emerge. In a sample of 120 insights, only 25 percent involved impasses. None of the 120 insights I studied emerged from the deliberate dreamy, let-your-mind-wander state so often encouraged.
5. Correlation doesn't prove causality, but many important insights started when someone noticed a coincidence.
6. People who gain insights often held flawed beliefs. What set them apart is that they were able to abandon these beliefs whereas others fixated on their flawed beliefs and were trapped by them.
7. The strategy of listing assumptions has never been shown to improve performance. It doesn't even make sense because the beliefs that trap

us are often based on hidden assumptions that we aren't aware we are making. Therefore, we would never list them.

8. When scientists run experiments and get results that support their hypotheses, they haven't gained any insights at all. Only when the results don't work out as expected do scientists have to seek insights. Other parts of the scientific method, such as just observing the phenomenon of interest, are richer sources of insight.

9. Claims that can't ever be wrong are usually pretty bland. Scientists would do better to make the most extreme claims they can defend. Unfortunately, too many scientists are so risk averse that they censor themselves.

10. Many challenging projects involve "wicked problems" that don't have a clear goal. The only path to success is to gain insights about the goal along the way. Locking in on the initial goal is likely to lead to failure.

11. There is no clear evidence that deliberate exposure to lots of diverse ideas will result in more insights.

12. A well-designed workstation may feel comfortable, but it will trap us in our traditional routines and make it harder to have insights about better ways to do the job. If the workstation filters out "irrelevant" cues, it may filter the cues that might spark insights.

The field of insight is marked by myths and superstitions. Only by exposing these outdated ideas can we expect to make progress in using our uniquely human talent to make discoveries and achieve insights.

—*November 25, 2014*

6.2 The Second Wave of Critical Thinking

A Balanced Approach to a Misunderstood Concept

The concept of critical thinking is clearly important. There is widespread acceptance that we would do better if there was more critical thinking. Society would benefit. Students would do better in schools. People would be more successful in their personal and professional lives.

We generally view critical thinking as making judgments based on the systematic analysis of evidence of some problem or topic, rather than relying on impulses, opinions, and emotions. That's the standard approach, which is the first wave of conceptualizing critical thinking.

While the concept of critical thinking can be traced back to Socrates and the Socratic dialogue, interest in training critical thinking skills in the United States rapidly grew after the 1983 publication of *A Nation at Risk*, which described declines in national academic performance and SAT scores.

However, there is a second wave, which is a more recent development. The second wave refers to thinking clearly about what is going on around us and not uncritically accepting what people tell us is happening. It's about thinking for ourselves, asking ourselves, "Is this explanation plausible?"

In his 1994 book *Re-Thinking Reason*, Kerry Walters explained how the first wave concentrated on logical reasoning and the "calculus of justification." The second wave appreciated the importance of imagination, creativity, intuition, and insight.

The first wave is about how we think. The second wave is about what we can discover.

Both waves have value. By disentangling them, perhaps we can find better ways to improve critical thinking and reach a more balanced view of it.

The first wave of critical thinking

The first wave is about trying to reduce errors and illogical reasoning. Critical thinking should be thorough and systematic, rigorous, consistent, logical, and it should rely on reliable evidence. In the System 1/System 2 formulation of cognition, the first wave aligns with System 2.

The first wave has received most of the attention thus far when it comes to critical thinking. I have reviewed some of this literature (Klein, 2011) to capture the kinds of guidance being offered: If we want to strengthen the first wave of critical thinking, we are advised to check our assumptions and to identify the areas of uncertainty that might cloud our judgments. We should worry about inconsistencies and should review our arguments and beliefs and assumptions to try to maintain internal consistency because otherwise we can fool ourselves and draw invalid conclusions.

All of these suggestions are undoubtedly familiar to readers. The Wikipedia entry on critical thinking offers a comprehensive summary of the different aspects of the first wave.

In my 2011 article, I also discussed the dangers of overemphasizing the processes described by the first wave. Most organizations concentrate on the first wave because it is easier to catch errors than to notice when insights got missed. However, we need to be careful not to put so many restrictions on reasoning and inferences that we inhibit creativity.

For example, if we are encouraged to consider all relevant hypotheses, the flood of possibilities may make it harder to judge what is going on. If we spend our time tracking assumptions and uncertainties, checking the pedigree of sources, and checking for logical inconsistencies, we may not have the remaining bandwidth to gain insights. If we require people to justify their conclusions, they will likely attend to cues that they can verbalize and ignore the tacit knowledge that is the core of expertise. Following the requirement for checking assumptions, maintaining internal consistency, and so forth may encourage a passive mindset of trying not to make mistakes rather than an active mindset of trying to make discoveries.

The second wave of critical thinking

The second wave encourages us to use our own judgment about what's happening in situations and what should be happening. Instead of blindly accepting the interpretations of others and passively following orders, we can do more to actively make sense of events.

We can be alert to weak signals that others aren't noticing. We can become curious about coincidences and possible connections. We can be sensitive to events that were supposed to happen but didn't. We can be more mindful. Curiosity appears to be a common denominator for all of these aspects of the second wave of critical thinking.

One aspect of critical thinking is a shift in mindset, from a procedural mindset to an investigative mindset. The procedural mindset is that all we need to do is to follow the procedures. Certainly, in most jobs, we need to learn the procedures. But sometimes the rules and procedures don't apply or would lead to poor outcomes. Procedures are necessary, but they aren't sufficient. We need to learn the procedures but shouldn't get trapped by them. We also need to look around.

This mindset shift, from procedural to investigative, has come up in many different professional settings that I study, such as child protective services. Caseworkers are responsible for keeping children safe after an incident or a report that suggests possible harm. Caseworkers are given training and even checklists for how to conduct site visits and interviews.

But that's not enough. You can't have checklists for what might be dangerous for a specific family in a specific home or living arrangement. A good caseworker needs to go beyond the procedures to imagine what might go wrong, what kinds of risks might emerge.

Here we are in the realm of detecting problems—anticipating dangers. There are no procedures for identifying danger. A caseworker who is a first-wave critical thinker might think his/her job was done after completing all the steps of the checklist and might miss trouble spots not covered in the checklist. When senior administrators in child protective services complain that young caseworkers aren't showing enough critical thinking, they refer to the second wave and being alert to the hazards in a specific home for a specific family.

The second wave of critical thinking also encourages us to question the goals we have been given. It is so easy to mindlessly pursue the official goals and objectives—the ones issued by our organization or by our boss. However, in complex and changing situations, these goals may be overtaken by events. Or we may be up against wicked problems with no definitive goals, and we'll need to revise the goals as we proceed. I have referred to this process as Management by Discovery: the need to adapt and improvise, not simply adapt the tactics for achieving the goals, but to rethink the goals themselves. Essay 9.10 elaborates more on this concept.

Conclusions

My purpose in writing this essay was to offer a broader perspective of critical thinking, encompassing both the first and the second waves. The first wave has initiated many thoughtful and useful ideas and programs (e.g., Halpern, 2007).

The second wave is an important balance to the first. The second wave develops programs and methods to prepare decision-makers to independently assess what is happening and what goals they should be pursuing. Hopefully, the future will see additional progress in strengthening both aspects, the first and second waves of critical thinking.

—May 26, 2020

6.3 The Different Forms of Insight

Insights Come in Several Varieties

In 1926, Graham Wallas described the four stages of insight: preparation, incubation, the flash of illumination, and verification. This model of insight tries to explain how people make discoveries that get them past impasses. For example, the 9-dot puzzle challenges people to connect all the dots with only four lines, without lifting pen from paper (see figure 6.2).

The 9-dot puzzle seems impossible. Most people struggle and many cannot find a solution. (A solution is shown at the end of this essay; see figure 6.4.)

What makes the puzzle so hard is that we have been trapping ourselves with flawed assumptions. We don't have to stay within the borders, and we don't have to change directions on a dot. And notice that the first-wave critical thinking exercise of listing all our assumptions wouldn't have helped us

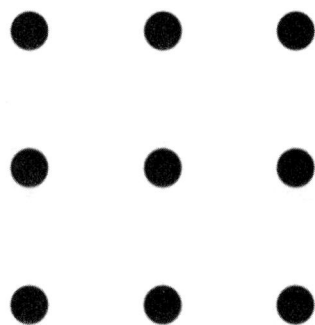

Figure 6.2
The 9-dot puzzle problem.

because we make these two assumptions (stay within the borders and change direction on a dot) unconsciously. It is difficult to list unconscious assumptions.

The impasse paradigm fits the Wallas model and is the most common method for studying insights. We can think of it as a correction path because we are correcting flawed assumptions to escape from an impasse. But this is only one form of insight.

Other types of insight don't involve impasses and don't require us to detect flawed assumptions. The second variety of insight hinges on spotting a contradiction—something that doesn't make sense. The "Anomaly Detection" essay in part 5 used the example of the police officer who noticed the driver of a new BMW flick his ashes. No impasse, no advance preparation, just a troubling anomaly.

The third variety of insight involves a connection, shown in figure 6.3. Think of Charles Darwin, who read a book by Malthus on competition for scarce resources, such as food; Darwin appreciated that his theory of evolutionary changes could be driven by survival of the fittest.

This third form, the connection insight, is illustrated by a news story about how to use mushrooms to protect the environment. This mushroom revelation also teaches us some important lessons about insights. The story started when a high school boy made an accidental observation while shoveling wood chips on his father's maple sugar farm in Vermont. That observation has evolved into an exciting technology for using mushrooms in place of the Styrofoam plastics we see all the time in packing peanuts and coffee cups. Styrofoam lasts almost forever, littering highways and oceans. The new mushroom technology, which is cheap to produce and safely

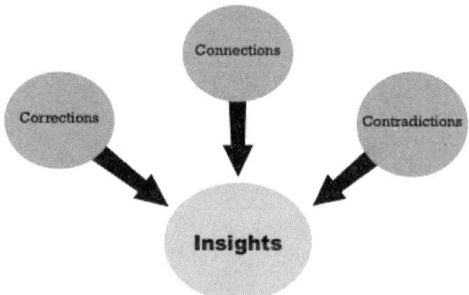

Figure 6.3
The Triple Path model of insight.

The Different Forms of Insight

biodegrades in a month, might someday replace Styrofoam as an insulation and packing material.

The short version of the discovery—for a fuller account see Ian Frazier's article, "Form and Fungus" in *The New Yorker* May 20, 2013—starts with Eben Bayer performing farm chores such as moving wood chips around. Even when the piles of wood chips were covered by a tarp, they still got wet; mushrooms would sprout and weave the chips together into clumps, making it easier for Eben to lift them with his pitchfork. Not an earth-shaking observation, not worth writing a scientific paper about. Just a passing lesson as Eben helped his father.

Fast-forward a few years and Eben was attending Rensselaer Polytechnic Institute (RPI) in Troy, New York. He had been given a course assignment to make insulation panels using perlite, a mineral that comes in large granules that settle, making it hard to apply uniform coatings. It was difficult to get the perlite to clump together, which made Eben remember his wood chips. So he ordered a cheap mushroom kit and mixed the spores with perlite, adding water and nutrients to let the mushrooms sprout. In a few days, he had achieved success. The mushroom strands had woven the perlite into a solid disk, the shape of the glass flask in which he had grown the mixture.

In his senior year at RPI, Eben showed this disk to another professor, in a course called "The Inventor's Studio." Eben wasn't sure what to do with the disk and hoped the professor would be impressed. He was. He immediately appreciated that Eben had invented a biological polymer that could replace Styrofoam and other synthetic polymers. Growing the mushroom compound requires minimal energy—you just mix the right kinds of mushroom spores with waste products, such as rice husks and corn stalks; put it in a mold to give it the shape you want; and turn off the lights. A few days later, it is ready. You stop it from growing by applying heat, which kills the mushroom strands. The professor helped Eben and his partner set up a small company that has the potential to become the biological version of Dow Chemical or DuPont.

Eben didn't run into an impasse about how to use mushrooms as a biological polymer because he wasn't trying to invent a replacement for Styrofoam. He didn't even understand the implications of his invention until his professor enlightened him. Wallas's account of insight doesn't work, at least in cases like this.

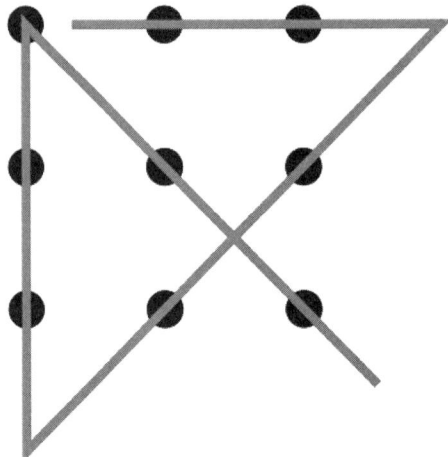

Figure 6.4
The 9-dot puzzle solution.

Insights don't necessarily depend on preparation. They don't necessarily help us get past impasses. If we want to understand insights, we'll need to broaden our perspective to take stories like this into account. We will need to appreciate that there are several pathways to achieving insight.

—June 12, 2013

6.4 Scientific Insights

Most Research Discoveries Aren't Where We Would Expect Them

How do scientists work? A common view is that they spend their time testing hypotheses: selecting a good hypothesis to test, designing a study with the right control groups, arranging the stimuli and conditions, collecting and analyzing the data. Then, if everything works out, the results will support the hypothesis, giving statistically significant differences between experimental and control groups, and the experiment can be written up and published. This is an ideal case.

But it has one big problem: a lack of insights. In this scenario, the researcher hasn't made any discoveries.

Where are the insights in the scientific process? Let's look at the "scientific method." There is no official definition of the scientific method, but I think most scientists would agree about the basic steps.

Step 1. Select the question or phenomenon. Lots of opportunities for insight here as scientists try to pin down a question or phenomenon to investigate, revise it, often changing it as they make discoveries about what they think is really going on.

Step 2. Observe and gather data directly. Again, lots of opportunities for insights as the observations add more detail and add unexpected wrinkles that contradict beliefs and/or connect with beliefs in unexpected ways. Careful observation often shakes scientists loose from their preconceptions.

Step 3. Interpretation. Build a story, theory, or hypothesis. The struggle to make sense of the observations often results in insights. Here is where new theories emerge.

Step 4. Use data to evaluate the theory. If this step proceeds smoothly, then no insights are generated. Scientists only formulate insights when the data do NOT conform with expectations and don't readily support the hypothesis. When that happens, researchers may be disappointed and frustrated, hoping that some error had crept into the analysis and that the data really do conform to the intended result. However, after further reflection, sometimes weeks or months later, the researcher may conclude that the phenomenon actually is more complex than originally imagined. Eventually, the researcher may be amused at how simplistic the original hypothesis was.

Step 5. Generalize. In stretching to apply the findings to new conditions and domains, scientists may acquire further insights.

Notice that the only place in the scientific method that fails to generate insights is the classical activity of testing a hypothesis and getting the desired results. The conventional view of research centers on the activity that is least likely to yield insights. And conventional views ignore the activities, particularly in the early stages of the scientific method, where insights are most likely to be found.

By dissecting the scientific process, we can see where insights happen. And where they don't.

—*February 3, 2014*

6.5 Cognitive Roadblocks

What Prevents Us from Having More Insights?

In the earlier essay, "The Different Forms of Insight," I described three different forms of insight: (a) making connections, (b) seeing contradictions, and (c) overcoming impasses by correcting flawed beliefs. I identified these different forms in a 2011 study in which I collected 120 examples of insight and then sorted them out. I was trying to understand how people arrive at insights.

But what can get in our way? What kinds of things *prevent* insights? To find some answers, I went back through these 120 accounts and found 30 cases in which 1 person had an important insight, while another person with the exact same information failed. For example, after Darwin presented his theory of evolution, T. H. Huxley reacted, "How extremely stupid not to have thought of that."

One such pairing involved Watson and Crick, who made a breakthrough about how genetic information is transmitted from parents to their offspring. Other scientists at the time possessed the same information as Watson and Crick. Remember that Watson and Crick never did a single study of their own, so they weren't holding anything back. But the other scientists, even ones who had collected the data that Watson and Crick used, got scooped.

Another pairing was the CIA's determination in October 1962 that the Soviet Union was preparing to place ballistic missiles in Cuba. John McCone, the director of the CIA, understood the implications of the photographs taken by the U-2 spy aircraft. However, Sherman Kent, a CIA specialist in Russian behavior, judged it highly unlikely that Nikita Khrushchev, the Soviet leader, would do anything so risky. Kent had all the same information as McCone, but he drew the opposite conclusion.

I reviewed each of the 30 pairs to try to identify the reasons why the uninspired person missed the discovery. I found several different types of barriers (see figure 6.5).

First, a number of people missed the insights because they tenaciously held onto flawed beliefs. Sherman Kent didn't think that Khrushchev would take any big risks; Kent had carefully studied the historical trends. But that study made him vulnerable to shifts in the trends. Watson and Crick had a few erroneous beliefs of their own, but they didn't become trapped by them.

Second, experience made a difference. People with a richer background could notice implications in the data that others missed. On the surface, Watson and Crick had less experience than the leading scientists of the day. They were the upstarts. However, many of the leading geneticists at the time didn't know biochemistry; they were just interested in the characteristics of genes. Likewise, the organic chemists who were studying DNA weren't interested in genetics. In contrast, Watson and Crick were a good collaborative team. They had the right blend of experience and complemented each

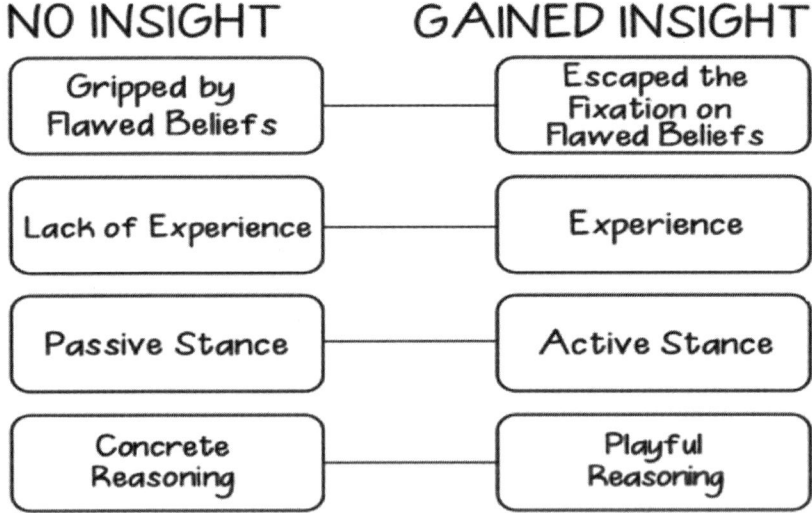

Figure 6.5
Four types of barriers.

other. Crick's background was in physics, X-ray diffraction methods, proteins, and gene function. Watson's background was in biology, phages (bacterial viruses), and bacterial genetics. Crick was the only crystallographer interested in genes. Watson was the only one coming out of a US-based phage group who was interested in DNA.

Third, the people who missed the insight were more likely to have a passive stance than an active one. Back to the DNA example. Rosalind Franklin had a fairly passive stance. She was going to carefully collect data before entering into any speculations, unlike Watson and Crick who were filled with wild speculations. Those wild speculations were indicators of an active stance.

Fourth, a fixation with concrete reasoning tended to restrict insights, while more playful styles relishing speculation and hypothetical reasoning increased them.

A reasoning style isn't something you can easily change, and experience isn't something you can readily obtain. But the other two factors do appear malleable. We may be able to take steps to become less fixated on our beliefs and more flexible in our thinking. And we may be able to become more mindful, taking an active stance more often.

—*June 18, 2013*

6.6 Popular Advice for Achieving Insights

Five Popular Ideas for Increasing Discoveries

Let's review five ideas for boosting insight that have been put forth by different authorities:

- Increase swirl
- Encourage failures
- Be open to new ideas
- Apply critical thinking
- Get into a quiet, meditative mood

Each of these ideas seems reasonable, useful, and worth trying. Nevertheless, I am not convinced by any of them. It may be worth examining my misgivings in order to see what a more effective strategy needs to achieve.

Increase swirl. Steven Johnson, in *Where Good Ideas Come From* (2010), has championed the notion that we can spark innovation and insights by exposing ourselves to lots of ideas, particularly unfamiliar ideas. Many others have come to the same conclusion. A number of companies designed their office layouts to mix up specialties, forcing the knowledge workers to bump into different types of specialties. The strategy of increasing swirl fits into the connection path in my model of insight: people make unexpected connections between ideas.

Nevertheless, I am uncomfortable. I doubt the anecdotal evidence because it's based on hindsight. If I am a mechanical engineer, and I have lunch with a friend who works in the optics department, and she describes a new project that gives rise to an insight, great. But what about all the lunches that didn't result in insights? It's like having a great idea while taking a shower and then doubling the number of showers you take as a way to double your chances of having more great ideas.

Another problem with the swirl strategy is that insights don't arise by increasing the combinations of ideas, because the more ideas we expose ourselves to, the more connections and the more useless combinations we have to sort through. In contrast, when an insight arises, we know right away. Sure, sometimes we're wrong and we find out later that the discovery won't work, but we aren't plowing through lots and lots of sterile combinations.

Encourage failures. I think the strategy of learning from failures is very important, so I do see merit in the advice to encourage failures and the slogans to fail fast to learn faster. The failure-based strategy was advocated by Karl Popper, the philosopher of science, who pointed out that no theory is perfect and so scientists should be trying to refute their own theories rather than defending them. However, despite this sage advice, scientists do not try to shoot down their own theories. We aren't built that way. The failure strategy doesn't match our psychological makeup. Personally, I hate failure. I have failed too often, and each time it takes a toll. Later, I can sometimes look back and diagnose why I failed, so I do learn a lot from my failures. But I never enjoy them and never set out to fail. I suspect few people are built to seek out failure. Therefore, this advice doesn't seem practical.

Be open to new ideas. Many advice manuals state some variation of this strategy to stay open-minded. And the advice makes good sense. People who are closed to new ideas are unlikely to have insights. The advice to keep an open mind seems to be particularly relevant to the contradiction path of insights, reminding us not to be too quick to dismiss evidence that doesn't fit our preconceptions.

What's the problem? Simply that the advice to be open doesn't seem all that powerful. It's not clear what we can do to keep open-minded. The advice is more of a slogan than a strategy.

And when I go back to my 120 examples of insight and look at the set of contradiction cases, I find something strange: in two-thirds of them, the person did NOT have an open mind but was skeptical of the conventional wisdom and was seeing events through that skeptical lens. Very different from an open mind.

Apply critical thinking. Laboratory-based studies of insight generally use some variation of the impasse paradigm: give the subjects a puzzle that traps them into making an unnecessary assumption. The impasse paradigm lines up with the correction path in my Triple Path model of insight (see figure 6.3).

The only way forward is to discover which assumption can be jettisoned. Therefore, the critical thinking approach (first wave) of listing assumptions seems spot on.

And yet I am dubious about the value of critical thinking for generating insights. One reason is that I am not aware of any evidence that if you follow critical thinking practices to list assumptions and sources of uncertainty you will have greater numbers of insights. A second reason is that even with laboratory tasks, the subjects are trapped by assumptions they are not even aware they are making.

Get into a quiet, meditative mood. If insights emerge from our subconscious mind, then we might be able to coax more of them into consciousness by giving them space—by quieting down all the clutter that usually fills our thoughts. The essay "Dreamy Insights" explains my misgivings about this advice because none of the 120 cases of insight I studied had emerged from this kind of deliberate incubation. (The essay also describes ways that incubation might occur.)

None of these five approaches seems very helpful. However, reviewing what is wrong with each of these suggestions may provide some ideas about what an effective insight strategy would have to achieve.

—*May 10, 2015*

6.7 Dreamy Insights

Can We Get in the Mood for Breakthroughs?

The popular view is that we can summon forth insights by entering into a dreamy state of mind, just letting our thoughts drift, such as in Kiefer and Constable's *The Art of Insight: How to Have More Aha! Moments* (2013). Calm and receptive moods are thought to give insights a place to land as they cross the boundary from our unconscious into our conscious awareness.

Some evidence supports this notion of an insight state of mind. John Kounios and Mark Beeman (2009) reviewed neuroscientific studies and found evidence of increased alpha-band activity, followed by increased gamma-band activity just before people solved puzzles. The alpha-band activity is linked to putting the brain in idle, and even inhibiting activity in brain areas, so this pattern does fit the notion of entering into a dreamy state.

In addition, the concept of a dreamy state fits the idea of incubation that Graham Wallas described in 1926. After trying to solve a problem and failing, people reported how the solution came to them suddenly when they ceased their efforts and engaged in recreational activities, such as taking a walk. The data on incubation are mixed—most studies report some incubation effect but at least a third of the studies failed to find any evidence that incubation increased insights.

Out of curiosity, I went back through my database of 120 examples of incidents to see how often people deliberately entered a dreamy state of mind in order to gain an insight. The answer was clear: Zero! Not a single person willed himself/herself into having an insight.

I found only five cases where the insight was preceded by incubation (none of these people was deliberately trying to gain an insight during that incubation period), versus 47 cases where no incubation was possible. One of those cases featured a wildland firefighter, Wagner Dodge, who had gotten trapped on a hill in Montana. A fire on the other side of a gulch had unexpectedly crossed over the gulch and was rapidly growing in intensity as it swept up the hill. Wagner Dodge and his crew were running for their lives, barely a minute ahead of the forest fire. Suddenly, Dodge had the insight to start an escape fire in front of him to burn off the grass, leaving only the ashes, which he could take refuge in. There was no time for incubation in cases like this. The other 68 cases in my sample were inconclusive.

My database included 22 cases where the insight was accidental—the person wasn't trying to solve any problem. There was no reason to get into a mood for insight in these cases.

I have also discussed how insights take different forms. One form is to notice a connection—these insights usually occur immediately upon receipt of new information. No dreamy, incubation state here. Another form is to notice a contradiction, also on receiving new information.

A third form is more promising—insights that arise when we escape from an impasse by discovering the unconscious assumption that's been trapping us. Think of the 9-dot problem. This impasse paradigm is the one used in neuroscience studies because it is so easy to schedule. This is the form of insight most likely to fit the "dreamy state of mind" strategy. However, many of the incidents in my database involved people who were desperate to find a solution, such as Wagner Dodge who was running for his life. That type of desperation doesn't fit with a dreamy state of mind.

As a result, I am unconvinced that we can deliberately promote insights by getting to a calm mental space. I think insights are more likely to arise when we adopt an active, rather than a passive mindset, and when we give rein to curiosity and speculation upon encountering something that doesn't fit our preconceptions.

Nevertheless, there might be some ways that incubation could work. If incubation lets us recover from mental fatigue, that points to the correction path—and to our struggles with an impasse. Incubation could work by sparking remote associations, and then we are dealing with the connection path and with joining different ideas. Incubation could make it easier to build on chance events, which points to the connection path and noticing the significance of unexpected cues, but it also touches on the contradiction path and musing about inconsistencies that have gained awareness through the chance events. Therefore, the different mechanisms for incubation might be linked to the three paths we take in gaining insights.

—*August 19, 2013*

6.8 Different Tactics for Making Discoveries

Each Path to Insight Calls for Its Own Techniques

My research uncovered three different pathways for gaining insights: making connections (and also seeing coincidences), spotting contradictions, and a correction path to discard flawed assumptions—often marked by a sense of creative desperation.

Each path has its own set of tactics for trying to gain insights. Each path has its own pitfalls. And each path opens up different methods and opportunities.

Connection path. The connection path works best if we can sustain an active mindset, not just running on automatic but being alert to nuances and implications. Langer (2014) would call it a mindful stance as opposed to a mindless, tuned-out stance. It is not clear how easy it is to be more mindful, in the moment. I suspect that we can become more mindful and present than we typically are.

When we shift to a more active mindset, we will also engage in more anticipatory thinking: imagining how events might unfold. We are not predicting the future, just sensing opportunities and risks we might not have otherwise noticed.

The active mindset helps us explore anomalies that we might otherwise dismiss, opening up new possibilities for gaining insights.

Steven Johnson has suggested that we would gain more insights by exposing ourselves to a greater variety of ideas. I am not convinced of this advice—it seems anecdotal. Nevertheless, such a strategy certainly fits the connection path.

Another suggestion is to try to shift into a tranquil mood that allows remote associations to form and gain consciousness by letting our minds wander. Again, I am skeptical because the tranquil, dreamy state seems counter to an active mindset. Also, in the sample of 120 insights that I studied, not a single one emerged through a deliberate attempt to shift into a meditative state. However, my suspicions may be unfounded, as discussed in the previous essay. For instance, the use of a tranquil, dreamy state to encourage remote associations fits within the connection path.

Contradiction path. For contradiction insights, we need to react differently to conflicts, confusions, problems, failures, miscalibrations. Our natural tendency is to paper over the differences, to smooth out the perturbances, to resolve the disagreement, in order to regain harmony on our team and harmony among our thoughts. However, contradictions require us to sharpen the disagreements and conflicts and take them more seriously. Contradiction insights flow more easily when we pursue the "what-ifs" instead of being impatient with idle speculation.

We often try to dismiss conflicts by explaining away the discrepancy, but contradiction insights only emerge when we take the discrepancy seriously and imagine the implications if the discrepancy was valid. The conflict often makes us uncomfortable because it implies that we haven't thought things out as clearly as we should. And that's the point. The conflict and confusion within a team are pointing us to the areas that haven't been thought out so well, exposing areas that contain opportunities for useful discoveries.

The Pre-mortem method, which I discuss in part 9, works so well because it deliberately invites disagreements. It invites the team members to surface doubts and inconsistencies. In a Pre-mortem, the team members independently list everything that worries them about a new plan or project. This method threatens the complacency of the group. Too often, complacency masquerades as harmony.

Correction path. This path, often born of creative desperation, aims to find a flawed assumption that is blocking a way forward. Simply listing our assumptions won't work because very often the critical assumption is one we are not even aware we are making. As with the contradiction path, one way forward is to become alert to anomalies and inconsistencies that may hold a clue to the flawed assumption.

Different Tactics for Making Discoveries 231

A more aggressive strategy is to deliberately try on different perspectives to see what might be learned. These trial perspectives might include viewing ourselves through the eyes of a competitor, viewing our situation through the eyes of a successor who is not tied to sunk costs that might be trapping us, and imagining that we are overlooking some weak signals.

—March 29, 2014

6.9　The Insight Stance

Boosting Your Insights

Maybe there is a way to increase our chances of making discoveries.

I have been examining a new strategy for boosting insights. I am calling it an Insight Stance. Before I explain what an Insight Stance is, I want to go over some of the thinking that got me there.

One thing I did was to try to learn lessons from existing approaches. Essay 6.6, "Popular Advice for Achieving Insights," listed some conventional suggestions for increasing insights and explained why I didn't think any of them would work. These limitations can help us see what an effective insight strategy needs to do. First, it should dramatically increase the success rate. Some of the strategies seek to generate lots of options. These may lead to more insights, but they'll also produce many bad ideas, so we'll have to do a lot of work to filter out all the ideas we can't use. A fruitful insight strategy won't produce lots of losers. Second, a good insight strategy will help us learn from failures without pretending that we love failures or want to learn fast by failing fast. Failures hurt, and while we can get smarter as we lick our wounds, it's better not to get wounded in the first place. Third, we may want to keep an open mind, but an open mind is too passive, and insights arise from being actively curious. Besides, sometimes we gain insights by being skeptical and contrarian.

Another source of ideas was when I contrasted people who gained insights with others who didn't. In my study of 120 insights, I found 30 incidents that included a contrasting "twin": a person who had the same information as the one who gained the insight but failed to make the discovery.

I compared the two people in each of these cases, the one who had the insight and the one who missed it. Here are the differences I spotted: The failure twin often got trapped by his/her flawed beliefs, whereas the person who gained the insight was able to escape from mistaken beliefs. In addition, the successful twin had an active mindset, whereas the failure twin was just passively doing his/her job without giving it much thought. Also, the successful twin seemed to relish speculating about how things might work differently, whereas the failure twin was often a concrete thinker and impatient with these flights of fancy.

The Insight Stance emerged from these observations. Before I describe it, I'd like you to adopt an inquiring mindset rather than a skeptical one. Skepticism comes naturally to many of us when we first encounter a new idea, but I'd like you to defer your skepticism for a bit. Once I explain the Insight Stance you can and should shift back into a critical mode. However, you'll get more out of this exercise by imagining how you might use the Insight Stance. It's like trying on new clothes—you want to start with enthusiasm.

The Insight Stance is a mental set we adopt for encountering new ideas and events. Others have advocated a meditative stance or letting our minds wander, but I am suggesting the reverse: we can adopt an active, curious mindset, preparing to be delighted by discoveries. Advocates of critical thinking (the first wave) encourage us to use a skeptical stance, and, again, the Insight Stance is just the opposite, promoting curiosity and exploration.

We can focus this mindset in a few ways.

a. Wonder about inconsistencies and anomalies instead of dismissing them or explaining them away. We don't want to get distracted by every anomaly, but we will spend a few seconds noticing anomalies or contradictions that might be important and thinking about what they might mean.

b. Wonder about coincidences, not every coincidence, but ones that seem promising.

c. Give a freer rein to our curiosity, spending a bit more time speculating about the implications of events or ideas that aren't on the main path we are pursuing.

d. Be alert to unexpected connections between ideas.

e. Notice leverage points that might help us when we get stuck, alternative ways to move forward when our usual problem-solving methods aren't working. These are all the different pathways that I identified when I analyzed the 120 cases in my research project. They are the pathways that lead to insights.

We can't sustain this Insight Stance indefinitely, but I think we can learn to enter into it more easily, more often, and for longer periods than usual. The Insight Stance might be a habit of mind that we can practice. One exercise is to actively celebrate the insights we have, the small ones, as well as the large ones. If you are like me, you spend a fair amount of mental energy brooding about stupid decisions and dumb mistakes. What if we devoted some more mental energy to noticing insights we've had and savoring our successes? These could be industrial-strength insights like a new idea for a product or service. Or they can be small-scale, like diagnosing why a cell phone is giving us trouble and fixing the problem. Or smaller scale yet.

A few days ago, I noticed some workmen in my apartment building fiddling with a door in the "C" wing. I came to a locked door to the staircase in the "B" wing, but when I punched in the code, the door didn't unlock. Very strange. I tried a few more times, then gave up and took the elevator. Later, as I passed the locked door to the "A" wing, I tried the code and again had no success. And then it hit me. The workman must have been fitting a new combination lock to the staircase in the "C" wing. Up to now, it was the only one that had allowed free entry. The men had been working in the vicinity of the "C" wing door—I hadn't paid much attention when I passed them. When they installed the new lock, they must have changed the code for the doors leading to the two other stairways because you want all the door locks to have the same entry code. And then I remembered reading an announcement that all residents needed to be more alert to intruders because some thieves had been spotted breaking into a car parked nearby on the street. Suddenly it all fit together. That's why the old code wasn't working. Sure enough, that afternoon we got a notice with the new code. This isn't a major insight, but it was a pleasing one.

We have these kinds of insights all the time. Let's take note of them, perhaps enter them in an insight diary. We want to encourage ourselves to enter into an Insight Stance more often.

The Insight Stance might counter the dread we experience when things don't go as planned. It should foster a sense of wonder and exploration as we are forced to—or rather, as we are allowed to—improvise and see what we can discover. That's one of the ways I distinguish experts from people who are merely proficient. The journeymen get frustrated when none of the standard techniques work. The experts get a sparkle in their eyes as they take on the new challenge. The Insight Stance is intended to promote that sparkle in all of us.

At the level of teams and organizations, you might be able to promote insights by altering the way you do business. For instance, many organizations run progress reviews every month for projects. The project leader gets up and shows how well the tasks are getting completed and how well the resources are being expended in keeping with the plan. But you can add an additional component to these progress reviews, especially if the project has to cope with vague goals and complex situations: ask the project leader, "What has happened since the last review that surprised you?" If the project leader answers, "No surprises, so you don't have to worry," that's when you should start worrying. You want a project leader who is alert to anomalies and ready to make adjustments and gain insights.

If you are a supervisor, what you want to do here is to encourage your project leaders to be on the lookout for anomalies and surprises. You want them to speculate about new goals that might result in greater success. You want them to consider departures from the plan rather than being locked into meeting milestones. You want them to be adaptive, not only in changing the plan but also in changing their thinking.

You can also change your stance about conflicts. Here is an example. During a recent seminar, I discussed how difficult it is for supervisors to communicate what they want. Subordinates frequently misunderstand. One person

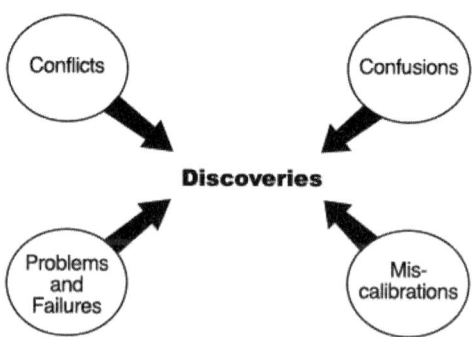

Figure 6.6
Discoveries.

in the group interjected that he knew just what I was talking about. The previous week he had that exact experience. He had given a task to someone on his staff, but when he checked back a few days later, the man had gotten it wrong. So he explained his intentions again. Very frustrating.

I asked this supervisor if he had questioned his staff member to see what the man thought was wanted, and the supervisor looked puzzled. "No," he said. "Why would I do that?" And I thought—because the staff member might have a flawed mental model of the work, and you could correct it. Or perhaps the directions you thought were so clear were in fact ambiguous, and you can learn a lesson about communicating your intentions.

People who can adopt this curiosity-oriented stance might find that they are fostering discoveries instead of resentment (see figure 6.6).

These two issues, progress reviews and confusions/conflicts, simply illustrate the kinds of activities organizations can engage in when they want to create a culture that encourages discoveries, as opposed to a culture that just wants to eradicate errors. Organizations have many ways to build on an Insight Stance. They have many opportunities to increase the insights of the workers and also the supervisors and leaders.

—*June 4, 2015*

6.10 Getting Unstuck

What to Do When You Need a Breakthrough
___

We all know the feeling of getting stuck: we need to solve a problem, but we don't see any daylight. Maybe the problem is unsolvable, but maybe, just maybe, there is a way out. Unfortunately, try as we may, we can't find it.

Chess players often face this challenge. They even have a name for the process—creative desperation.

However, getting past an impasse isn't always a game. In 1949, Wagner Dodge led a team of smokejumpers who got trapped by a forest fire in Montana. They raced as fast as possible uphill, but the fire was rapidly gaining on them, and Dodge realized his team could never outrun it. Then he had an insight. Looking at the heavy dry grass all around him, he realized that he could set a fire that would burn the grass ahead, depriving the fire of fuel. Barely a minute before the forest fire engulfed him, he used his canteen to wet his handkerchief, held it over his face, dove into the ashes of the escape fire he had started, and saved his life.

Aron Ralston faced a life-and-death impasse when his right hand became trapped by a small boulder that pinned him to the side of a canyon. He spent several days, hoping someone would rescue him, but no one came. He used his knife to try to chisel a gap between the boulder and the canyon wall and pull his hand free, to no avail. Out of food, out of water, weak with exhaustion, he made the decision to cut off his hand in order to escape from the trap. But by now his knife was too dull. He couldn't cut through the bone. He was done for. He threw a small involuntary tantrum, flailing around, and as he flailed, he noticed the bone in his arm bend. And in that instant, he realized that he didn't have to cut through the bone—he could snap it! His insight let him escape from his canyon trap.

Most psychological studies of insight rely on impasse problems. Not the life-and-death kind, but small impasses that fit into a laboratory, like the two-string problem: finding a way to join two strings that are hanging from the ceiling but are too far apart. Most subjects in these kinds of experiments get stuck and stay stuck, failing to notice the pair of pliers lying on the ground, along with other items, such as a book of matches, an extension cord, and some books. The subjects don't see that they can tie the pliers to one of the strings and get it swinging while they take hold of the other string. But some subjects have the insight and use the pliers to solve the problem.

In my book *Seeing What Others Don't: The Remarkable Ways We Gain Insights*, I pointed out that these kinds of impasse situations weren't the only path to insight. We also achieve insights by noticing connections and contradictions. In fact, in the sample of 120 real-life insights that I studied, this creative desperation path, as I called it, was much less frequent than the other two.

Nevertheless, impasse problems can be very important—as we see in the Wagner Dodge and Aron Ralston examples. This path is the only one of the three insight paths in which the person is deliberately searching for a solution. What can we learn from people who have succeeded? To investigate this path further, I went back to the 120 insight examples I had compiled and identified 25 incidents of impasses that got overcome. I added two more that weren't part of the original sample (Aron Ralston was one) for a total of 27.

Looking through the 27 cases for a common theme, I found one: the impasse was created when the person asked the wrong question. The insight came when the person replaced the original question with a better one. Wagner Dodge was fixated on outrunning the forest fire, but the life-saving question was how to keep the fire from engulfing him. Aron Ralston was fixated on using his dull knife to cut through his bone, but the life-saving question was how to separate the portion of bone connected to his hand from the portion connected to his elbow.

The shift to a new question often includes a shift to a higher-level goal: not getting engulfed by fire rather than outrunning the fire, disconnecting the forearm bone rather than cutting through it.

When we shift to a better question, we spot leverage points we hadn't noticed before: the escape fire, the snapping of the bone. In fact, seeing the leverage point is part of the process of shifting to the new question. When

Aron Ralston threw his tantrum, he noticed the bone in his forearm bending, which was the hint he needed to recast his question.

Hints are very important. A total of 18 out of the 27 impasse incidents I studied depended on people noticing hints that suggested a better question and a new leverage point. We can't just will ourselves to shift to a better question—we need to be open to hints. One suggestion for handling impasses is to adopt an active, curious mindset to increase the chance of noticing these hints. Even for toy problems like the two-string task, researchers found that if they "accidentally" brushed against one of the strings and set it swinging, that hint helped a lot of the subjects change from the question of how to grasp both strings to the better question of how to get one of the strings to swing—at which point they noticed the pliers.

Two other impasse incidents out of the 27 I studied were solved by a "shake the tree" strategy of finding a way to probe the situation to uncover an essential hint. The protagonists in these incidents manufactured their own hints.

For five of the 27 impasse incidents, the solution was to shift to a better question, but I couldn't detect any hint in the account of the incident. The Wagner Dodge incident fell into this category. The idea of an escape fire just came to him. Perhaps as he was running through the grass, he thought how much quicker he could run if he didn't have the grass slowing him down, which might have given him a hint about removing the grass and thereby removing the fuel for the fire. But that's just my own speculation.

In the final two impasse incidents, the person adopted a skeptical mindset. In one case, the person tried to make an argument for a belief that was opposite to one she was holding. The other case involved a computer technician who systematically worked through every facet of the system to find why an internet connection had failed—along the lines of the critical thinking program of listing and testing assumptions.

—*June 1, 2016*

6.11 The Discovery Platform

A Tool for Exploring Intelligent Systems

How do you examine things that are so complex and opaque that even their designers don't understand how they work?

My colleague Shane Mueller and I had a chance to do just that. This essay describes our project as a case study and hopefully as a source of ideas that can be used in different settings.

Here's what happened. Shane and I, together with Robert Hoffman, the third member of our team, have been working on a DARPA (Defense Advanced Research Projects Agency) program called Explainable Artificial Intelligence (XAI). I've described it in an earlier essay, in part 4. The XAI program arranged for 11 international groups of AI experts who have been trying to make it easier for people using their systems to understand how the systems arrive at recommendations and decisions. And this is tricky. The designers of the AI systems don't fully understand their outputs because the systems rely on machine learning, which means that they absorb hundreds of thousands, sometimes millions of examples and tune themselves to digest these examples, but the tuning is invisible to the designers.

I was discussing this problem with Bill Ferguson, one of the leaders of the BBN/Raytheon project. Bill was trying to figure out the kinds of images and questions his AI system did well with and the kinds it failed at. So he went through his database and identified three rules of thumb. Once Bill told people using his AI system about these rules of thumb, these users improved their performance.

When I heard about that, I figured I could use Bill's approach, and his database, and apply it to other AI systems. I would have a Discovery Platform—a basis for making discoveries about AI systems. It seemed very straightforward, a clear path to success.

Except that it was a bad idea. Bill disliked the database and interface he was using. They were designed for analyzing performance data, not for making discoveries. Therefore, Bill's system was an example of what NOT to do, rather than a prototype for a Discovery Platform.

But this bad idea was also an opportunity. Knowing some of the limitations of Bill's system gave us a chance to design something we think is better. Something that would help designers, and users, get a better understanding of how a specific system works, where it fails, why it fails, and perhaps even workarounds to overcome the failure.

Interviews with Ferguson captured some of the features needed for a Discovery Platform:

Commonalities and patterns. Bill wanted to examine commonalities to spot general themes. "Hmmm, my AI system is getting location questions right—oh, I see, it is relying on extra cues, like a kitchen usually has a sink, a refrigerator, a stove."

Exceptions. It had to make it easier to find exceptions, anomalies, and outliers and show the actual images so that the designers could perhaps notice something important.

Failures. It should make it easy to pull out failures—cases the user got wrong so that the designers could diagnose the reasons for these failures. For example, "I notice that a key object is obscured in most/all of these photographs."

Contrasts. These might be cases the AI system failed at that it usually got right. For example, Ferguson studied photographs of soccer (which his AI typically nailed) that were mislabeled and noticed that they were all indoor soccer games. You can also contrast cases that were AI successes with cases that were AI failures. Bill wanted to have better ways to easily set up contrasts.

Confusions. Bill wanted to be able to look at high confusion classes because something might be brewing there.

Representations and instances. Thumbnails. Showing the photographs instead of hiding them. Ferguson needed to study individual photographs.

Shuttling. Bill wanted to easily shuttle back and forth between a statistical view and the specific instances.

The Discovery Platform

This all seemed too complicated to ever achieve, but that's one reason I like to work with Shane. In short order, Shane had built a system that did these things. When we demonstrated it to Bill Ferguson and his colleagues, they felt how "sticky" it was, in that it was hard for them to stop playing around with it and trying new things. It was hard for them not to use it to make discoveries.

You can watch the YouTube video: https://youtu.be/qRQb-fa0N5A.

You can also access the system itself and play around with it (obereed.net:3838/mnist). The code is open source, so if you are an AI developer who wants to use it on your own classification system, you can download it at https://github.com/stmueller/xai-discovery-platform.

I hope that the principles of the Discovery Platform can apply more generally, beyond AI systems, to support speculative thinking and exploration in other contexts.

Acknowledgment and disclaimer: This material is approved for public release. Distribution is unlimited. This material is based on research sponsored by the Air Force Research Lab (AFRL) under agreement FA8650-17-2-7711. The views and conclusions contained herein are those of the authors and should not be interpreted as necessarily representing the official policies or endorsement, either expressed or implied, of AFRL or the US government.

—March 25, 2021

6.12 Reflections

One of the most exciting sources of power we have is to arrive at insights—sudden, unexpected discoveries and radical changes in our mental models. In contrast to the many researchers and consultants and practitioners who just want to find ways to reduce errors, the Naturalistic Decision Making community also wants to learn more about insights and the process of speculative thinking. We want to learn a few things: Where do insights come from? What can interfere with insights? Are there ways to increase insights?

People have many beliefs about these topics, so part 6 began with a test—a 12-item insight test. I assume you have read this part already and you know the easy scoring method: all of the items were false. Many common beliefs about insights are incorrect, and the reasons they are incorrect provide us with guidance in gaining a better understanding of insights.

Gaining insights may be seen as a form of critical thinking—part of a second wave of conceptualizing critical thinking. Admittedly, this may be a stretch, but on the other hand, it may be a valuable expansion of the notion of critical thinking. The first wave seems too relentless about the down arrow in the equation, about reducing errors.

The core of part 6 is the description of the three different pathways leading to insights. This framework seems to be an important contribution to understanding where insights come from: connections, contradictions, and corrections.

What can interfere with insights? Many things: getting trapped by flawed beliefs, the problem of fixation errors we've encountered previously, lack of expertise, a passive mindset as opposed to an active one, and a cognitive style favoring concrete thinking rather than speculative thinking.

The last question taken up by this part is whether there are ways to increase insights. The popular literature suggests different approaches (increasing swirl, encouraging failures, being open to new ideas, applying critical thinking, and getting into a dreamy mood), but I am skeptical about each of them. However, I am not ready to jettison the idea of incubation just yet. The evidence for incubation is mixed, and the incidents I studied don't support incubation as a deliberate strategy. Nevertheless, I kind of believe in incubation, and I personally try to take advantage of it, like working on a difficult conceptual task before going to sleep, hoping that something will pop out when I wake up the next morning.

Part 6 ended with some of my own ideas for increasing insights. I don't have hard evidence that these ideas work—I am just throwing them out there. I am particularly enthusiastic about adopting an Insight Stance (essay 6.9). Some of these ideas link up with my earlier suggestion about breaking free from fixation by attending to anomalies and hints instead of explaining them away in order to escape from fixation. Some other ideas for promoting more insights were about tactics that teams and organizations can use to promote insights, but you will see in part 8 that I am skeptical about the ability of organizations to foster insights. Part 6 closed with a description of a Discovery Platform, which I think can be a very useful tool for helping researchers and developers achieve insights into the workings of the systems they use.

7 Getting Stronger—Training

Overview

Training programs often try to teach procedures—the rules to follow when carrying out a task and the steps needed to follow those rules. They also teach explicit knowledge—the information and facts we need to learn and remember in order to perform the steps.

As I have stated many times in previous parts of this book, I appreciate the value of procedural training.

However, I think we can go much further. The cognitive dimension opens up an important opportunity to promote expertise by helping students and trainees acquire the tacit knowledge that is essential for mastering a job. That means developing perceptual skills, compiling a richer set of patterns, strengthening mental models and mindsets.

When we get better at seeing cognition, even as people perform procedures, we can become more effective trainers and more effective training developers. Our exercises and materials can have a greater impact.

In this way, trainees should be able to become better decision-makers, better able to make sense of confusing situations, better problem-solvers, and better at adapting to unforeseen events that could never be included in the procedural training manuals.

From my perspective, the cognitive dimension is one of the missing pieces of training and education. It's missing because cognition is invisible, whereas performance and behaviors are so easily observed and measured. It's missing because many professionals reject the concept of expertise. It's missing because training professionals worry that they themselves lack expertise or are apprehensive because they don't know how to help trainees achieve expertise.

Of course, skilled teachers and trainers have already been seeing cognition and applying the cognitive dimension, and I have learned what I can from their examples and their discoveries. My assessment about a procedural mindset is directed at the views that I have seen in too many training programs, and the complaints I have heard from those who have gotten frustrated with the limited scope of these programs.

The training community has ignored the cognitive dimension long enough. It's time to provide that community with ideas and methods they can put into practice. The essays in this part are an attempt to move in that direction.

Essay 7.1, "Common Confusions about Teaching," is intended to loosen readers up by tackling some of the prevalent but mistaken beliefs.

The second essay, "Training versus Evaluation," keeps the pressure on. It argues that training and evaluation are really in conflict, so efforts to combine them will make training less effective.

And while readers are still off balance, essay 7.3, pushes you even further, asking "Is Teaching Overrated?" This question is not a gimmick. The essay suggests that we need to change our mindset from thinking about *teaching* to thinking about *learning* and that we have to see learners as engaged in self-explanation. That's an important perspective to maintain.

That perspective is illustrated by essay 7.4, "Training as if Your Life Depended on It." This case study illustrates how a well-constructed scenario can unleash the power of self-motivated trainees. In this incident, the trainees were miners who needed to find ways to stay safe in the face of a dangerous accident.

How can training professionals start to make the transition from a procedural approach to one that includes the cognitive dimension? Essay 7.5, "Cognitive Coaching," describes some ways to help others gain expertise. Essay 7.6, "Teaching through Insights," shows how teaching can be viewed, not as a means of conveying information but as a way to promote insights on the part of the trainees and students.

Essay 7.7 introduces a tool to identify the cognitive challenges of a job: "The Cognitive Audit." And essay 7.8, "Cognitizing a Scenario," suggests ways to inject these requirements into existing training exercises.

The concept of mindsets plays a central role in these essays, but what do mindsets consist of? Essay 7.9, "Mindsets," suggests a practical way to think about mindsets. Training and education become much more effective

Getting Stronger

when the trainers and instructors can achieve a mindset shift that favors curiosity and a sense of wonder. The tenth essay, "How to Harness Curiosity," describes how curiosity functions, the kinds of things that interfere with curiosity, and several ideas for getting trainees and students to exhibit greater curiosity.

The following essay (7.11), "Getting Smarter," presents a set of tips for ways to become smarter, or at least to gain more expertise that can result in greater decision success.

Essay 7.12, "Bring It On!," describes another important mindset shift: welcoming challenges instead of fearing and avoiding them. This stance is valuable in a classroom and in many other situations as well.

Essay 7.13, "Changing the Mindset of the Marines," offers a case study of how scenario exercises helped to change the mindset of a very large organization—the US Marine Corps.

7.1 Common Confusions about Teaching

Do You Fall into One of These Five Traps?*

Whether in a children's classroom, a military school, or a corporate training program, these five questionable ideas are widely held and put into practice—to the detriment of students and trainees. Most of these claims are more complicated than people realize, and some of them are flat-out wrong.

A number of you reading this post may hold some of these beliefs. If so, it is time to rethink them.

Claim 1: Accommodate learning styles. There is a widespread belief that each individual has a preferred learning style and learns better if instruction is tuned to that particular learning style. Boser (2019) found that 97 percent of the teachers and educators surveyed bought into this learning styles myth.

Most systematic reviews of the published research find little or no empirical evidence to support the belief that if you present instruction geared to a student's learning style you improve their learning (Coffield et al., 2004; Pashler et al., 2009; Willingham, Hughes, & Dobolyi, 2015).

And that holds whether you emphasize a preferred sensory modality (visual, auditory, kinetic) or a personality type (e.g., sensing type individuals prefer concrete, practical facts while intuitive type individuals prefer exploring concepts, extrapolating data, and finding patterns).

There's also no evidence for the idea that you should accommodate personality types as right-brained or left-brained. The right-brain/left-brain

---

*This post is a collaborative effort with Herb Bell, a cognitive psychologist whose research interests include training and skilled performance.

concept is simply hare-brained. Both sides of the brain operate cooperatively in verbal and spatial tasks. Boser found that 77 percent of the teachers surveyed bought into this right-/left-brain myth.

Claim 2: Try to speed up the learning curve. It's not that simple. What matters is how well people perform the work *after* the training is completed, not how quickly they acquired the knowledge/skill in the classroom. When you add challenges and make the learning more difficult, you slow down the learning curve, but you often produce richer mental models and improve how much the person remembers and applies afterward (McDaniel & Butler, 2011).

Claim 3: Use a building block approach. Start with simple concepts and build on those.

The problem here is that this tidy sequential approach doesn't always get the job done. If the "job" is performing that particular task/procedure, then the building block tactic does work. However, if the "job" is to solve real-world problems, knowing which task/procedure to perform and when, then the building block approach isn't ideal. Research shows (Gopher et al., 1994; Hall et al., 1994; Kornell & Bjork, 2008; Rohrer et al., 2015) that nonsequential ordering results in better transfer although the initial learning may be slower (see Claim 2).

The building block approach usually teaches a skill independent of the broader context in which it will have to be applied. Textbook writers often compound the problem by presenting homework assignments blocked by the type of method, so students just follow the same pattern and don't need to think through what method to use with each item.

Of course, students and trainees need some mastery of basic elements to start with. However, most training programs wait too long to introduce decision problems, so trainees think that all they have to do is learn the procedures.

Claim 4: Repetitions breed comprehension. Repetitions give us a sense of familiarity, and we may equate familiarity with understanding. For example, "I had to read the chapter three times, but I finally feel that I really understand it." This claim confuses familiarity with understanding—the rereading fallacy. Essay 7.3, "Is Teaching Overrated," goes into more detail about why active and constructive learning counts for much more than repetitions.

Claim 5: Try to reduce class size. Yes, learning suffers when classes are too large. But instructor quality matters much more than class size. A highly skilled instructor with a large class will get better results than a poor instructor with a small class. Therefore, school districts and training programs would do better by getting higher-quality instructors than by shrinking class sizes. An essay titled the "Opportunity Myth" (TNTP, 2018) explained that highly skilled instructors can teach more effectively, provide more appropriate assignments, increase engagement, and raise expectations.

Once a claim takes hold, it is difficult to dislodge. The claims take hold because they are so convenient: If you are a teacher, it's easier to focus on learning styles than to diagnose why individual students are struggling. Speeding up the learning curve lets you train in less time. Sequencing the training lets you deal with one topic at a time, putting less strain on you. Familiarity is a low-effort substitution for insight. Reducing class size is easier to manage than upskilling teachers.

We believe that educators, trainers, and learners need to stop hamstringing themselves with popular ideas that turn out to be limited and even wrong.

—*September 1, 2020*

7.2 Training versus Evaluation

It's a Mistake to Do Both Simultaneously

Several years ago, I heard a story about a southeast Texas petrochemical plant that tried to put some of my company's decision scenario methods into action. The lead instructor designed several scenarios and then gave them to two newly promoted panel operators. The two men had been working outside in the plant, checking valves, calibrating sensors, performing routine maintenance. Both had been promoted to work inside—on the panel controlling the unit.

One of the men was very impressive—he was highly confident, and others readily trusted his judgment. The second man was much more hesitant. He wasn't as sure of himself, and the managers wondered if he was ready to take on the challenge of running subsystems of the plant.

The lead instructor walked both of them, independently, through the decision scenarios. To his surprise, the first man struggled. He got the right answers, but his reasoning wasn't sharp. He was nowhere as prepared as they'd thought. The second man, however, did very well. He definitely understood the logic of plant operations and troubleshooting. He "got it," to use the language of the plant.

Accordingly, the plant welcomed the second man into the ranks of the other panel operators. But the managers sent the first man back outside. He needed another year before he'd be ready to be a panel operator.

From that point on, no one in the plant would do any more of these decision scenarios. No one had realized that the scenarios would be used for evaluation. The scenarios had been billed as training exercises. Even the plant managers thought of them as training exercises. It was only after they saw the results that the managers applied the scenarios as an evaluation tool.

And so ended the introduction of decision scenario training at this plant. Too late, the plant discovered that it was a mistake to use the same scenario activities for training and for evaluation.

I tucked this odd story away, but then recently, I began to reflect on it because of instances I heard about people washing out of a training program. Stories about trainees who couldn't keep up, about supervisors who scrutinized the trainees to determine which ones could be allowed to continue.

That's when the light came on for me. A number of training programs, perhaps most of them, combine training with evaluation. The trainees are being assessed while they are trying to master the skills and the material—and that practice is counterproductive.

If I am a trainee, and I know that supervisors are assessing my performance, I am going into a defensive mode. I am trying not to make any mistakes. My primary goal is to make it through training without getting terminated. I am not trying to learn as much as possible. I am not trying to explore different strategies. I am not attempting to learn from my mistakes. None of these. If I can wash out during the training, it really isn't training, is it?

Now you see why training and evaluation do not mix, and why programs that do both are making a mistake.

Is there a way around this dilemma? I think so. Make it clear to trainees that none of their performance will count regarding retention in the program. They are free to experiment as much as they like.

They will be evaluated—on designated trials labeled as such in advance. No surprises. These trials and events will be separate from the training activities.

The difference between training and evaluation also applies to schools. Children dread tests because they are evaluated on the results. Tests can also be valuable opportunities to learn but only when the grade doesn't count. In fact, these learning opportunities shouldn't be graded. The individual problems should be graded in order to provide feedback, but there is no need to tabulate an overall score. Tests can become exciting opportunities instead of nerve-wracking trials.

When there is a need for testing to assign overall scores, these tests can be labeled as such and kept separate from the learning experiences.

Perhaps we can learn the lesson from the cautionary story out of a Texas petrochemical plant.

—*February 5, 2018*

7.3 Is Teaching Overrated?

It May Be Better to Help Learners Engage in Self-Explaining

We are all familiar with the notion of a master teacher—a person who holds the class spellbound, who clearly explains very complicated ideas, who inspires students to work hard.

In support of this notion, many studies have shown that a highly experienced, highly effective teacher can boost the performance of the students by six months or even a year, compared to comparable students taught by a mediocre teacher.

But perhaps our emphasis on teaching is misguided.

That's my assessment of the work of Micki Chi and her colleagues. Their interest is in learning: what a person learns and how strongly that learning takes hold. They find, in repeated studies, that what matters the most is getting the learner to self-explain, not in exposing the learner to a master explainer/tutor/teacher.

In one study, Chi, Roy, & Hausman (2008) found that a tutor-centered approach (as opposed to a learner-centered approach) resulted in little learning:

- There was no benefit when the tutor initiated an interaction with the learner.
- There was no benefit when the tutor injected high-quality comments.
- There was no benefit when the tutor adapted as needed to help the learner.

Worse yet, Chi, Roy, and Hausmann showed that novice tutors couldn't accurately gauge whether a learner understood the material. Several previous studies had found that even skilled teachers weren't very accurate at assessing learners' understanding. If skilled tutors, working one-on-one, face-to-face, cannot adequately judge what learners are comprehending, it's unlikely that those tutors can adapt their instructional tactics to determine how and when to deliver explanations, feedback, questions and to select the next problem for the learner to work on.

The Chi, Roy, and Hausmann research involved tutors, not classroom teachers or corporate trainers. But I think the research findings might well hold across different settings. Therefore, instead of a tutor-centered approach, Chi and her colleagues favor a learner-centered approach that encourages students and trainees to engage in self-explaining, rather than in passive attempts to memorize the material. Chi & Wylie (2014) have described a general scheme for increasing learning as students shift into self-explaining, moving from passive to active and then to a constructive, and finally to an interactive stance.

The research by Chi and her colleagues over the past few decades suggests a few important principles:

- Make the learning active. Reduce (or eliminate) the time the learner has to spend listening to an explanation or a lecture. The point here is to avoid putting learners in a passive mode. Even when learners are watching a video, you want to see them doing things like taking notes, writing down steps, posing questions. That's what Chi means by active learning—interacting with the material instead of sitting back and trying to absorb it.
- Make the learning constructive. You want the learners to be trying to self-explain, not to try to memorize what's been presented. Some learners think that the way to study from a textbook is to read the material again and again, hoping that most of it will stick. That strategy doesn't work very well—it's better for the learners to be questioning the text, writing notes in the margins, seeing connections with earlier material. Sometimes you may even want to omit critical details as a way of provoking the learners to fill in these details themselves.
- Tutoring sessions work best when the tutor is not continually explaining things but instead is scaffolding for the learners: posing questions, giving prompts and hints, making statements with a fill-in-the-blank format. Chi et al. (2004) have listed 14 different forms of scaffolding.
- Scaffolding comments work best when they are short, perhaps 30 words, and not sliding into explanations. They invite relevant reactions. (Explanations tend to be long, averaging 66 words.)

- Errors are a prime opportunity for learning. Good tutors/teachers take advantage of errors. But they do NOT just correct the error. They use it as a way to have a dialogue with the learner about the flawed beliefs that led to the error.

Chi and her colleagues are not claiming that teaching skills don't matter. After all, skilled tutors and master teachers do make a difference. They can answer questions when the learner gets stuck. They can motivate learners to work harder. They can scaffold to encourage self-explaining. They can provide feedback to alert learners to flaws in their mental models and judge when to provide the feedback and in what form. Good teaching can be quite valuable. But it isn't sufficient.

Too many people equate teaching and learning, and they assume that good teaching equals good learning—or at least leads directly and efficiently to it. Even teaching programs that recognize that the teacher has to understand the learning needs of the students seem to fall into that trap. Get the teaching right and the learning will necessarily follow.

Chi's insight is breaking that flawed assumption and focusing on learning as a distinct activity from teaching. For Chi, the real issue is how to promote the most learning: by encouraging learners to take an active, curious, constructive stance of self-explaining.

—*May 5, 2020*

7.4 Training as if Your Life Depended on It

How Reluctant Trainees Became Super Motivated

One of the most innovative cognitive training companies I know is WTRI (Workplace Technology Research Inc.), which is run by my friends Lia DiBello, Dave Lehmann, and Sterling Chamberlain. I met with them in San Diego in 2018 and heard this story.

WTRI had been brought in to put on some training for Rio Tinto, the second-largest metals and mining corporation in the world. The training was tested at an exercise in an underground mine. The training seemed fairly mundane, and the miners didn't see any reason to spend two whole days on it. They were highly experienced and knew their jobs well. They complained loudly about having to go through the WTRI training and complied only because upper management insisted.

But they hadn't encountered the kind of training WTRI had designed—highly realistic scenarios presented in a virtual world, with each miner acting alone to make critical and time-pressured decisions. The virtual world layout had been carefully designed to match the actual layout of the mine as it will likely be in 2025, so some of it was very familiar, and some of it was new, but part of a well-known plan. In fact, it was the future layout the miners were engaged in building in real life. This was no cookie-cutter exercise. The miners felt that this was the real thing.

Their stated mission at the start of the Day 1 scenario was for the crews to get their assignments in a team meeting at the start of the shift, to practice finding work areas in the new underground territory they'd be exploring without getting lost, finish their assigned tasks and radio any reportable issues to their shift boss. When their task was completed, they would radio to the shift boss for another assignment, find that area, and so on. They believed they were practicing being efficient in a large underground environment.

Each trainee was alone in a room with a computer, wearing a headset and navigating the virtual world with a joystick. However, they were not alone in the virtual world. They could only see the others through the virtual world—but the others were people they actually worked with. Their shift boss was their actual shift boss. They were assigned tasks that they would be doing in real life. They had a radio in the virtual world for communication. The younger miners saw that it could be similar to a massive multiplayer online game they might play. After about 20 minutes inworld, the radio chatter indicated that they were fully immersed, cracking jokes like they do on the real radio, asking each other where others were, reporting safety hazards they found, and asking for direction on some tasks. There were about 30–35 people inworld together at the same time, not including the people logged in to run the show.

What they didn't expect was that once deep in the virtual mine, an upset would occur at some point, 45 minutes or an hour into the session. Usually, this was a fire in some random area of the mine. The actual training goal was to improve decision-making following an accident that required the miners to evacuate or, if that wasn't possible, to move quickly to a safe area with adequate ventilation, food, and water. The real purpose of the exercise, which the trainees hadn't been told about, was to see how they handled the emergency. In the virtual world, the underground tunnels filled with smoke and visibility got very poor. If they were near a fire, the noise was deafening. The lights on their helmets bounced off the smoke and haze, and the view could be deceptive; they could easily get lost or miss signs. Their avatars' performance degraded; without oxygen, their avatars were soon on the ground, unable to get up, with only minutes left to live. They had rebreathers that gave them about 30 minutes of air, but they had to decide when to put them on and then pick an exit path, or a path that took only 30 minutes to reach a rescue chamber.

Before the exercise, all participants were briefed on the procedures and what parts of the mine were too far from the exits to reach safely. They were all briefed on the locations of rescue chambers and the reasons for going to them. Rescue chambers are crowded and unpleasant underground boxes for sustaining small groups of people with food, air, and water until help can arrive. Understandably, people do not want to end up there. Sometimes they easily get to one and find it is already full.

It turned out that all the miners believed they knew how to get out of the mine safely, and none believed they needed to go to a rescue chamber. This was not the case. During the exercise, many of the participants (i.e., their avatars) did not make it out alive. Some died because they misjudged how long their air would last and thought they had enough time to go back looking for others they could hear calling for help. It was heartbreaking to hear (see figure 7.1).

Everyone was dismayed by the results—the WTRI team, the upper management, and the miners themselves. Most surprising was the emotional toll. Even though no one actually died, the workers were quite traumatized by the experience, realizing that about 30 percent of the miners would have perished if this was an actual fire and that the loss of life was entirely preventable. That kind of outcome gets your attention if you are a miner.

The training was scheduled for two days. That's pretty typical for WTRI. The first day is a realistic scenario to serve as a reality check and demonstrate to the trainees that their current way of doing business or thinking about the issues isn't going to work. The second day is to allow the trainees, while still in a state of shock, to drastically revise their mental model and their approach in order to become much more effective.

For this mining exercise, the second day was scheduled to start at 8:00 a.m. Given the unusually high level of complaints about having to do the first day of training, the WTRI team wasn't sure what to expect. On the second day, they got to the training site early, around 7:15 a.m., which was a very good idea because the miners had shown up at 7:00 a.m.! An hour

Figure 7.1
Mining simulation.
Source: Lia DiBello/WTRI, used with permission.

early. To say the trainees were motivated would be an understatement. They had just gone through a near-death experience the first day, especially the 30 percent who had died in the simulation. Their braggadocio was gone.

The second day of training was free of bellyaching and whining. It was all business. The miners were determined to diagnose what was wrong with their approach, and how they needed to rethink their response. Needless to say, the second day of the exercise resulted in a dramatic improvement. Everyone escaped safely. Those who escaped safely the first day escaped twice as fast the second day. They reported that they automatically made a mental note of the nearest exit and rescue chamber for every work area they were assigned to. Unlike the first day, during Day 2, they planned their escape route carefully, especially the ones who had run out of rebreather capacity the first time through. They didn't want that to happen to them again, not in the training exercise. Not ever. They vividly remembered how frightening it had been to be lost during the first event, even though they knew it was just a simulation. And listening to others over the radio—others who were not getting to safety in time—really heightened the emotional reaction. They talked about how much this experience had changed them, how frightening it had been because of their overconfidence even when their assumptions were wrong. They also talked about how upsetting it had been to get lost or to hear the voices of others who were lost.

How do you turn a bunch of gripers into grimly determined trainees? Not by speeches. Not by issuing values statements. Not by citing safety statistics. But by letting the trainees see for themselves that they aren't nearly as good as they thought and by letting them experience the panic that comes with failure. WTRI's research shows that carefully designed virtual worlds may be a way to accomplish that outcome.

When the WTRI research team returned eight months later for follow-up interviews, they found the effect had endured in the people who worked underground. The miners reported that they look at the underground space very differently now. The first thing they do in an unfamiliar mine is imagine a problem and mentally simulate getting to safety. Some said they are more aware of hazards as well, things that might cause a problem, such as a fire.

The initial virtual world disaster experience was enough to create a mindset shift—perhaps in this case we could call it a "mine-set" shift—to be much more sensitive to issues of danger and self-protection.

—*March 4, 2018*

7.5 Cognitive Coaching

Six Mindset Shifts Trainers Should Make

Most trainers and coaches mean well. It's just that many of them hold mistaken beliefs about cognitive skills such as better decision-making, accurate sensemaking, more creative improvising, and faster detection of problems.

Underlying all of these skills is the attainment of expertise. Too many trainers and coaches don't understand these kinds of cognitive abilities. As a result, they rely on instructional techniques that can actually get in the way of successful performance and the development of expertise.

This essay explores ways to help trainers and coaches become more effective in developing cognitive skills. Trainers and coaches have other responsibilities—motivating people, evaluating them, and so forth. We aren't going to get into these responsibilities here. Our topic is how to get people up to speed so that they think more clearly and show more mental agility.

This essay is aimed at trainers and coaches in industry, sports, first responders (e.g., police and firefighters), military, healthcare, petrochemical plant operators. All of these communities can benefit from having their trainers do a better job.

The essay is divided into two sections. The first section examines the mindset shifts trainers and coaches will need to make. The second section provides some suggestions for trainers and coaches about what to watch out for as they adopt the new mindsets.

Part I: Changing mindsets
Mindsets shape what we see, shape our interpretations, and shape our reactions. Most mindsets can be boiled down to a core belief. Therefore, by

attacking a flawed belief, we can achieve a mindset shift. If a person is trapped by a dysfunctional belief, we can show that person the limits and inadequacies of the belief while describing an alternate belief that is more promising.

Here are six mindset shifts that should help trainers and coaches improve cognitive skills.

1. *From criticism to curiosity.* The belief in question is that the job of the trainer is to spot mistakes and correct them right away. One senior trainer told me that this was his mindset starting out, but over the years, he had learned to be curious. Early in his career as a trainer, if someone made a mistake, he would happily rebuke them, which felt good but didn't seem to be achieving very much. Over time, his mindset shifted, and now if someone makes a mistake, he wonders why and tries to get to the bottom of it, working with the trainee to figure it out. This new mindset has made him much more successful. Too many trainers are just annoyed by mistakes rather than seeing them as opportunities. These trainers interpret mistakes as signs that the trainee wasn't paying attention, or didn't care, or maybe that the trainer did a poor job. With the criticism-oriented mindset, mistakes are blemishes. However, the curiosity-oriented mindset views mistakes as opportunities. If the trainer adopts a curiosity-oriented mindset, s/he can hopefully figure out what is confusing the trainee and help to clarify the trainee's thinking. Trainers should be seeking to harvest mistakes, not avoid them or make trainees feel guilty about making them.

2. *From following procedures to gaining tacit knowledge.* The belief in question is that virtually all jobs can be boiled down to procedures and steps, and the job of the trainer is to teach these steps. While procedures are important and necessary, they aren't sufficient. Expertise is not a matter of following steps. Just about all challenging tasks have too many contingencies and possibilities to be handled by procedures. Expertise is about what we do when the procedures don't clearly apply—when we have to use our judgment. Expertise is about gaining tacit knowledge—knowledge that can't be captured by procedures and steps. Tacit knowledge includes noticing subtle cues, seeing patterns, spotting anomalies, and using our mental models of how things work and how they don't work—what we have described as the cognitive dimension. Trainees want

to buy in to the *procedures* belief—they want to take refuge in learning more and more procedures, adding them to their toolbox, trusting that procedures will take care of just about any problem they might face. The trainer has to help the trainee get beyond this procedural mindset and move on to the path to expertise.

3. *From getting through the material to encouraging curiosity.* The belief in question is that most of what the trainee needs to learn is in the PowerPoints and lecture material. Therefore, the trainer has to make sure s/he gets through all this material. Class discussions and questions just chew up time and get in the way of covering the material. As a result, trainers often unwittingly block curiosity on the part of the trainees. They squash curiosity in a few ways (I am indebted to Ed Noble at Nova Chemicals for these observations): They discourage questions. They use ridicule, even with facial expressions, to make trainees afraid of looking dumb. They overwhelm the trainees with details. They introduce so much complexity so early that the trainee stops being curious and retreats into a passive stance of desperately trying to remember most of the material being shotgunned. There are many ways to stifle curiosity. Good trainers have learned to control their tendencies that diminish the curiosity of their students.

4. *From providing thorough explanations to providing focused explanations.* The belief in question is that the trainer should be lecturing trainees with all the details and contingencies that might come up. As we saw in the previous paragraph, excessive details and complexity can stifle curiosity. Good trainers have mastered the skill of diagnosing the reasons why trainees are confused or surprised. Instead of spewing a canned lecture, the good trainers can diagnose why the trainee is surprised—what belief has been violated, what assumption has been called into question. Then the good trainers can speak directly to that belief, that part of the trainee's mental model that needs adjustment. The trainers are asking themselves, "What assumption are these trainees making that is hanging them up?" Good trainers can provide a focused explanation instead of a comprehensive one.

5. *From explaining to discovering.* The belief in question is that the job of the trainer is to explain things. Often that is the case, but trainees learn more when they discover things for themselves. The challenge for trainers and

coaches is to craft exercises and experiences that enable discoveries. That is much harder than just offering an explanation.

6. *From evaluating to training.* The belief in question is that during the training period the trainers should assess which trainees are struggling and should be dropped from the program—the trainers can save everyone a lot of effort by culling those who aren't a good fit. The problem with this approach is that it severely interferes with training, as I explained in essay 7.3. If I know you are watching me to see if I measure up, I am going to be super defensive and guarded during training. I am going to be careful not to get caught doing anything stupid. I am NOT going to be exploring different strategies. I am NOT going to be eager to get feedback on what I did wrong. If I do get critical feedback, I am going to try to make excuses rather than take it in. By combining training with personnel evaluation, organizations interfere with the training process. Organizations do need to evaluate performance. Rather than mix evaluation and training, they would do better to set up special test trials and tell the trainees which these are. In this way, trainees know when they have to be on their guard and when they can relax and learn as much as possible.

Part II: Gaining expertise

Expertise is based on tacit knowledge. That is why it is hard to describe or notice, as explained in part 5. What can trainers and coaches do? Here are a few suggestions.

Subtle cues. Be on the lookout for visual, auditory, and even tactile cues (e.g., mechanical vibrations) that the trainees need to notice. It's hard for trainers, for experts, for anyone, to clearly explain what subtle cues they are picking up on. That's why trainers find it so tempting to simply explain the procedures. But these subtle cues are critical, so trainers can try to be alert to them during operations and bring them to the trainees' attention. Even if the trainee can't make a perceptual discrimination, knowing that experts can make this discrimination can motivate the trainee to practice. (See the work of Anders Ericsson on deliberate practice.) One navy electronic warfare coordinator (EWC) I interviewed explained that in his early career, he couldn't distinguish the signal profiles of two large aircraft—it might have been a KC-135 and a Boeing 737 (I don't remember). He knew that the experienced EWCs could tell the difference in signal signature, and so he became determined to do the same. Therefore, whenever an airplane of that approximate size appeared, he became extra vigilant trying to predict which it was, a KC-135 or a Boeing 737, and then he used other sources to check on his judgment. In less time than he expected, he acquired the skill he needed.

Hindsight perspective. Another exercise for identifying relevant cues is to use an After-Action Review of a situation, regardless of whether the trainee handled it well or poorly. The trainer can ask, "With hindsight, what should you have been paying more attention to?"

Anticipating. Instead of hindsight, what about using foresight. Many trainees get captured by what is happening right in front of them and fail to think ahead. Trainers can pause the action and ask, "What is likely to be going on in x number of minutes?" In this way, the trainer can try to encourage a prospective mindset, a habit of mind to imagine what might happen next, either a likely turn of events or a dangerous turn of events.

Shifting focus. Here is another mindset shift the trainer can try to foster—seeing the big picture. Trainees often get captivated by the micro-details of what they are working on, tunneling into the specifics, and forget to look up and take stock of what else is going on. The skilled decision-makers have learned from experience, often bitter experience, to shake loose of the micro-details and come up for air every now and again. This shifting focus is another habit of mind to try to inculcate. The trainer might be on the lookout for times when the trainee is staying micro for too long and can encourage a temporary shift in focus. Even better, if possible, the trainer can introduce an event in the scenario or simulation to "punish" the trainee who failed to scan the big picture frequently enough.

Fixation. We all have the tendency to fixate. When we are trying to make sense of a confusing situation, we usually cast about for explanations, and the first one that seems plausible captures us. Instead of telling students to keep an open mind, which is bad advice, trainers can be on the lookout for times when a trainee jumps to a conclusion and then holds on to it even though it is incorrect. Remember—there's no shame in jumping to the wrong initial hypothesis. Fixation is a problem when we hold on to that incorrect hypothesis despite mounting evidence that it is wrong. Fixation happens when we explain away the anomalous evidence rather than becoming worried or at least curious. Therefore, the trainer can try to cultivate a habit of mind to become curious about anomalies instead of discarding them. If a trainee is going down a garden path, impervious to warning signs, the trainer can note all the warning signs the trainee missed and use the After-Action Review to let trainees discover how they blinded themselves. Trainees who have just messed up are usually very open to tracing where they went wrong, as we saw in essay 7.4 with the miners who had to die a virtual death in order to take their safety seriously.

Hypothesis testing. To help trainees adopt the curiosity-oriented habit of mind discussed in the previous paragraph, instructors can discuss afterward what types of tests the trainees could have performed. What kinds of data were readily available to test that initial hypothesis? What kinds of changes were expected if that hypothesis was correct—and did they happen? The skilled decision-makers I have observed were very good at testing their hypotheses when they noticed some discrepancies.

Workarounds. The stronger our procedural mindset the stronger our belief that there is a "right" procedure to handle all kinds of difficult conditions, and our job is to recall what that procedure is. But if we want people to be more resilient, we want them to be aware of alternate tactics. We want them to notice possibilities. Instructors can monitor their trainees to see how flexible they are, and how aware of workarounds. In After-Action Reviews, when the pressure is off, instructors can go back over the incidents and reflect with the trainees about other options and about contingencies in case the typical actions are blocked.

In conclusion, this essay has described six mindset shifts that can help trainers do a better job of getting cognitive skills across and a set of practices to go along with these mindset shifts. The essay has concentrated on working with trainees during normal operations, but the ideas are also relevant to the classroom, to simulation exercises, and to scenario-based training.

Note: The ideas in this essay are built around conversations with Joseph Borders and Ron Besuijen during a project we collaborated on to delve into the mental models of panel operators in petrochemical plants. This project was sponsored by Dave Strobhar and Lisa Via, at Beville Engineering, for the Center for Operator Performance.

—*September 29, 2018*

7.6 Teaching through Insights

Strategies for Insight-Centered Instruction

What would it look like to view teaching as a process of creating insights?

I have been thinking about this for the past year, ever since receiving an email from Steffan Elis on July 31, 2014:

> Thanks so much for your book [*Seeing What Others Don't*] that I just finished reading. It really opened my eyes to the world of insights and provided some concrete thinking to something that feels like it happens by chance or involuntarily.
>
> I am a teacher and hopefully the awareness of how people gain insights means I can build these principles into my day-to-day teaching to help the children gain insights and make connections/search out contradictions in their learning. In addition, as I think about my role as a leader in school it'll help me develop the staff I work with to become even better teachers. Very useful summer reading.

Steffan's comments got me speculating about the link between insights and education.

Some classroom activities such as vocabulary and arithmetic drills (e.g., memorizing multiplication tables), don't have anything to do with insights. I am not dismissing multiplication tables—these kinds of operations need to become automatic. But the memorization task is different from the discovery process.

In contrast, approaches such as Problem-Based Learning and the Deweyan program of experiential education do seem like a platform for insights. Decades ago, Lauren Resnick and Robert Glaser, at the Learning Research and Development Center at the University of Pittsburgh, examined the discovery process needed to learn topics such as arithmetic. Science education has long considered concepts such as restructuring and tuning that have their origins in Jean Piaget's description of accommodation, as well as Karl Popper's ideas of fallibilism.

Also, classroom methods such as the use of Cuisenaire rods to help young students get a feel for basic arithmetical operations can be a springboard for discoveries and insights.

Classroom instructors have long tapped into techniques for encouraging insights, even if they didn't always use that terminology. Here is a well-known example. Deborah Ball, currently the dean of the School of Education at the University of Michigan, was teaching a third-grade math class. One of the students, Sean, explained that "6" was both an even and an odd number. Instead of correcting Sean, Ball took his assertion seriously and respectfully, and asked him to explain his comment. Sean said that 6 was made of three pairs of 2. "Six" contained a "2" element, making it an even number, and a "3" element, making it an odd number.

Sean's comment was a healthy sign of an engaged student exploring a possible inconsistency. (It also strikes me as the comment of a smart aleck trying to show the teacher up, but that's a valuable and engaged attitude and should be encouraged.) Ball opened a class discussion of what it means to be an even number, and the class generated a definition of an odd number: there is one left over if it is grouped by twos. Even Sean accepted that definition. The class supported Sean by creating a new category, called "Sean numbers," for cases like 6 and 10 that had an odd number of groupings of two. The example shows how a teacher, and a class, can diagnose a flawed idea and arrive at a richer mental model. In this incident, Deborah Ball let Sean correct his own thinking. Later, Ball explained that teaching depends on what the students think, not what the teacher thinks. Ball has gone on to create a test for teachers, to help them diagnose the flawed beliefs of students who give incorrect answers.

In this essay, I want to explore ways to use recent findings on the nature of insight to offer a few helpful classroom principles.

Before we get going, let's review some of the things we've learned about insights. I define insights as unexpected shifts in the way we understand things. Our understanding is based on our beliefs, and our beliefs combine to form a mental model of how things work. Insights change that mental model, either by adding new and important beliefs into the mix or by getting us to discard beliefs that are wrong or misleading. When we have an insight, it changes the way we understand. The insight can also change our ideas about what actions we can take, the cues we should be noticing, the goals we are pursuing, and the feelings we have.

Further, essay 6.3 explained that there seem to be three different pathways to gain insights: by connecting new information to our mental model, by taking contradictory data seriously instead of discarding them, and by finding assumptions that are getting in our way.

Now we can sketch out some ideas about Insight-Centered Instruction.

Diagnosis. Teaching isn't just adding more and more knowledge to what students already know. Early mental models are likely to be buggy—to contain flaws. Teachers need to help young learners revise their existing beliefs. And that means being curious about why students get the wrong answers. Wrong answers reveal flawed beliefs and are an opportunity to diagnose problems. The Sean example shows how a teacher can use a wrong answer—that 6 is both odd and even—to deepen the student's and the class's understanding. Insight-Centered Instruction is less fixated on getting students to state the right answers and more patient with incorrect answers, more curious about the reasoning behind them, and more respectful of the student gripped by them.

Unlearning. Teachers can help students unlearn flawed beliefs in a few ways. In the Sean example, the teacher didn't try to correct Sean but simply invited the class to respond. As a result, Sean abandoned a flawed mental model of odd and even numbers, and other students may have also corrected their beliefs. As long as Sean, and perhaps others, held erroneous beliefs, they were going to have trouble progressing. Another strategy is for the teacher to create cognitive conflict by presenting disconfirming information, letting the students struggle to sort out the inconsistencies, losing faith in the flawed belief as they struggle. Teachers can identify or suggest alternative beliefs, making it less scary to give up a wrong-headed idea. Teachers can use analogs; one science education study addressed the counterintuitive notion that a table exerts an upward force on a book that is resting on it. The teachers placed a book on students' outstretched palms, so the students could feel that they were pressing upward, as a start for thinking about the wooden table. The teachers balanced books on springs and on wooden planks, so the idea of a table exerting an upward force became less strange.

Feedback. The notion of feedback is, in itself, not particularly novel to the field of instruction. However, feedback is not very helpful if the learner doesn't understand it or grasp its connection to the actions just taken, so instructors will be tempted to spell out the implications. But some research (Schmidt & Wulf, 1997) suggests that having the teacher provide the feedback can be counterproductive. It can speed up the learning process but slow down the transfer process. Learners may start depending on having feedback dished out and digested for them, rather than building skills for finding and interpreting feedback for themselves. This is one of the reasons given for experiential learning in which students do acquire and make sense of their own feedback. In the Sean example, if the teacher had simply corrected Sean, she would have left his flawed beliefs intact.

Knowledge shields. These pose an additional difficulty when it comes to feedback. Several researchers (Chinn & Brewer, 1993) have demonstrated the ways that we resist feedback or any kind of information that conflicts with our beliefs. These knowledge shields allow us to preserve our mental models by dismissing the inconsistencies: We may ignore the new data. We may find some minor flaw that lets us reject the data. We may put the data on hold for the time being until we find a way to make sense of them. We may reinterpret the data so that they aren't so troublesome. We may make a cosmetic change to our beliefs in token compliance with the anomalous data. To make Insight-Centered Instruction work, teachers need to expect that students will use knowledge shields to preserve their mental models. Deborah Ball was not distressed that Sean tried to hold onto his view that 6 was both odd and even. She didn't want Sean to succumb to the group pressure to parrot the right answer. She wanted him to genuinely arrive at a deeper sense of what constitutes an odd or an even number.

Pathways to insight. My research has uncovered three pathways, and each comes into play in the classroom.

One pathway is forming connections. Students are often energetic at suggesting connections, most of which are minimally relevant. Rather than discouraging these flights of fancy, teachers might see them as valuable tendencies of engaged learners and discuss how to tell which connections are more fruitful than others.

A second pathway involves contradictions. Some students are on the lookout for inconsistencies, especially inconsistencies on the part of the teacher. Such behavior can be annoying, but the tendency itself is also a sign of an engaged learner. One study found that the best students were alert to anomalies and were stimulated by them, in contrast to unsuccessful students who sought to avoid the conflicting evidence as requiring too much of a cognitive burden. Some teachers will present an erroneous idea and challenge students to shoot it down. Or else teachers can use a student's erroneous idea, such as 6 being both odd and even, as a springboard for a class discussion.

The third pathway is to deliberately try to overcome a barrier by discovering assumptions that are trapping us. These discoveries are often highly exciting. Actually, all three of the insight pathways can be exciting because the end result, the "aha" moment, has such an emotional charge. One benefit of Insight-Centered Instruction is to take advantage of the insight rush that people experience when they make a discovery.

The Insight Stance. Teachers may be able to boost insights by encouraging students to adopt a stance or mindset that is driven by curiosity rather than a fear of getting a wrong answer. Teachers can help students notice the insights they have and encourage more of them. Teachers can suggest that students pick up on connections and on contradictions, and when students get stuck, the teacher can help them to reexamine the assumptions they are making.

Notice how Deborah Ball tried to promote an Insight Stance in her students. She treated Sean's wrong-headed comment with respect. She encouraged the class to explore the contradiction to see what could be learned. She approved of the idea of Sean numbers, a useless concept but still a novel discovery that the class had made.

I imagine some seasoned teachers will roll their eyes at the notion of encouraging an active, curious mindset and recoil at the idea of students posing one question after another. An obvious response is to tell them to stop with the questions and just listen to the material in order to get through the lesson. I can sympathize with that impulse, but it makes me uneasy. Skilled teachers seem to be able to encourage productive kinds of curiosity without having to stifle their students.

Insight-Centered Instruction seems well-suited to topics such as arithmetic, mathematics, and science. It may also be useful for other areas such as literature, trying to make discoveries about the motivations of people and their varying perspectives. Teachers may find it valuable to work on social insights that address confusions and conflicts. In history class, teachers can challenge classes to sort out why leaders acted in the way they did, and why groups and movements arose or failed to endure.

Teaching does depend on transmitting information and mastering material. Promoting insights is just part of the process. Too many teachers seem to be insensitive to insights and impatient with their students. Insight-Centered Instruction seeks a different balance, one that tries to foster insights when possible and appreciates their value within the educational process.

Good teachers challenge students in the ways I have described. The perspective on Insight-Centered Instruction would have its greatest benefit with less-skilled teachers who lack the patience or the inclination to diagnose problems and resolve them. Insight-Centered Instruction could help these teachers see the value of helping students build richer mental models and adopt a mindset for seeking discoveries.

—*July 29, 2015*

7.7 The Cognitive Audit

A Guide to Identifying the Cognitive Training Challenges of Complex Tasks

Many training programs center on the procedures people should follow, and this makes sense because procedures are essential, they are the tried-and-true means of performing a task well. By relying on procedures, instructors can determine if the trainee is making progress and learning how to do the task.

But procedures, while necessary, are often insufficient. Sometimes there are no procedures for complex tasks, and even when we can establish a set of procedures, trainees need to acquire the tacit knowledge (perceptual skills, pattern repertoire, rich mental models) to handle tough cases. Training has to push beyond procedures—it has to include cognitive skills to enable better decisions, more accurate sensemaking, more rapid problem detection, ability to handle uncertainty and ambiguity, and to manage risks.

How can instructors inject cognitive skills into their training programs?

A tool I call the "Cognitive Audit" might be useful. It is a method to assess which cognitive training requirements an instructor might want to address. The tool builds on previous concepts, such as tacit knowledge (Polanyi, 1958), the description of macrocognition (Klein et al., 2003), and on the Knowledge Audit (Militello & Hutton, 1998; Klein & Militello, 2004).

But the Cognitive Audit goes beyond these precursors by incorporating what my colleagues and I have learned about cognitive skills training from our ShadowBox projects.

What differentiates the Cognitive Audit from its predecessors is that it includes *trainable* cognitive skills. The other frameworks identify aspects of expertise and are very important, but many of these aspects are not directly trainable. For example, the Cognitive Audit does not include decision-making, which is not trainable. It doesn't include sensemaking, which is not a general skill that can be trained. Further, the Cognitive Audit does not include gaining a sense of typicality (which enables someone to detect an anomaly)—this is part of tacit knowledge, but it is not trainable. Finally, the Cognitive Audit does not include elements of the Knowledge Audit which are useful in doing a cognitive task analysis, but which don't appear to me to be trainable cognitive skills.

Of course, cognitive training, using ShadowBox or other techniques, should help people improve their decision-making and sensemaking because trainees will gain richer mental models, better mindsets, and more expertise. It's just that these outcomes cannot be directly trained as skills.

What's left? Here are some cognitive training requirements that may be relevant for a training program. They are the components of the Cognitive Audit. If you are seeking to cognitize an instructional program, you might start by determining which of these is particularly important for gaining expertise. These components do appear to be trainable.

Mindsets. These are often single beliefs that affect the way a person understands and manages situations. For example, a training program might help a person shift from a procedural mindset to a problem-solving mindset. In law enforcement, you might want to design training scenarios that help people shift to a mindset of trying to build trust in each civilian encounter.

Boundary conditions for procedures. Procedures are usually essential, but for cognitive training, you may want to describe the boundary conditions for following procedures—the conditions under which someone might abandon the procedures or modify them.

Goal trade-offs. It is fine to describe the relevant goals for a job, but the hard part is when we have to manage goal trade-offs, because there are usually several goals to juggle, and these may be in conflict with each other. Practice is needed in making these trade-offs.

Job smarts. This component comes directly from the Knowledge Audit—the tricks of the trade that people need to learn to perform their work efficiently.

Workarounds. The ability to improvise depends on experience and resourcefulness and is not directly trainable, but what is trainable, I believe, is a mindset of being adaptable versus clinging to procedures. This requirement was part of the original Knowledge Audit. Many of the Tactical Decision Games published in the *Marine Corps Gazette* feature a requirement to adapt or replace a plan in order to work around an unforeseen barrier.

Managing uncertainty and ambiguity. This component is also about training a mindset shift. I do not think there is a general skill for managing uncertainty—the training has to do with making decisions despite uncertainty as opposed to delaying in the hope of gaining more clarity.

Problem detection and diagnosis. Decision-makers can benefit greatly by spotting weak signals and detecting problems at an early stage (Klein, Pliske, Crandall & Woods, 2005). There is no reason to believe that problem detection is a general skill. Rather, the skill is in the mindset to attend to weak signals and imagine their significance. Another part of problem detection is for decision-makers to gain the experience to anticipate what the weak signals might imply.

Attention management. What to notice, what to ignore? With experience, people get better at allocating their attention, which is why it appears to be a trainable skill and was mentioned in Knowledge Audit. One of the variants of ShadowBox, detecting cues in a video, gets directly at attention management skills.

Perceptual discrimination. Experts have learned to distinguish subtle cues that novices don't pick up, as discussed by Klein & Hoffman (1992) and by Klein (1998).

Common ground and coordination/predictability. Teams improve their coordination as they gain more experience working together because the team members learn to predict each other's responses and achieve greater common ground (Klein, Feltovich, Bradshaw et al. 2005). They also get better at noticing when common ground is eroding. Therefore predictability and common ground become important training requirements.

The Cognitive Audit may be useful for appraising training requirements for a given activity and for guiding scenario development and training strategy. When working with existing scenarios, the Cognitive Audit might suggest ways to "cognitize" these scenarios—ways to modify the scenarios to tap into the components described in this essay. That is the topic of the next essay.

—*July 7, 2017*

7.8 Cognitizing a Scenario

Developing High-Impact Training Scenarios

Too many training scenarios get stuck in the issue of what course of action to adopt at different decision points. Of course, selecting a course of action is extremely important, but often the selection depends on how people read the situation, what they notice, what they infer, and these considerations don't make it into the scenario. And they can. That's what "cognitizing" a scenario is all about—creating a training scenario that taps into these kinds of behind-the-scenes mental activities.

Instead of fixating training scenarios on what to do, we can use them to raise issues about how to think. Instead of making scenarios more difficult by adding to the crisis and the demands—the Armageddon approach that builds in more and more challenges until the decision-maker is overwhelmed—we can increase difficulty in more realistic ways by introducing ambiguity, subtle cues, and even erroneous data.

Essay 7.7 described how a Cognitive Audit could be used to make training scenarios more cognitively demanding. I listed a set of trainable skills: changing mindsets, exploring boundary conditions for procedures, making trade-offs between competing goals, introducing tricks of the trade, performing workarounds, managing uncertainty and ambiguity, detecting and diagnosing problems, managing attention, making perceptual discriminations, and gaining coordination through repairing common ground.

But there is more to cognitizing a scenario than identifying the cognitive training requirements. As my colleagues and I have developed ShadowBox training materials, we have found ways to modify existing scenarios—they are the kinds of injects that would make a routine scenario more mentally demanding.

Ambiguity. Find ways to introduce ambiguity about what is going on.

Misleading information. Toss in some erroneous data to see if the trainee catches how these data don't fit the rest of the picture.

Missing information. In an age of information-on-demand, stress the trainee by leaving some blanks. Many people are severely reluctant to make decisions without having all the relevant information—they will have to learn to act despite uncertainty.

Information overload. In an age of information-on-demand, provide excessive amounts of information, more information than can be examined to make a timely decision so that the trainee learns how to decide what not to examine.

Violated expectancies. Set the trainee up with certain expectations and see how long it takes, how much contrary evidence, before the trainee reframes the situation. (Many trainees may never rethink the situation and will remain stuck until you end the session.)

Outdated orders. Give the trainee a clear set of marching orders—a clear Commander's Intent—but have it be overtaken by events to see whether the trainee adapts his or her goals.

Time pressure. Put the trainee under time stress to make critical decisions under uncertainty.

Competing goals. There is never just one goal, and anytime you have more than one goal, you have the potential for goal conflicts. See how the trainee handles these goal conflicts.

Problem detection. Introduce the first signs of trouble in a very subtle way, perhaps obscured by more dramatic events, to see if the trainee picks up the problem when it is still minor enough to be easily managed.

These suggestions for cognitizing scenarios can be used to spice up conventional training scenarios and make them more difficult, more compelling, and more useful for preparing trainees to handle complex and uncertain situations.

—*August 6, 2017*

7.9 Mindsets

What They Are and Why They Matter

A *mindset* is a belief that orients the way we handle situations—the way we sort out what is going on and what we should do. Our mindsets help us spot opportunities, but they can also trap us in self-defeating cycles.

This essay isn't about all the beliefs we might hold. It is about the beliefs that make a difference in our lives—the beliefs that distinguish people who are successful at what they do versus those who continually struggle.

The Stanford University psychologist Carol Dweck (2006) popularized the idea of mindsets by contrasting different beliefs about where our abilities come from. If we have a *fixed mindset* and think that our ability is innate, then a failure can be unsettling because it makes us doubt how good we are. In contrast, if we have a growth mindset, then we expect that we can improve our ability—and a failure, therefore, shows us what we need to work on.

People with a fixed mindset are out to prove themselves and may get very defensive when someone suggests they made a mistake—in other words, they measure themselves by their failures. People with a growth mindset, on the other hand, often show perseverance and resilience when they've committed errors—they become more motivated to work harder. You can imagine how much having a fixed or growth mindset can affect our lives.

My investigation of the nature of insight turned up a major difference between people (and organizations) who concentrate on ways to reduce errors versus others who, in addition to worrying about errors, are also excited about chances to make discoveries. The preoccupation with errors—the belief that the only way to improve performance is by reducing errors—seems to fit the fixed mindset paradigm and the interest in discoveries—the belief that performance improvements depend both on cutting errors and on making insights—maps onto the growth mindset.

Other types of mindset can also make a big difference.

Once my wife Helen and I studied police officers, soldiers, and marines who had shown outstanding skills in dealing with civilians. We wanted to see what set them apart from colleagues who typically intimidated civilians to get them to comply. We discovered that these "Good Strangers" (as they were called) shared one trait—they all had a mindset that their colleagues didn't.

Sure, they worried about their own safety and that of their buddies. Sure, they wanted to achieve the mission and to follow the rules. But in addition, the Good Strangers sought to gain the trust of civilians. One police officer explained to us that in every encounter with civilians, even when he was arresting a lawbreaker, he tried to conduct himself so that the civilian trusted him more at the end of the encounter than at the beginning. He believed that being a professional meant doing his job in a way that fostered trust. Think back to your encounters with police—I suspect some of these encounters did not increase your trust in the officer.

We found a fourth important mindset in our work with police and military. Many of them believed that the way to get someone to do what you want is to command obedience, through intimidation or in other ways. But the Good Strangers believed that they often could get cooperation voluntarily. It took skill, as well as more time, but it had a long-term payoff—it built trust.

Mindsets aren't just any beliefs. They are beliefs that orient our reactions and tendencies. They serve a number of cognitive functions. They let us frame situations: they direct our attention to the most important cues so that we're not overwhelmed with information. They suggest sensible goals so that we know what we should be trying to achieve. They prime us with reasonable courses of action so that we don't have to puzzle out what to do. When our mindsets become habitual, they define who we are and who we can become.

Here is another mindset that emerged from a project my research team, headed by Emily Newsome, did with child protective services caseworkers. The mediocre caseworkers believed that their job was to follow procedures, but the best caseworkers saw the job as continually solving problems.

We found this same contrast between following procedures versus solving problems in other groups, such as nurses and petrochemical plant operators. We also found it in another study of police officers. Recent academy graduates tried to add to their playbook, believing that if they learned enough procedures, they could do the job.

In contrast, the seasoned police officers appreciated that there were never enough procedures, and they had to be ready to solve unique problems. In fact, some of the seasoned police officers got a little bored when everything went too smoothly. They appreciated a good challenge—obviously, they had a growth mindset.

One of the most powerful aspects of mindsets is how quickly they can be shifted and how powerful the consequences can be. Unlike skills that need to be practiced again and again, mindsets sometimes show dramatic shifts. Reading Dweck's book *Mindset* for an hour or two is enough to alter our beliefs about our abilities and motivate us to change to the growth mindset. In my work with police officers, I heard several stories of officers who expected to demand obedience—until they saw a supervisor speaking quietly and getting compliance.

One police officer remembered an event, decades earlier, at the beginning of his career. It was a dark night in a dangerous neighborhood. He and his supervisor, Raymond (both white), had spotted a Black suspect and were closing in to make the arrest. On the way, they passed a mildly inebriated homeless Black man sitting on a stoop, and the man whispered, "He's got a gun, Raymond." Sure enough, the suspect was armed, and they were able to make the arrest safely.

Afterward, our informant asked his supervisor why the vagrant had warned them. Raymond explained that the man was harmless; he tried to look out for him and get him to shelters when necessary. In that instant, the rookie officer decided he wanted to have that kind of Good Stranger relationship with the people in the community. He wanted them to trust him and look out for him, rather than fear him.

Of course, it doesn't always go this easily—some of the police and military I encountered were just too determined to take no unnecessary risks. And I suspect some of the people Dweck has encountered couldn't let go of their fear of failure. But others are able to shift their beliefs and mindsets.

Dweck tells the story of Jimmy, a junior high school student who had shown little interest in his classes until he sat through a session describing the growth mindset. Afterward, when the rest of the class had left, he tearfully asked Dweck, "You mean I don't have to be dumb?" From that point, Jimmy became a hard-working student. Mindsets are powerful, and shifting them can be sudden and transformative.

—*May 1, 2016*

7.10 How to Harness Curiosity

Curious? You're Not the Only One

Curiosity is a powerful force in our lives. But what is it? How does it work? And how can we do a better job of harnessing its power? In this essay, I explore each of these questions.

What is it? Very simply, it is wanting to know something. It may sound trivial, yet curiosity can exert intense force on us—we often work hard to satisfy our curiosity despite being hungry, thirsty, or sleepy.

Curiosity can stop us in our tracks—even when we're goal-oriented, perhaps writing an essay like this one. If we are foolish enough to leave a web browser open and the right click-bait appears, off we go down the rabbit hole.

But curiosity can also be quite brittle. Loewenstein (1994) observed that in a supermarket checkout line, we may become intensely curious about the latest news regarding a movie star's marital woes, but this curiosity disappears as soon as we step forward and away from the tabloids.

How does curiosity work? Researchers have studied curiosity for decades. (See Loewenstein for an excellent literature summary.)

Different things can trigger our curiosity, as shown in the diagram (figure 7.2).

- A violated expectancy—something surprises us, something we didn't expect and cannot explain.
- A puzzle we're trying to solve or a mystery novel that is gripping us.
- Missing or even inaccessible information—Loewenstein points out how we strain to eavesdrop on conversations or yearn to know what made

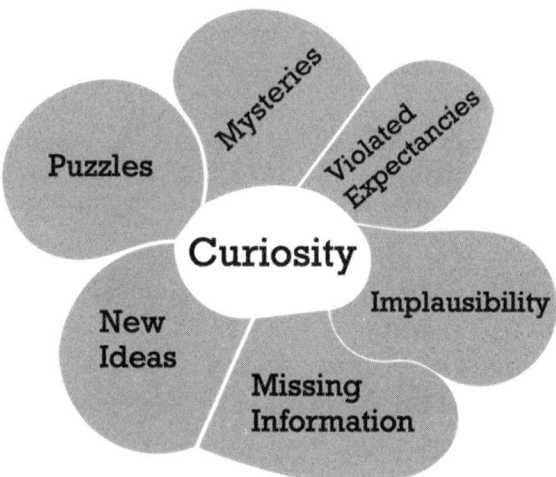

Figure 7.2
Curiosity.

someone chuckle while reading a magazine. We get frustrated by the tip-of-the-tongue phenomenon, maddened by our inability to remember something we know that we know.

- A chance to gain new ideas—perhaps by probing the part of a story that doesn't seem plausible to us so that we gather more information and make assumptions. For example, counterfactuals fascinate us. What would have happened in history if (fill in the blank)?

Loewenstein's own model features an information gap between what we know versus what we want to know. Underlying all of these triggers, curiosity is driven by our tendency for sensemaking—to find order, to discover patterns and intentions.

Blocking curiosity. Unfortunately, plenty of things can get in the way.

- Overconfidence—we may think we know more than we do.
- Being so self-absorbed that we are unaware of our surroundings.
- Negative emotions, such as guilt, fear, and anxiety, and external pressures, such as threats and punishment, all can diminish our curiosity.
- Getting an external reward rather than working on a task because it interests us.

Instructors often stifle curiosity without meaning to by asking yes/no questions, or insisting that there are right answers, or emphasizing memorization, or being too quick to correct student mistakes, or paying more attention to what a trainee is doing rather than why. Instructors can flood students with details, introducing too much complexity too early, which can unnerve students who may give up and resort to memorization.

Sometimes, instructors discourage questions and class discussions because they want to get through all the material. And there's no shortage of instructors who enjoy making students feel stupid, perhaps using ridicule.

Surprisingly, teachers can inhibit curiosity by providing explanations that are too complete, leaving no space for students to engage in self-explanation.

Harnessing curiosity. Good teachers have lots of ways to make their students curious: You can pose questions. You can present situations with unknown outcomes—and you can make the curiosity more intense by asking students to make predictions. You can reduce anxiety by showing students that the gap in their knowledge isn't out of reach. You can quiz students about how a process works instead of just having them learn its steps.

Counterintuitively, it may not be a good idea to call for students to ask questions! Too often, that leads to an uncomfortable silence or a shallow question desperately posed to end that silence. It's better to pose questions to the students, which primes the pump.

Perhaps the most important thing teachers can do is to be curious themselves—to wonder what caused a student to make a mistake. And that takes a shift in mindset, from being critical of mistakes to being curious about them.

—*December 3, 2020*

7.11 Getting Smarter

Nine Tips for Gaining Expertise

What can we do to get up to speed more effectively? In previous essays, I examined ways to identify who is an expert (part 5), as well as cognitive coaching (part 7)—mindset shifts that trainers need to make to do a better job of building expertise in the trainees.

This essay is about what any individual can do, without any coaches. I have been pondering this topic for decades. I even wrote a book about it, *The Power of Intuition* (2005), but that was more than a decade ago. Based on my experiences in the past four years with ShadowBox training (Klein & Borders, 2016), I think I have learned some things. Some of the tips in this essay just repeat ideas from the 2005 book, but others are new. Some of the tips come from a book by Hoffman et al. (2014) *Accelerated Expertise*—a very valuable overview of research in this area. Other tips can be found in an article by Fadde & Klein (2012).

In my view, expertise depends on tacit knowledge rather than explicit knowledge of facts, rules, and procedures. By tacit knowledge I mean the perceptual skills required to make fine discriminations, to detect patterns, to judge familiarity (and therefore to notice anomalies), to draw on a rich mental model of causal relations. These are the items under the waterline in the diagram (figure 7.3).

So how can we strengthen our tacit knowledge? Here are nine ideas we can put into practice.

1. Seek feedback. I am continually surprised by professionals who think all they need to do is show up at work and magically they will get better. They

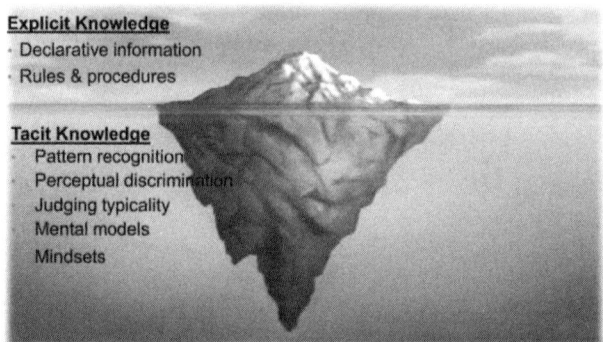

Figure 7.3
Tacit versus explicit knowledge.

don't give a thought to getting feedback, or else they find excuses—it's too hard, too labor-intensive, too many privacy restrictions, and on and on. Yes, it is often hard to get feedback, but many people just don't even try. And when they do, they settle for feedback on explicit knowledge (facts, rules, procedures) rather than tacit knowledge. In *Streetlights and Shadows* (Klein, 2009), I discuss all the reasons that feedback is not trivial to obtain or to interpret, and my advice is that we shouldn't be satisfied with outcome feedback. Instead, we can seek process feedback. If I want to improve at archery, I need feedback about where each arrow lands (outcome feedback) but I also need feedback about my form (process feedback). If I am engaged in underwriting large investments, I won't get feedback on how the endeavor played out for years, perhaps decades. But I can get feedback on the way I made my estimates and the types of variables I included or ignored. Without feedback, especially process feedback, we cannot make much progress.

2. Consult with experts. Meaningful feedback comes from experts who will take the time to help us. Who is an expert? See my earlier essay on identifying experts in part 5. We can get their thoughts on the actions we've chosen. We can also get their views on the processes we went through. I know that experts can be intimidating, and we don't want to pester them too often. We also run a risk in even asking for feedback because we are making ourselves vulnerable. On the other hand, many experts appreciate being singled out for assistance and may take a stronger interest in helping us advance.

But we shouldn't waste the experts' time with useless questions like, "How am I doing?" We're likely to get useless answers, like "Just fine. Keep it up." Instead, we should be specific. We should ask about a particular incident, a tough situation. See how the experts made sense of it. What goals would they have prioritized? What questions do they ask that we haven't even considered? What were they noticing that we had ignored? What do they think of the strategy we pursued? Here we are getting into valuable on-the-job training centered on actual cases. We are engaging in a fruitful dialogue. We are not simply asking for advice but probing the thinking of the experts and pressing back if we don't agree with them in order to make them think more deeply themselves.

3. Vicarious experiences. It is easier and safer to learn from other people's experiences and mistakes than our own, and as long as we are having dialogues with experts, we can ask them about their tough cases—what made these cases so tough? With hindsight, what would the experts have done differently? What do they wish they had been paying more attention to right from the start?

4. Curiosity. Obviously, curiosity is a powerful motivator for learning and for gaining expertise. I have come across some ways that curiosity gets squashed so we can be alert to these to see if they are taking a toll. They include worrying so much about making mistakes that we are afraid to explore things. Or having a compulsive attitude of wanting to study all the material rather than taking side explorations into topics that seem interesting or strange. Or being afraid to ask questions in a class for fear of looking stupid. The previous essay, "How to Harness Curiosity," elaborates on the topic of curiosity.

5. A growth mindset. Carol Dweck (2006) has distinguished a fixed mindset (I am either good at a skill or not) from a growth mindset (with practice, I can get better and possibly even get very good). Clearly, a growth mindset can help motivate us to gain expertise. There are mixed reports about whether Dweck's findings can be replicated, but they still make sense to me.

6. Overcoming a procedural mindset. So many of us are captured by the belief that even complex tasks can be broken down into procedures, and if we just master the procedures, we will become experts. As I have stated in the past, procedures are often necessary but are rarely sufficient. Procedures don't reflect tacit knowledge that is the core of expertise. To gain expertise, we need to shift from a procedural mindset to one that is sensitive to tacit knowledge and curiosity. We also should shift from a procedural mindset to a problem-solving mindset, and that means being alert to what is happening in a situation and what is needed rather than adopting a checklist stance of following the official routine for getting the job done.

7. Harvesting mistakes. Countless self-help manuals advise us to make use of mistakes in order to grow, encouraging us to welcome mistakes as opportunities. True enough, but that advice just isn't realistic. I hate making mistakes. I don't feel grateful when I make them. They eat at me until I can figure out why I made them and what I should have done.

That's how mistakes motivate me—not by welcoming them but by mulling them over and feeling annoyed with myself, usually for several days, until I am able to make sense of them and discover what I should have been noticing or inferring or doing. After all, if I can't be smart in hindsight, I can never be smart.

Failures alone are just punishment—we need to diagnose the reasons for the failures.

8. Adapt and discover. When people tell me about trips they have come back from, they don't describe all the flights and hotel reservations that worked out smoothly. Instead, they tell me about the glitches—missed connections because of weather delays, hotels that somehow lost the reservation information—and how they solved their problems. They are usually very proud of themselves for their ability to adapt. That doesn't mean we don't need to prepare carefully—it does mean that we don't have to come unglued when the preparations don't work out as we expected. In my experience, experts in a field sometimes seem to relish challenges that fall outside the normal procedures.

Perhaps we can develop a mindset that appreciates these opportunities to stretch, to surprise ourselves with our resourcefulness. We might even think of modeling this mindset with our children in the hope of making them more resilient. Once I was taking one of my grandsons, Koby, by bus to a restaurant, and Koby became alarmed that we were getting lost. Instead of trying to convince Koby not to worry, I turned it into a game: If we were getting lost, how could we figure out where we needed to be heading? How could we reorient? Were there other ways to get to the restaurant besides using a bus? I think Koby was a little disappointed when the bus actually took us to the restaurant.

9. Don't let evaluation interfere with training. When an instructor is judging our performance, we naturally tighten up and try to avoid making mistakes. Even without an instructor, when we are evaluating ourselves, it is hard to grant ourselves the freedom to explore a task or a situation.

That's it, for now. Nine tips on ways we can pursue mastery and expertise.

—*November 6, 2018*

7.12 Bring It On!

Learning to Welcome Obstacles Instead of Dreading Them

I recently heard a story about a nursery teacher meeting with parents prior to the first day of school. One of the parents commented, "How hard your job must be, with all these 4-year-olds disobeying instructions. Life would be so much easier if they just did what they were told."

The teacher disagreed. She explained that she views her class as a place where children learn to become more civilized. It's where they gradually give up their oppositional tendencies. That's how she sees her job. She welcomes their disobedience and views it as an opportunity to gradually move them toward cooperation.

I was struck by this story and realized that what I considered an obstacle this teacher regarded as a gift. It was a mindset shift for me, and it has changed the way I engage with my grandchildren. Instead of getting irritated by their disobedience (and they are all real sweethearts), I get curious. "It's not fair," one of them will insist, and I will ask what they mean by "fair." I know that this can become tedious for them, and I try not to overdo it. My goal is to defuse their sense of injustice, to help them think about what is a just resolution to a dispute, and to calm them down. At the very least, it calms me down. I think it makes me a better grandfather than I would have been otherwise.

In some ways, this mindset shift might be banal—along the lines of "make the best of it." But I think it rises above cliché. The teacher was saying that "this is my job, and I can do it best if I get these opportunities—if the children act out so that I have a chance to help them grow up. I want them acting out in my classroom because that's my skill and my profession, to help them mature." Unlike many of their parents, this teacher could not be goaded into becoming angry or authoritarian. She could show the children that the games they played to antagonize their parents wouldn't have any effect on her.

The teacher's story reminded me of experts in a number of professional fields that I study. I thought about a police officer who told me that he used to get angry when someone he was arresting would curse at him or resist his orders. Now, he looks forward to this resistance because it lets him test his ability to gain voluntary cooperation, and it lets him try out new methods to de-escalate the encounter.

Or consider people making a sales pitch. They'd like to get instant buy-in and usually get frustrated when the potential customer seems unconvinced. Maybe they can see the resistance as a challenge and a chance to learn about this customer, a chance to educate the customer, and at least a chance to hone their strategy for future customers. They can find out more about the customer's perspective, and they can see if there are any parts of their message that do seem to resonate with the customer.

There are two aspects of this mindset shift, from seeing difficulties as obstacles to seeing them as opportunities. The internal aspect of the shift is about the chance to gain skills. The external aspect of the shift is to help the people around us.

Once again, we are reminded of the lessons to be learned in kindergarten—or in this case prekindergarten.

—*September 6, 2019*

7.13 Changing the Mindset of the Marines

A Case Study in Fostering Critical Thinking

In part 6, I presented an essay on the second wave of critical thinking—sizing up situations for ourselves rather than uncritically accepting what we are told.

Can this type of critical thinking be taught? I think so because I have seen it happen in the US Marine Corps. I have seen the marines make a mindset shift from a procedural mindset to an investigative mindset fueled by curiosity. This mindset shift has encouraged marines to question the goals they are given rather than mindlessly pursuing them.

In complex situations such as combat or even peacekeeping missions, the stated goals may be overtaken by events, or, more often, the goals may be so ill-defined that they'll have to be clarified while they are being pursued.

How did this transformation happen?

In the 1980s, the US Marine Corps (USMC) underwent a dramatic institutional and operational reformation in response to the dysfunction of the Vietnam War. It was known as the Maneuver Warfare movement. As part of that movement, then-captain John Schmitt and a few colleagues introduced Tactical Decision Games (TDGs) as a way to build decision-making skills. TDGs are mini-scenarios centered on a map showing the terrain and the location of friendly forces and the possible location of enemy forces. The TDG contains a dilemma, a need to make a decision about how to proceed despite uncertainty and ambiguity. It is a way to practice the kinds of decisions that leaders might face in combat.

Starting in 1990, the *Marine Corps Gazette*, the corps's professional journal, published a new TDG every month and encouraged readers to submit solutions, some of which would be published two months later. One of the TDG themes, never explicitly stated to Schmitt's readers, was about questioning goals. These TDG exercises would begin with an order to be carried out, and then the TDG scenario would take an unexpected turn that rendered that order obsolete. What would the marines do?

Historically, questioning orders was not a part of Marine Corps operations or culture. Marines had a reputation for accomplishing the mission at all costs. But Schmitt and his colleagues felt that this mindless obedience wasn't in the best interest of the Marine Corps. Without announcing his agenda, Schmitt simply published these and other types of TDGs.

Schmitt wondered if the TDGs had any impact. So, after four years of writing TDGs, he decided to run a little study. He dug up his very first TDG, from April 1990, "Enemy Over the Bridge." It featured an order that no longer made sense. The protagonist is a battalion commander ordered to move his battalion into an assembly area to prepare for an attack the next day across a bridge held by friendly forces. However, upon approaching the assembly area, the battalion commander discovers that it is already occupied—by enemy forces! He also learns that that bridge is undefended and that enemy forces are pouring across it.

Schmitt evaluated the solutions sent in by Gazette readers. The submitted solutions fell into four main groups: (1) attack the assembly area (the most common solution—in keeping with the stated mission), (2) hunker down and defend in place, (3) report the situation and wait for orders, and (4) attack to recapture the bridge, which Schmitt argues is the best decision because the assembly area has no essential value, whereas the bridge is the critical terrain.

Then in 1993, Schmitt wrote a new TDG, "Action at Oxford," that was intended to pose essentially the same dilemma as "Enemy Over the Bridge." This time, however, the written solutions that marines sent in all converged: ignore the instructions given by higher headquarters and address the unexpected problem (analogous to the bridge in "Enemy Over the Bridge"). Most solutions made a point of informing higher headquarters, but no one suggested waiting to ask for guidance. And no one advocated holding on to the original goal, which had been the most common response four years earlier.

It would seem that TDGs had, at least in part, changed the mindset of the marines who read and commented on them, and perhaps changed the culture of the USMC. Senior leaders in the Marine Corps had been promoting a shift to Maneuver Warfare, and the TDGs helped to change the mindset of marines from bullishly following orders to being critical thinkers ready to shift goals as the situation played out.

—*July 30, 2020*

7.14 Reflections

Part 7 consisted of three sections. The essays in the first portion were contrarian, raising questions about a number of cherished beliefs regarding teaching and training. None of these challenges had all that much to do with the cognitive dimension or Naturalistic Decision Making, but the essays were fun to write and, more important, should have been fun to read and perhaps even useful. Essay 7.1 attacked the idea of learning styles, attacked the strategy of speeding up the learning curve, attacked the building block approach, attacked the value of repetitions, and, for good measure, attacked the notion that schools should try to reduce class size. It's unlikely that you bought into all of these attacks, and some of them may have left you sputtering, but I think a good case should be made for each.

Part 7 explained why it's a bad idea to mix training and evaluation. If someone can wash out during a training period, it probably wasn't a very good training period. In my opinion, essay 7.3 was the most outrageous in this part, arguing that teaching is overrated. I wouldn't have the courage to make this claim myself, but Micki Chi, whose work I respect greatly, has shown that learning and self-explaining matter more than good teaching, and I find her arguments convincing. The takeaway of these essays is that we shouldn't get fixated on the teaching process and on things like speeding up the learning curve. Instead, we should be paying attention to what people learn and how deeply they learn it.

The second portion of part 7 described different ideas for applying the cognitive dimension to teaching and training. These essays covered the use of virtual worlds that are designed to correct flawed mental models, shifts in the mindsets of coaches and trainers, types of tacit knowledge that coaches and trainers can try to convey, envisioning training as an opportunity for gaining insights, a cognitive audit to help trainers focus on important cognitive requirements instead of performance measures, and advice for converting training scenarios so that they capture and emphasize the important cognitive challenges of a task. The essays in this bloc of part 7 should have given you a stronger cognitive orientation to training as opposed to a behavioral orientation.

The last section of part 7 took the cognitive orientation further by examining what can be done to help instructors and trainees and learners shift their mindsets. This theme of mindset shifts was introduced in essay 7.5, but here we went deeper into what that means. The concept of mindsets in education was popularized by Carol Dweck, who distinguished fixed versus growth mindsets. However, part 7 shows how the mindset concept can be expanded well beyond fixed versus growth. Several of the mindset shifts that emerge again and again have to do with encouraging learners and instructors to become more curious, and you now have a set of ideas for harnessing curiosity. You can also be thinking about mindset shifts that might improve decision-making. One of my favorite essays, 7.12, described a counterintuitive mindset of a gifted teacher. She didn't dread the misbehaviors of her nursery school students—she kind of welcomed those misbehaviors because they gave her a chance to reorient the children. I don't know how readers will respond to this idea, but I found it refreshing and inspiring and liberating.

And speaking of liberation, the final essay in this part described how decision scenarios might have contributed to the liberation of the marines, freeing them to make their own assessments of dangerous situations rather than being trapped by the expectation that they are supposed to follow orders regardless of whether the orders make sense. This third section of part 7 should have given you an expanded concept of mindset shifts. And part 7 should have deepened your understanding of the cognitive dimension by showing how that dimension plays out with regard to training and education.

8 Other Minds—Teamwork

Overview

When we apply the cognitive dimension to teams and organizations, we are trying to "see cognition" in others. The better we can do this, the more successful we should become. It isn't easy, however. Some claim it may be impossible and that when we think we are doing it, we are deluding ourselves. Many seem to be disinterested in seeing cognition in others—either because the chances of success and accuracy are so low, or because they don't think they have the skills. Or because they are genuinely uninterested in how others think, believing that all it takes is for each person to do his/her job and not worry about the others. I disagree with this last viewpoint and have difficulty with the others, but I can understand why there would be some resistance to the idea of seeing cognition in others. Nevertheless, the rewards are great, and I think there are ways for people to improve.

The core of what we need to improve is our perspective taking—our ability to accurately identify how another person is thinking. How that person is interpreting the same situation we have been trying to make sense of. What that person's mindset is. What that person is likely to notice and, perhaps more important, likely to ignore or to become confused about. With a perspective-taking mindset we should be less quick to conclude that another person is stupid if that person disagrees with us. Instead, we should wonder, ever so slightly, what is motivating that different perspective? Maybe the other person knows something we don't or doesn't have some knowledge that we possess. Maybe that person has different goals and priorities than we do—goals and priorities we hadn't considered. Maybe the person's values are different, lacking or undervaluing some of our values or being guided by values that don't matter very much to us. Maybe the person is sizing up the situation differently than we are. There is a lot to consider here, which is daunting, but also a lot to be curious about, which can be intriguing.

One reason for trying to strengthen perspective-taking skills is to coordinate better with others. The essence of coordination is predictability. The more accurately I can predict your actions, the smoother our coordination. One common way to increase predictability is to have us both follow the same game plan, the same doctrine, the same best practices. However, when faced with ambiguity and complexity and confusion, the game plans and doctrine and best practices start to erode, and that's when it pays for us to appreciate how our teammates think and not just what is the next step they're supposed to follow in the checklist.

Another challenge to coordination is when we have a breakdown in common ground. This breakdown can arise when teammates have different viewpoints; or, worse, when they don't realize they have different viewpoints; or, worst of all, when they fool themselves into believing they are on the same wavelength even though they aren't. Many serious accidents occur as a result of common ground breakdowns. Unfortunately, we can't eliminate these breakdowns. We can't set up common ground at the start of a mission or project and be sure that it will continue all the way through. By getting better at perspective taking, however, we can get better at spotting common ground breakdowns and taking corrective action before it is too late.

Or we can continue to be oblivious and fail to take even simple actions to recalibrate. Here is a recent example. I was scheduled to put on a Zoom workshop with a customer headquartered in the United Kingdom. I am located on the East Coast of the United States, eastern time. A week earlier, the time zone in the United States had shifted into daylight savings time. The workshop was scheduled to begin at 10:00 a.m. eastern daylight time (EDT), 3:00 p.m. in the United Kingdom. So far so good.

So far not so good. The customer had not realized that this daylight savings time shift had occurred in the United States (second Sunday in March). It wasn't scheduled to shift in the United Kingdom until the last Sunday in March. Therefore, the customer sent out a Zoom link for a 3:00 p.m. start in London, which was now an 11:00 a.m. start, eastern time, an hour later than the original plan. I was unaware of this glitch until the night before the workshop, as I checked all the communications and read the Zoom link more carefully.

Here is the email trail that ensued between me, Paul (my prime client), Regina (his contact at the company paying for the workshop), and Anna (assistant to Regina). (These are not their real names.) The emails started with the one I sent the night before the workshop. Pay close attention to the word "original" as in "original time," because to me this meant 10:00 a.m. EDT and 3:00 p.m. in London. However, Paul and Regina kept referring to the Zoom announcement as setting the original time, even though that announcement stated 11:00 a.m. EDT, which was different from the 10:00 a.m. EDT starting time we had originally agreed upon. None of us, Paul, Regina, or me, seemed to have noticed how the original time had changed for the United States, even though it stayed the same in London. That's how common ground breakdowns get started.

Gary: I just noticed that the Zoom link for tomorrow is for 11:00 a.m. EDT, which is an hour later than we had originally planned. What shall we do? Keep the original time or shift to the later time? I can make the change, but I don't want to confuse participants who might have carved out their schedule for the time we originally stated.

Paul: Regina, Gary kindly just pointed out that the invite is showing an hour earlier [sic] start than discussed. Just realized that this is the only week per year that EST versus UK time are only four hours apart and not five, hence the mistake.

Would you rather keep the time in the invite, as people may already have taken this into account, alternately would you like us to change the invite?

Regina: Hi Paul, my sincere apologies!!! Can we keep the original time? I hope I don't cause too much trouble. It might be problem changing since there's so many people involved. I really appreciate if you can accommodate this. Let me know. Sorry again.

Paul: LOL!!! I.e. leave invite as is?

Regina: By original time I mean the one that is now in everyone's schedules.

Paul: Yes, the one in everyone's schedules.

Regina: Exactly.

Paul: Invite stays as is looking forward to tomorrow.

Regina: Great, thank you. We're all looking forward to tomorrow as well!

Gary: Just to be precise: What is the original time? Specifically, what time (EDT) are we starting tomorrow?

Paul: So, by original Regina meant what is currently in the diary. She has confirmed that she doesn't want this changed given the number of people that now have it in their diary.

I do hope that is okay, and we very sorry [*sic*] for the confusion.

Gary: Just to be precise: What is the original time? Specifically, what time (EDT) are we starting tomorrow? [Yes, I repeated this statement because it had gotten no useful response. This time it got a response, but still not a useful one.]

Paul: (to Gary, copying Anna): The original time we stated in the invitation.

Gary: So that would be: 11:00 a.m. EDT to 2:00 p.m. EDT. Correct?

Anna: Good morning, Gary. My sincere apologies for the inconvenience. The meeting is due to start at 11 a.m. ET now; will this be OK?

Gary: Yes. 11:00 a.m. EDT it is.

It would have taken so little to resolve the common ground breakdown—a simple statement of the exact time, EDT, we were starting, but it took many emails, and the intervention of an assistant, to make this happen. Part of the confusion is the word "original" as in "the original time," because the original time in the United Kingdom was not the original time in the United States, although Paul and Regina seemed unaware of this issue. And to add more confusion, one of the workshop participants was from Canada, which uses the same arrangement for daylight savings time as the United States, at least for almost all of its provinces. And several other participants were located in different countries, including one in South America. Fortunately, we got the starting time calibrated, and the workshop went off very well.

This example involves just a few people. What about scaling up to organizations? There are a great many implications for the cognitive dimension at that level. This part discusses just two of those implications, the reactions to insights and the reactions to warnings. The news is not very good on either front.

Now to preview the essays in part 8.

Essay 8.1, "The Power to Read Minds," reviews a very discouraging set of experiments showing that people cannot accurately take someone else's perspective. The studies are well designed and executed. The analyses are clear. Nevertheless, I don't think we should accept the conclusions.

In essay 8.2, "Can We Train Perspective-Taking Skills?," I argue that we can, and I present some ideas for how we might do that.

The next essay, 8.3, "The Camera Grip," presents an example of what can happen if we make the effort to describe our own perspective to someone else.

Essay 8.4, "Switch!," describes a simple game that families can play at dinner to help their children build a mindset of taking another person's perspective.

Teams have to make decisions together and can use a variety of different strategies. The movie *The Martian* (starring Matt Damon) depicted a popular strategy—letting each team member decide for himself/herself whether to undertake a risky mission. Essay 8.5, "Don't Decide Like Martians," explains why this is a bad idea and what the team should have done.

Essay 8.6, "Cutting Down on Confusion," presents a simple strategy that teams and organizations can use to reduce the potential for confusion.

What can we do when we get entangled in a dispute? Essay 8.7, "How to Defuse a Dispute," offers some suggestions.

Essay 8.8, "Is COVID-19 a Black Swan Event?," shows that it isn't and that black swan events are less common than people imagine. They seem like black swans because organizations are so skilled at ignoring all the early warnings they receive.

And here is the bad news. Essay 8.9, "Insights versus Organizations," explains why even though organizations *claim* they want more insights, even though they *believe* they want more insights, they actually don't for reasons that are difficult to change.

8.1 The Power to Read Minds

Why Perspective Taking Still Matters

> Across a wide variety of experimental tests, involving relationships that ranged from strangers to spouses, we found no evidence that perspective taking systematically increased one's ability to accurately understand the mind of another person compared with a control condition.
>
> —Eyal, Steffel, and Epley, "Perspective Mistaking: Accurately Understanding the Mind of Another Requires Getting Perspective, Not Taking Perspective," p. 567

This statement summarizes the disheartening conclusion reached by Eyal, Steffel, & Epley (2018) based on no fewer than 25 experiments that they conducted to explore different ways to promote perspective taking. Not a single experiment showed any benefit of perspective taking on accurately predicting the reactions, attitudes, or beliefs of others. Case closed.

Or is it?

In this essay, I take a deeper look at the process of mind reading, or, as it is called in the scientific literature, perspective taking. (Note: When I refer to "mind reading," I am not talking about mystical powers or extrasensory perception.) And I take a deeper look at the Eyal et al. research. But let's start by quickly considering some of the ways that a perspective-taking skill can help us.

Potential benefits of perspective taking

If we could read people's minds, even to a small extent, we'd accrue many benefits. I've been interested in perspective taking for over 20 years and included a chapter, "The Power to Read Minds," in my 1998 book *Sources of Power*.

Gladwell (2014) attempted to explain the thinking of David Koresh in the confrontation between the federal government (the Bureau of Alcohol, Tobacco, and Firearms (ATF) and the FBI) and Koresh's Branch Davidians in Waco Texas in 1993. The confrontation ended badly. Koresh and his followers died, and the FBI and ATF agents, including FBI negotiators, showed themselves to be dangerously incompetent. The media accounts of this standoff made Koresh's actions seem incomprehensible. After reading Gladwell's analysis, the Branch Davidians made much more sense. Unfortunately, the FBI was unable to read Koresh's mind, labeled him as irrational, and dealt with him accordingly.

Most of those reading this essay can think of their own examples of successful and unsuccessful perspective taking. There's no disagreement about the value of perspective taking (mind reading), if only it worked.

Eyal, Steffel, and Epley have concluded that it doesn't work.

The Eyal, Steffel, and Epley research project

Eyal et al. reported 25 studies that they had conducted.

Some studies used laboratory tasks such as judging emotions from photographs of faces or body postures, spotting real versus fake smiles from short video snippets, or identifying whether or not a person was lying based on a short video.

Other studies were more naturalistic, using actual partners such as married couples, romantic partners, and friends. The task was to predict the partner's preferences regarding activities, movies, jokes, videos, art, and opinions. In these studies, the people in the perspective-taking condition were asked to put themselves in their partner's shoes. The participants in the control group were simply told, "We would like you to use whatever strategy you think is best" (p. 559).

As I stated at the beginning of this essay, Eyal, Steffel, and Epley did not find any evidence that having people engage in perspective taking improved the accuracy of their predictions or assessments. "Our experiments found no evidence that the cognitive effort of imagining oneself in another person's shoes, studied so widely in the psychological literature, increases a person's ability to accurately understand another's mind" (p. 550).

There's a lot that I like about the Eyal, Steffel, and Epley article. I'm highly impressed by the number of studies they ran, the care with which they conducted these studies, and the care they used in analyzing their data.

I'm also impressed by the clarity of their conclusions. No hedging, no hiding behind caveats, no "further research is needed" defensiveness. They reached a strong conclusion and they put it out there. I'd like to see more of that kind of courage and confidence in scientific reporting.

Nevertheless, I think their primary conclusion is wrong.

Did they actually show that perspective taking has no effect?

The experimental group was simply asked to take the target's perspective. That's all. For example, "While watching the pictures, please think about the person in the picture. Try to adopt the perspective of the person in the picture as if you were the person who is answering the question. Do your best to adopt his or her perspective, putting yourself into the other person's shoes as if you were that person. Remember that the person in the picture may have a different perspective than you do as the viewer of the picture" (p. 552).

The control group was not given any specific instructions and had the same task as the experimental group (e.g., to try to identify the emotion of the person in the picture, or describe what the person was thinking/feeling, or to predict some aspects of the person's preferences).

However, the control participants may have tried to take the perspective of the person in the picture, even though they were not asked to do so. They were not told *not* to engage in perspective taking. Since the task was to predict what the other person was thinking, it seems reasonable that they might try to take the other person's perspective.

Therefore, the experimental/control contrast is not clean. Both groups may have been engaging in perspective taking, which would explain why the researchers found no differences between them. Eyal, Steffel, and Epley briefly acknowledge this point at the end of their article, "participants in the control conditions of our experiments were already making inferences about another person's perspective" (p. 568), but they don't expand on the ramifications of this observation.

As a result, I don't think that the research demonstrated that perspective taking had no effect, even though this is what the authors claim. The research merely demonstrated that the perspective-taking *instructions* didn't achieve much—that these *instructions* were insufficient to boost the experimental group over the control group. The research tells us nothing about the *value* of perspective taking.

The authors seem to understand this—on page 566, they acknowledge that several other studies have shown that people are more accurate in understanding others than random chance, even though they're not perfectly accurate.

The issue isn't whether people can use perspective taking to increase accuracy—it is whether *explicit instructions* have any effect. The research clearly demonstrates that the instructions did not make a difference, even though many of us might expect that they would.

Conclusions

In all sorts of situations, we try to take the perspectives of others, and I suspect we do a reasonably accurate job. Merely having a conversation with another person requires that we speculate about what the person knows, what the person wants to know, and what the person can understand.

In fact, we become frustrated when the other person does a poor job of perspective taking. We become impatient when the other person goes into excessive detail, explaining things to us that we already know, and that the person should anticipate we know. On the flip side, we can get irritated when the other person is too cryptic and fails to give us some necessary details. Our frustration suggests that we expect reasonably accurate levels of perspective taking.

For me, the real question is what it might take to build perspective-taking skills. That's the topic of my next essay, "Can We Train Perspective-Taking Skills?"

—*February 11, 2020*

8.2 Can We Train Perspective-Taking Skills?

Some Ideas for Developing the Ability to Take the Perspective of Another Person

What might it take to build perspective-taking skills? In this essay, I present several suggestions.

Practice and feedback

These are the staples of training. We can let people practice and give them feedback. This advice doesn't seem so unusual. It's how people acquire skills. We could even use the tasks that Eyal, Steffel, and Epley employed: have people perform various tasks, make their predictions, and get feedback.

Diagnosis

We could guide people to try to diagnose the reasons for inaccurate predictions, perhaps identifying cues and patterns they might have missed so that in the future they might be more alert to those kinds of cues and patterns.

The diagnosis might discover mismatches between the thinking of the predictor (the person doing the predicting) and the "predictee" (the person whose behavior is being predicted). Here is a short checklist of the types of mismatches to consider:

- Mismatch in knowledge—one person knows things the other doesn't
- Mismatch in priorities—differences in the goals of each person

- Mismatch in situation awareness—the two people are sizing up the situation differently
- Mismatch in mindsets—each person has a different belief about what is called for in the situation

Calibration

Scenario methods such as ShadowBox (Klein & Borders, 2016) could be very effective for building perspective-taking skills. We could give team members a challenging scenario that contains choice points asking each person what s/he would do (from a set of options) and what s/he expected the other person would do. We wouldn't need to gather responses from experts—we could use the reactions of the two partners. We would let them try to predict the behavior of the other and then allow them to study the actual choices made and the rationale statements backing up these choices/predictions.

Role-playing and role reversals

We can use exercises such as role reversals that place people in contrasting perspectives. For example, a military commander explained to me how he would turn the map around to see the battleground from the vantage of the adversary.

I also remember hearing about a Marine Corps force-on-force field exercise. The first day of the training was about attacking an adversary's position. A separate group was to play the role of the adversary, but through a scheduling error, that group never showed up. Therefore, one of the training groups was given the assignment of being the adversary, defending against an attack. They were the "designated defenders," facing each of the different teams mounting attacks, and they were very irritated—they were never going to have a chance to practice how to conduct an attack.

The next day, all the groups were tested on their ability to conduct an attack, and, to everyone's surprise, the "designated defenders" came out on top. Learning how to defend against different tactics provided them with the perspective-taking skills to be highly effective attackers, even though they never had a chance to conduct any practice attacks of their own.

In a team context, just practicing together can be useful for anticipating what the others are going to do. However, training can go further, flagging instances of miscoordination and using the mismatch checklist presented earlier to discuss how the team members were seeing things differently.

In adversarial conditions, reviewing historical data on the opponent can be helpful. During World War II, Patton, watching Rommel's force attack, growled, "You beautiful bastard, I read your book."

Conclusion

These are just a few ideas for how we might train perspective-taking skills. Doubtless, there are many others. The most basic tactic is to provide participants with feedback.

Researchers might also examine individual differences. Some people may be better at perspective taking than others. Some people may benefit more from training than others.

I am much more optimistic than Eyal, Steffel, and Epley. I see some exciting possibilities for fostering skills and helping people become better at taking the perspective of others.

—*February 16, 2020*

8.3 The Camera Grip

A Case Study of the Power of Appreciation

My brother Dennis is a writer, director, and producer in Hollywood. Several decades ago, Dennis was running *Buffalo Bill*, a half-hour TV comedy series starring Dabney Coleman and featuring Geena Davis. Dennis was the producer of the series. He wrote most of the show's episodes and directed some of them.

As the showrunner, his attention was not only on the actors but also the crew, and even the grips—"grip" being the term for the man (and in that era, the crews for TV and movies were exclusively male) whose job it was to do all heavy and, at times, even dangerous physical work on a film set. Grips were generally regarded as grunts and laborers, the lowest on the crews' totem pole of roles, status, and respect.

The first week of the series, Dennis noticed a grip who was pushing one of the show's three-camera rigs, which are cameras on wheels. Controlling each rig was a camera operator and focus puller.

This particular grip's rig carried the B-camera, the most important one. The B-camera was the middle camera. It had a wider angle than the (side) A and C cameras, and so this man moved around the stage much more than the other two camera grips because he was continually trying for the best angle on the actors in the scene. And the actors were constantly moving around and forming new tableaux.

He was a burly, middle-aged fellow who, despite his bulk, maneuvered the heavy camera rig with ease. He wheeled it across the stage smoothly and swiftly, perfectly executing the appropriate moves, like a ballet dancer.

He always hit his marks, all the while laughing very hard at the show, yet laughing silently because Dennis decided to shoot this show without an audience. Therefore the set had to be very quiet.

This multi-camera-but-with-no-audience strategy (which Dennis would use again for another half-hour TV series he later co-created and produced: *The Larry Sanders Show*) cut down on expenses by being quick. Dennis also believed that by excluding a studio audience, the actors would play their parts more as the characters and less as performers pushing to get laughs from the crowd.

For Dennis, this camera grip on rig B, tasked with listening to the lines, *was* the audience. And the shaking of the man's big belly as he bent over and maneuvered the camera rig told Dennis just how funny or not funny his writing was at every point in the script.

Dennis found the camera grip's laughter inspiring. Late at night, alone in his office writing the scripts for the show, Dennis would work very hard to come up with ideas and lines that were sufficiently funny they would make the B-camera grip laugh so hard he would miss his mark.

Dennis never succeeded. He thinks he came close on several occasions, but that's as far as he got. Fortunately for the show.

And then one week Dennis showed up on the set only to see a new grip on B-camera!

Dennis asked the cinematographer, "What happened to the other guy?" Dennis didn't even know the B-camera grip's name. He was told that the grip had taken a job on *The Bob Newhart Show*. That series was filmed on the other side of the massive lot and was shot before a live audience, which meant the crew there worked three days a week, whereas *Buffalo Bill* only filmed two days a week. The grip could make much more money by taking the *Newhart* job.

That day, during the *Buffalo Bill* crew's lunch break, Dennis walked all the way across the lot to the *Newhart* set. He went over to the grip, said hello, shook the man's hand, and explained to him how much he'd enjoyed working with him and how much pleasure he got watching him laugh. Dennis even confessed to the grip that he often thought of him late at night, writing his scripts, trying to come up with something so funny as to make the grip laugh too hard, hoping to trip him up.

Dennis said he knew that the new job paid substantially better than *Buffalo Bill*, and he fully understood why the grip had taken it. Dennis said he'd come by only because he wanted to thank the man for his terrific work and wish him well at his new show.

And that was that.

Except that on Monday of the following week, when filming started on the new episode, Dennis saw that the grip had returned to *Buffalo Bill* and was once again muscling the B-camera.

—*May 3, 2018*

8.4 Switch!

Helping Children See Different Perspectives

It's easy to explain why perspective taking is important, and it's relatively easy to formulate methods that should help, but the hard part is personal: being able to imagine a viewpoint other than our own. Some people are very concrete thinkers and just can't do the hypothetical thinking needed to try on a different set of assumptions. Some people are so competitive that they lock into their views and can't let go, even for a few moments. Others are used to seeing the world using right/wrong, good/bad dichotomies and are uncomfortable imagining that their opponents might have some valid reasons for their views. This suggestion to take the adversary's perspective can be very difficult to carry out.

Maybe the perspective-taking skill is something we can introduce to children. Not young children, but teenagers and even pre-teens. That way they'll be ready when they become adults, ready to sympathize and empathize and cooperate.

Here's a game I played with my daughters as they were growing up. I started when they were about 8 and 11. We'd be having dinner, and we'd get into a friendly argument. I was often losing these arguments because I tended to take extreme positions just to keep the discussion exciting. I would see my daughters grinning because they had me cornered. Then I would hold up my hand and say, "Switch!" The game was for them to immediately change positions and argue for my point of view, and I'd have to argue theirs. My wife Helen was supposed to be a neutral observer but usually became a cheerleader when the daughters argued my original views better than I had.

My daughters got very good at this game—they were actually better than I was. Once the "Switch!" was thrown, they had no hesitation in making a 180-degree turn. They might initially groan because they were just about to win the debate, but they relished the challenge of doing a better job of presenting my viewpoint than I had. And they occasionally called "Switch!" themselves, to keep me on my toes. Anyone could call "Switch!," and it had to be without warning.

I think it helped that we used the "Switch!" game for impersonal arguments, such as social and political issues. Later on, when the switching was ingrained in our family culture, we occasionally used it on personal conflicts.

Did the "Switch!" game make any difference? I don't know. But my younger daughter Rebecca once described a sixth-grade class project to interview people in the community about different social issues. Rebecca and her partner chose the topic of abortion and were given a list of people who were pro-life or pro-choice. Both girls were advocates for choice. Rebecca's friend recoiled at the notion of interviewing anyone with anti-abortion views. In contrast, Rebecca was excited by the chance to hear the other side, so that's how they split the list, with the friend talking with people who held the same views that she did and Rebecca interviewing the pro-life advocates. I don't think the Switch! game we played was responsible for Rebecca's choice, but it may have given her the enthusiasm for encountering a perspective that had seemed incomprehensible.

Recently, I asked my older daughter, Devorah, what she thought of the game. Without hesitation, she explained her firm conviction that "Switch!" helped her become the professional she is today. She feels that she has an edge over others in her profession—design research—because the "Switch!" game helped her learn how to quickly and smoothly decenter and take another perspective.

These are just anecdotes. I don't have any evidence about the effectiveness of the Switch! game. If you try this out with your children or with others, I hope you will make some useful discoveries.

—April 1, 2016

8.5 Don't Decide Like Martians

The Most Common Team Decision Strategy Is Probably the Worst

Individual decisions are hard enough, but team decisions can be even more difficult because we have to wrestle with competing agendas, competing interpretations, and arbitrary methods for capturing the intentions of the team members.

There are common methods for teams to arrive at a decision: The leader can simply assert authority. The team can try to broker a course of action that reflects the desires of the members—a consensus. Or the team can vote.

Now let's increase the stakes. Let's imagine that there are life-and-death consequences for the entire team. Many leaders would understandably refuse to assert authority—they would want the team members to weigh in on their readiness to take the risk.

And let's imagine that the decision is go/no-go rather than something that can be moderated. Now we can't rely on a brokered compromise.

That leaves one option: a vote. But how should the team carry out that vote?

The issue comes up in settings like the following. We are cross-country skiing the back country with a group of friends. The safest terrain is very flat, but that doesn't offer much excitement. We go looking for hills that will be fun to glide down, the steeper the better, up to a point. And now we have reached that point. The steepness of the hills in front of us, and the heaviness of the snowpack, pose a risk of an avalanche. Should we take that risk, or back off? Safety protocol is to take the pulse of the group, to see who wants to proceed and who doesn't. Safety protocol is to vote so that any squeamish team member has a veto.

However, consider some typical voting scenarios. Hands up if you want to chance it—and now hands up if you want the group to withdraw. Or else poll each team member one at a time. Voting puts enormous social pressure to conform. Voting puts pressure not to disappoint the risk seekers who have come all this way for adventure. It puts pressure not to seem like a wimp. Most of the time these votes are a sham.

The better way to vote is to make the choices confidential. Each team member can be given 1 black and 1 white bead. Each member would select one bead (say, the white bead for backing off or the black for continuing) and put it in an opaque bag so that no one can see any of the votes. The team members would put the other bead in a second bag for discards. Once each team member has voted, the leader publicly displays the contents of the first bag so the team can see what it chose—it can see if there are any white beads.

I recently watched the film *The Martian* and was troubled. (Spoiler alert—if you haven't seen the film but intend to, you might want to stop reading and come back to this piece later.) I enjoyed the movie and recommend it, but I didn't like the message it sent about team decision-making. Faced with the life-and-death decision about whether to go back to Mars for their stranded comrade (Matt Damon), the spaceship team used the typical voting scheme—a public statement. Those most likely to opt for the rescue went first, building up social pressure on the waverers. Thus, the team arrived at a unanimous vote on an extremely risky decision.

I am not complaining about the realism of the procedure. My complaint is with the way the film modeled poor team decision-making. Team members with realistic apprehension were railroaded into taking a large gamble with their lives. I fear that lives will be lost as moviegoers emulate what they watched on screen and get trapped in untenable conditions should they have to make their own life-and-death team decisions.

I am not opposed to heroism, as long as people choose for themselves. I am opposed to bullying others into taking risks they want to avoid.

Hopefully, audience members can ignore the predictable Hollywood ending of *The Martian* and perhaps imagine alternative endings in which the team meets with disaster. Compare *The Martian* with another recent movie, the documentary film *Everest*. (Same spoiler alert as before.) Rob Hall, the mountaineering team leader, accepted all the responsibility. He broke his own inviolable rule about everyone who hadn't summitted by

2:00 p.m., turning back. By proceeding he managed to kill himself and several members of his expedition. I suspect that if the decision to press on was put to a *Martian*-style vote, the expedition would have voted to go for the summit. *Everest* didn't glorify excessive risk-taking. Instead, it left its audience reflecting on the consequences of overconfidence and of not wanting to disappoint others.

Let's not pretend that we are invincible Hollywood heroes. Let's not decide like Martians.

—*November 6, 2015*

8.6 Cutting Down on Confusion

A Strategy for Spotting and Dismantling Verbal Land Mines

Language is a means for communication, but it can also be a means for miscommunication.

This essay is not about mild confusions, such as transposing digits in a telephone number or forgetting an appointment. The topic is the kind of profound confusion that leaves all the parties to a conversation shaking their heads, if not their fists, and arguing about what went wrong. This essay is about breakdowns in common ground.

These breakdowns are insidious because each person erroneously believes s/he is on the same wavelength as the other. They may not discover their error until it is too late to avoid damage.

Here's an example. Many years ago, I was invited to a meeting on helping the army train officers for leadership and decision-making. At the meeting, an army colonel explained that during the 1990–1991 Desert Storm campaign, many small unit leaders had to be removed because of poor leadership skills. A representative from an army laboratory jumped in and described the new three-part leadership training program his laboratory had just completed. Next, a technology developer explained how his organization's new virtual environment platform could be perfect for presenting the training. Everyone in the room was enthusiastic about this new project. Everyone but me.

I asked the colonel to explain the kinds of leadership problems that were plaguing him. He confessed that he didn't know. All that the records stated was that lieutenants and captains had to be removed because of leadership problems. I pressed further. "That could be micromanagement or lack of management. Excessive strictness or excessive permissiveness. Being too punitive or too soft. Don't you have any more details?" He admitted that he didn't.

I explained that the term "leadership problem" was so vague it could cover anything. And because we didn't know what the real problem was, how could we be confident about what training program was even relevant here? What bothered me wasn't that the people in the room had different notions of "leadership problem" but that they all believed they had the same notion. They were getting ready to commit large sums of money to a training program that might have zero relevance to the army's needs.

I thought about this incident recently when I met with a friend, a physician who had just resigned her position with a hospital. She'd been hired to take over safety operations and transform the hospital into a safety-conscious exemplar. Now, several years later, she was still bitter about how the higher administrators had blocked her initiatives. "They weren't really serious about wanting to promote safety," she complained. I disagreed. I didn't think they had misled her. They were sincere, but their concept of "safety culture" didn't mesh with hers. Only when she hit them with new ideas did the mismatch become clear.

What's the solution? I think what's needed is a two-step strategy. Step 1 is to identify the verbal landmines that can trigger a common ground breakdown. A program to combat leadership problems—that's a trigger. So is a hospital position to install a safety culture. Or an agreement to remodel an office. Or to raise a child to be a good citizen. These cases all contain verbal landmines.

Step 2 is to dismantle the verbal landmines once we spot them. A way to do that is to use stories. Stories and examples can rescue us from the ambiguities of language. When I was a college freshman, the first course I took was Intro to Philosophy, and the first reading assignment was a Plato dialogue, *Euthyphro*. In this dialogue, Socrates carries on a conversation with Euthyphro, a leading citizen of Athens. Socrates asks Euthyphro if he knows what "piety" means. Euthyphro explains that it is hard to put it in words and wants to give Socrates some examples, but Socrates waves him off. He wants it in words. Euthyphro tries, and stumbles, and fails. Socrates is able to show that Euthyphro really doesn't understand the concept of "piety." Chalk one up for Socrates.

However, many years later as I thought back to this dialogue, I realized that Euthyphro was trying to use stories and examples—the technical term is an "ostensive definition." By rejecting examples, Socrates shut the door on the power of stories. Stories are concrete, whereas language is notoriously slippery. In my army example, I was asking the colonel for stories of leadership problems so that our group could calibrate on the same types of failure.

I suggested to my physician friend that in future job interviews, even if the hospital administrators insist that they want a safety culture, she could try to anchor the discussion by offering some examples of safety changes other hospitals have made. She can explain that she wants to understand the administrators' comfort zone. She may try to stretch their comfort zone, but if her ideas are clearly out of their comfort zone, she is just setting herself up for failure and setting the hospital up for frustration. In contrast to the usual exchange of platitudes and empty values statements, she can have a more meaningful conversation about specific cases—how they fit the hospital's plans and how they might be incompatible with the hospital's needs.

This two-step strategy doesn't have to take a lot of work. We just need to train ourselves to notice the slippery terms when we make an arrangement, and then spend a few minutes pinning these terms down with stories and examples. We can invite our colleagues to add their stories. It's not a guaranteed solution—we can't inoculate ourselves against all confusions. The two-step strategy is only for confusions that might lead to common ground breakdowns between people. But it might prevent a lot of unnecessary misunderstandings.

—*November 2, 2014*

8.7 How to Defuse a Dispute

Five Strategies for Managing Disagreements

Recently, a client conducted a small group session using a ShadowBox decision training scenario that my colleagues and I had developed and bumped into a dilemma. For the first decision point, six people picked one option and the other two picked a different option. What do you do when the group doesn't neatly line up? My client explained how the majority, the six group members, put pressure on the other two to change their minds, but that didn't go over very well. Afterward, she called me for advice.

A typical approach is to stifle the disagreement by trying to convince the outliers through majority rules, using authority, using threats, coercion, and so forth. That's what my client's group had done. If this sounds heavy-handed, it's the way lots of democracies work: the powerful group gets to impose its will on the weak, within bounds. (Athenian democracy didn't work that way. As Paul Woodruff explained in *First Democracy* [2006], the majority was expected to find a compromise.). But majority rule didn't work out well for my client. As is often the case, it created resentment and weakened the harmony of the group.

What can we do when we encounter an interpersonal disagreement, in a group or even face-to-face with another person? Here are a few strategies. They all depend on perspective taking—being able to see the dispute from the vantage point of the other side.

1. Be curious. In my conversation with my client, I suggested that next time she use a different strategy: to be curious. What were the reasons given by the two dissenters? Why did they care about their positions? Maybe they can convince the majority. (Remember what Henry Fonda did in the movie *12 Angry Men* to convince the other 11 jurors.) Or maybe if the majority shares its reasons in a careful way, the minority members may voluntarily change their position. We've all encountered people who ask for our reasons just to attack them. "I just want to learn why you are taking that position," they'll say, and once you explain, they pounce on you. That sort of dialogue isn't very constructive. I think it works better to take dissenters seriously and treat them with respect. We need to ask questions whose answers we don't already know.

2. Repair common ground. A lot of the disagreements I see aren't substantive but are caused by confusion. Very often people use the same terms to mean different things. The argument can become very heated, but the protagonists are talking past each other. In the previous essay, "Cutting Down on Confusion," I described a conflict in which a friend was hired by a hospital to create a safety culture, only to find that the administrators didn't give her the backing they promised. She felt betrayed. However, her ideas of a safety culture were very different from those of the administrators. They each used the term "safety culture," but with different expectations. Terms like "safety culture" are common ground landmines, just waiting to be tripped. The strategy here is first to be alert to these landmines. If the disagreement hinges on this type of misunderstanding, maybe it can be defused. Sometimes we can avoid a common ground landmine by pinning down our terms, not with words, and certainly not with metrics but with examples so that each party has a more concrete image of what is expected.

3. Sort out knowledge differences. Sometimes one party knows something that the other side doesn't. One party may be laboring under constraints and restrictions that the others aren't aware of. By listening carefully, we might be able to defuse disagreements by making information available. We can ask ourselves, "Is there something the others don't know? Or are they assuming I know something of which I am ignorant?"

4. Appreciate motivation differences. Rivals in a dispute may have some overlapping goals but certainly will have a lot of separate goals. They're never going to line up the same way, but they can gain a deeper understanding of differences in their priorities. Sometimes people won't be candid about their goals, or may not fully understand their own goals, but sympathetic efforts to contrast each party's goals might work better than assuming that everyone has the same motives.

5. Discover flawed beliefs. If we listen carefully to the opposite side, maybe we can spot errors in their thinking, erroneous or unnecessary assumptions they are making. And if we explain our own position, maybe others can notice mistakes we are making. People often get defensive about such flaws, so they need to be described tactfully. Sincere questions are often the best way forward.

This list is not exhaustive. I am sure readers can generate other techniques they find useful. Some strategies may require professional skills. For example, Jay Rothman, a specialist in conflict resolution, believes that many disagreements stem from deeply rooted identity issues that should be surfaced and acknowledged in order to make progress. Each party needs to hear how the conflict reflects the identity dynamics of the other. The purpose of this essay is not to review the entire field but simply to show that there are approaches other than the majority imposing its will.

All of these strategies can be useful when parties who would like to work better together are blocked by honest disagreements.

But not all disagreements are honest. Too often, people engage in dishonest disagreements. One of the parties may be holding a grudge or may feel antagonism. That person may be searching for ways to demean the other, impugn the other's motives and character, disqualify the judgments and competence of the other. The specific disagreement is just a vehicle for launching an attack. The festering antagonism seeks expression as a disagreement. None of the five strategies described in this essay will be useful with dishonest disagreements because the intent is to use the dispute as a weapon, not to resolve it.

The line between honest and dishonest disagreements blurs when an honest disagreement becomes heated and gives rise to antagonism, a desire to win the debate at almost all costs. Too many arguments become inflamed in this way. That's why it's important to try to de-escalate the dispute before it gets out of control.

—March 1, 2016

8.8 Is COVID-19 a Black Swan Event?

Maybe Black Swans Don't Really Exist

If there was ever a black swan event, it would be the COVID-19 pandemic. Taleb (2007) has described how an unexpected event can wipe out all our plans and preparations.

As we are all painfully aware, prior to the pandemic, everything was proceeding smoothly in November and December 2019 and into February 2020. The US economy continued its upward swing. The Dow Jones and the S&P 500 recorded all-time highs on February 12, 2020.

Then it hit. Starting on February 24, the stock market went into free fall. Not only did we have a collapsed US and global economy, but we were also locked down, fearful of venturing from our homes, wondering what had happened to us and how long it would take to return to normal—wondering what normal meant anymore.

However, I do not think the pandemic was a true black swan. I used to buy into Taleb's arguments. I used to believe the concept of black swans was very valuable. But I don't anymore.

I know that many people enthusiastically apply the concept of black swans, and that's a problem because some of the most common reactions to black swans are not particularly helpful. Even worse, applying the idea of black swans may get in the way of using more effective tactics to detect problems in time to head them off or at least mitigate them.

Let's start with the question of whether the pandemic was a black swan event. It turns out that epidemiologists have been warning of pandemics for many years, so they weren't surprised. And some epidemiologists sounded the warning about COVID-19 once the picture from Wuhan, China, started to become clear. The Centers for Disease Control and Prevention learned about the Wuhan outbreak in December. The World Health Organization issued a warning on January 5, 2020.

Therefore, the pandemic was not an unexpected event. Alarm bells for the COVID-19 outbreak were starting to ring in January. Therefore, I don't think the collapse of mid-February was a black swan. Even Taleb has stated that COVID-19 was not a black swan event.

Going further, when I have investigated other "unexpected" catastrophes, such as the 9/11 attacks, or the stock market collapse of 2007–2008, or the "unexpected" fall of the Berlin Wall in 1989, or the Yom Kippur War of 1973, when Israel was "unexpectedly" attacked by Egypt and Syria, I always find individuals who did sound a warning.

These events did not come out of nowhere. They were predictable—because people predicted them. That's why I no longer believe in black swans. (To be sure, there are some truly unexpected events, but they seem to be very infrequent and usually don't involve the high-profile catastrophes we worry about.)

This may seem like an academic argument, but it does have a practical impact. One type of response to the notion of black swans is for countries and organizations to invest more in data-gathering technologies and apply Big Data analysis techniques to try to pick up the earliest warning signs. Technology to the rescue—except that this investment doesn't seem to pay off very much, if ever.

The belief in black swans comes with a delusion that once informed about a threat, we will expeditiously take action. And we know that this isn't true. From my perspective, the problem isn't the lack of data, but the complacency of the decision-makers.

Along with that complacency comes what I think is the real problem: silencing the people who try to sound an alarm. They get silenced because their message is inconvenient, and because the events they are warning us about are fairly novel. I remember hearing one story in which a junior intelligence analyst issued a warning about a coup in a certain country, but his supervisor refused to pass the message up the chain in her agency because that country hadn't ever had a coup before, so it seemed to be unlikely. Three days later, the country had its first-ever coup. When I heard that story, I wondered why the US government was funding that agency because it seemed determined to only issue warnings that were obvious to everyone involved.

That's why I question the attempt to spot black swan events using technology. Why invest in technology when decision-makers are determined to ignore bad news? Why invest in technology if decision-makers are determined to marginalize the bearers of that bad news, because their news is so inconvenient, and because the dangers they are describing seem so implausible and improbable?

We don't need a wider array of detectors. Countries and organizations already have people sounding the alarms. These people are just not getting heard.

Of course, most alarms are false. We can't respond to every alarm, or else we'd paralyze ourselves.

Therefore, we should develop protocols for *listening* to the alarmists, even though we won't necessarily act on their warnings. We should develop exercises to shake decision-makers out of their knee-jerk dismissals of improbable warnings. We should prepare drills for helping decision-makers anticipate the consequences of the events being flagged and to track the trajectories of these events to gauge their significance. If the warning has merit, we should notice more and more confirmations, and here we can deploy technology to focus data-gathering on the warnings that deserve attention.

However, we are unlikely to do any of these things as long as we continue to believe in black swans.

—*May 11, 2020*

8.9 Insights versus Organizations

How Organizations Reduce Insights

Most organizations claim—and sincerely believe—that they want to increase insights and put them to use. We shouldn't let that sincerity fool us.

Organizations inadvertently suppress the insights of their workers, and they do it in ways that are ingrained and invisible. Organizations stifle insights because of forces locked deep inside their DNA: they value predictability, they recoil from surprises, and they crave perfection, the absence of errors. In their zeal to reduce uncertainty and minimize errors, organizations fall into the predictability trap and the perfection trap.

The *predictability trap* is to arrange projects to run as smoothly as possible. Managers carefully map out the steps that will carry them successfully from start to finish. They set up a timeline showing when each step starts and finishes. They calculate the resources to allocate to each step—the dollars they will spend and/or the hours they will need. When the plan gets disturbed, managers can quickly detect the perturbation and reprogram resources so that progress isn't slowed. The job of managers is much easier if they can accurately predict the workflow, resources, and schedules. Their job is easier if they can accurately gauge progress in moving toward the official project goal.

Insight is the opposite of predictable. Insights are disruptive. They come without warning, take forms that are unexpected, and open up unimagined opportunities. They are disorganizing. Insights disrupt progress reviews because they reshape tasks and even revise goals. They carry risks—unseen pitfalls that can get managers in trouble.

In 2012, Mueller, Melwani, & Goncalo published a study of why people have an aversion to creativity, even though they claim to want creative ideas. The researchers found that if an idea is novel, people automatically assume it isn't practical, reliable, or error-free. Novel ideas are associated with failures. Creativity was connected in the participants' minds with uncertainty. When people were motivated to reduce uncertainty, they gave lower evaluations to creative ideas. Managers dislike uncertainty and unpredictability, and therefore distrust creativity.

Organizations treat disruptive insights and innovations with suspicion. Witness the initial hostile reactions to the telephone, to Google's search engine, to VisiCalc, to the Xerox 914 copier.

The *perfection trap* is to try to reduce or eliminate errors. Organizations naturally gravitate toward reducing errors. Errors are easy to define, easy to measure, and relatively easy to manage.

The quest for perfection, error-free performance, is right up there with the quest for predictability. These are both inherent in running an organization that depends on managing people and projects. In well-ordered situations, with clear goals and standards, and stable conditions, the pursuit of perfection makes sense. But not when we face complex and chaotic conditions.

Organizations have lots of reasons to dislike errors—they can pose severe safety risks; they disrupt coordination; they lead to waste; they reduce the chance for project success; they erode the culture; they can result in bad publicity. Managers are continually checking to see if workers meet their performance standards. When managers find deviations, they quickly respond to get everything back on track. It's much easier and less frustrating to manage by reducing errors than to try to boost insights. Managers know how to spot errors. They don't know how to encourage insights other than hanging inspirational posters on the walls.

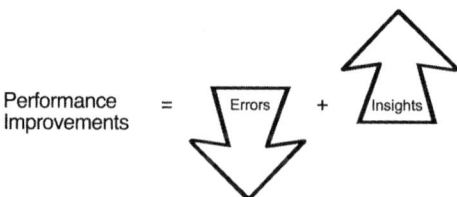

Figure 8.1
Two arrows to improve performance.

Unfortunately, the actions that organizations take to reduce errors can actually impede insights. They drain the attention and energy of the employees into error-reduction rituals that crowd out the mindset needed for insights.

The performance equation in figure 8.1 shows that to improve performance, we need to do two things. The down arrow shows that we want to reduce errors and uncertainty. The up arrow is what we want to increase—insights. To improve performance we need to reduce errors and uncertainty, and we also need to increase insights.

Most organizations lean too far toward the down arrow. They care more about reducing errors and uncertainty than making discoveries. These forces—the desire for predictability and perfection—aren't values that organizations choose. They seem to be inherent in the very nature of organizations.

—*July 3, 2013*

8.10 Reflections

The ability to see cognition extends to seeing cognition in others—and being able to take their perspective. These are the takeaways for part 8. The first two essays explored the skill of perspective taking and made some suggestions about how perspective-taking skills might be trained: basic practice and feedback, diagnosis for inaccurate perspective taking, a short checklist of possible reasons for a mismatch (mismatch in knowledge, or priorities, or situation awareness, or mindsets), and role-playing exercises. The essays are very enthusiastic about the likely effectiveness of perspective-taking training and the effects this kind of training might have on teamwork. However, these speculations are short on data, even if they are long on enthusiasm, and many attempts to boost perspective-taking skills have fizzled, so there is a lot of work to be done here.

The next essays in part 8 continued this spirit of enthusiasm. I described the impact of letting people (a camera grip in this case) know they are appreciated. I shared the rules of a dinner game that I played with my children to foster perspective taking by unexpectedly requiring them to argue the opposite side in a debate. I used a movie (*The Martian*) to suggest a decision strategy to increase the safety of a team or group by letting cautious members vote anonymously. I explained the problem created when common ground breaks down in a team or group and offered a two-step strategy: identify the potential verbal landmines, and then use stories to dismantle these landmines. I described a set of strategies we can use to manage disagreements so that the dispute doesn't escalate: We can be curious about the views of people taking a different side in the dispute. We can be prepared to repair common ground because many heated disputes really stem from common ground breakdowns rather than disagreements about substantive issues. We can be alert to disagreements caused by mismatches in what the people know, or mismatches in motivations. Sometimes we can trace the disagreement to flawed beliefs, ideally the flawed beliefs of our opponents but occasionally, and embarrassingly, our own flawed beliefs.

The essay on COVID-19 provided yet another suggestion—that we can become more resilient and faster to spot problems, not by investing in warnings and alarms capabilities but simply by listening to people within our organizations. This suggestion cuts costs and speeds the warnings. For many crises, those who tried to sound the alarm were ignored.

Unfortunately, part 8 ended on a discouraging note. Organizations may claim to want more insights and discoveries but they are fooling themselves. Forces inherent in organizations act to stifle insights, not to promote them. Insights are disruptive and disorganizing, and therefore threaten the systematic ways that organizations function. Organizations strive for perfection by eliminating errors, which interferes with the messiness needed to foster insights. I am not sure there is much to do to counter this organizational tendency.

9 Making Waves—Tools and Tactics for Improvement

Overview

This part is devoted to essays describing methods and recommendations. These are tools and techniques to let you apply the ideas covered in the previous parts. Those parts did include some methods, but here in part 9, the spotlight is on practical advice.

Part 9 is titled "Making Waves" to reflect the Naturalistic Decision Making (NDM) image from the first part (see figure 9.1), to remind you of the themes of the cognitive dimension. The methods described in part 9 are intended to help you handle the complexities of natural settings.

Part 9 is a culmination of the concepts presented earlier. Part 9 is the WIIFM part, "What's in It for Me?" What does the cognitive dimension buy us? But part 9 also reinforces the skill of seeing cognition by showing different ways of putting that skill into action.

There are 13 essays here. The first set of essays address ways for individuals to do better, and the second set of essays are aimed at ways for organizations to improve.

Essay 9.1, "Naturalistic Decision Making Tools," is an introduction to this part. I provide a listing of 42 tools that NDM researchers and practitioners have developed and use and recommend to others. Several of the other essays in this part expand on some of these NDM tools.

The next six essays cover tools and tactics for helping individuals.

"When to Consult Your Intuition," essay 9.2, contrasts my views with those of Danny Kahneman. The conclusions I reach may surprise you, although I find them pretty reasonable.

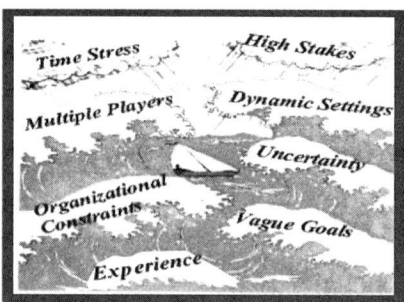

Figure 9.1
Decision-making waves.

The next essay (9.3), "Know Yourself," takes a serious look at a long-standing and fairly meaningless recommendation and puts it into a different perspective—hopefully a more useful one.

In essay 9.4, "Are You Pursuing a Pipe Dream?," I take aim at the conventional cliché favored by so many graduation speakers, to follow your passion. If nothing else, this essay may help to make future graduation ceremonies more endurable.

The next two essays are about a technique, the Causal Landscape, for representing causal complexity in a manageable way. Essay 9.5, "The Causal Landscape," is a synthesis of two essays I had originally written on the topic. Essay 9.6, "Why Did Hillary Lose the Election?" presents an illustration of the Causal Landscape in trying to understand the 2016 presidential election.

Essay 9.7, "Is Wanting to Change Enough?," was written by Devorah Klein and Gretchen Wustrack, based on projects and research they had conducted when they worked at IDEO, the design and innovation company. The answer to the question is that merely wanting to change is not sufficient. If your goal is to create enduring changes, you need to consider a number of factors, and this essay shows how that might happen.

Part 9 switches gears at this point, from advice for an individual to advice for organizations.

Essay 9.8, "The Pre-mortem Method," describes a technique that I developed in the late 1980s. I designed it for my own company, and I have been astonished at how well-known it has become and how widely it is used, even though I have written very little about it and never publicized it.

"The Decision Scorecard," essay 9.9, presents an idea for making personnel evaluations more interesting and more meaningful.

Essay 9.10, "Management by Discovery," offers a framework for planning when faced with wicked problems, as well as confusion and ambiguity about the situations we face and the goals we want to accomplish.

In essay 9.11, "The Nine Levers Organizations Can Use for Better Performance," I catalog the opportunities that organizations have available to change the behaviors of the workers. It's not just training and incentives. Leaders and managers have a much broader set of tactics available than they might imagine.

The next essay (9.12), "Turning Policy into Practice," explains why merely issuing policy statements is usually insufficient and suggests some ways to get these policy statements to stick.

There are a lot of suggestions in part 9—can people really take action to produce large and lasting change in their organizations? Essay 9.13, "The Difference-Makers," describes four individuals who succeeded in making lasting changes in their organizations, not by force of personality but by identifying leverage points. This essay is an echo of essay 9.7, "Is Wanting to Change Enough?" Both are about creating lasting changes. Essay 9.13 is pitched at the organizational level rather than the individual level and might inspire you to take bold actions to improve the organizations you work with.

9.1 Naturalistic Decision Making Tools

A Compilation of the Methods Developed by the NDM Community

Recently, I polled many of the leaders of the Naturalistic Decision Making (NDM) community about the tools and methods they've developed and used. By "tool" I meant something that could be used to get a job done, including conceptual models. However, we did not include methods that are primarily designed for doing laboratory research involving controlled experiments.

The following colleagues helped me to identify all these tools (in alphabetical order): Cindy Dominguez, Julie Gore, Robert Hoffman, Devorah Klein, Laura Militello, Brian Moon, Emilie Roth, Jan Maarten Schraagen, and Neelam Naikar.

The result was a list of 42 methods, many more than I had expected. But after all, the NDM community has been going strong since 1989.

The tools fell into nine categories. You can find the complete set of tools, along with a key reference for each, on the NDM Association website, at naturalisticdecisionmaking.org. Adam Zaremsky took the lead in adding the short descriptors and references.

Knowledge elicitation tools, primarily methods for doing cognitive task analysis, such as the Critical Decision Method, the Situation Awareness Record, Applied Cognitive Task Analysis (ACTA), the Knowledge Audit, the Cognitive Audit, and Concept Maps.

Cognitive specifications and representations, such as the Cognitive Requirements Table, the Critical Cue Inventory, the Cognimeter, Integrated Cognitive

Analyses for Human-Machine Teaming, Contextual Activity Templates, and Diagrams of Work Organization Possibilities.

Training approaches, including the ShadowBox technique, Tactical Decision Games, Artificial Intelligence Quotient, On-the-Job Training, and Cognitive After-Action Review Guide for Observers.

Design methods (e.g., Decision-Centered Design, Principles for Collaborative Automation, and Principles of Human-Centered Computing).

Evaluation techniques such as Sero!, Concept Maps, Decision-Making Record, Work-Centered Evaluation.

Teamwork aids (e.g., the Situation Awareness Calibration questions, the Cultural Lens model).

Risk assessment methods: the Pre-mortem.

Measurement techniques such as macrocognitive measures, Hoffman's "performance assessment by order statistics," and four scales for explainable artificial intelligence.

Conceptual descriptions. These are models like the Recognition-Primed Decision model that have been used in a variety of ways.

Undoubtedly this compilation will expand in the years to come, but it seems useful to have it on hand as a reference and guide.

—*April 5, 2021*

9.2 When to Consult Your Intuition

Should Your Intuitions Come before or after Your Analyses?

Danny Kahneman and I have different views on the way to use intuition.

We both agree that when informed by feedback and experience, in a reasonably coherent setting, intuitions can be valuable (Kahneman & Klein, 2009). My research with firefighters and other types of decision-makers (Klein, 1998) has shown the importance of intuitive judgments. Kahneman's early work with the Israel Defense Forces (IDF; see Kahneman, 2011) convinced him of the value of intuitions. Kahneman's experience is particularly relevant here, so let's examine it in more detail.

In the 1950s, the IDF relied on trained evaluators to conduct a 15- to 20-minute interview to form a general impression of how well a recruit would do in the army. However, the IDF found that these predictions had little value for predicting a recruit's future success. That's why the IDF asked Kahneman to come up with something better. To replace the interview, Kahneman devised a more objective procedure that had the interviewers use a set of objective criteria to evaluate recruits on six different dimensions (e.g., responsibility and sociability). Kahneman made this interview as factual as possible to overcome any halo effect. He wanted the interviewers to turn off their intuition. When they resisted, Kahneman relented and added a final question, after all the objective data were collected, to use their intuition to imagine the recruit as a soldier and assign a global rating on a 5-point scale. As Kahneman expected, the new objective interview greatly increased predictive accuracy over the previous method.

But, to Kahneman's surprise, that final global intuitive rating did just as well. The final method included both the objective and the intuitive parts. The IDF is still using Kahneman's methodology today.

What is telling about this project is that when the interviewers just gave a global rating, their accuracy was terrible. But when they made global judgments after collecting the factual material, their global judgments were very good. Gathering the objective data improved their intuitions. That's why Kahneman wants you to use intuitive judgments after you collect the objective data, not before.

My perspective, as described in the Recognition-Primed Decision model, is that we start with intuitions, in the form of pattern matching, and then step back and do a deliberate and conscious evaluation, perhaps going through a mental simulation of what might happen if we take an action.

Which of us is right?

I think that's the wrong question. When faced with divergent views, a better question would be: Under what conditions should you start with your intuitions, and under what conditions should you delay your intuitions to the end?

I can see the benefits of doing the analyses first, breaking the choice down into smaller chunks, using objective markers where possible, and making judgments on those. You can be more accurate in making finer judgments about a set of candidates, looking at their experience level, their ability to manage stress, their performance on different test batteries, their readiness to show initiative, than you can in making an overall judgment about whether to promote the individual. If the global intuition came first, it would color the judgments on the individual dimensions. Once you decide a candidate is not suitable, you are going to have trouble making fair assessments of the individual features. In Kahneman's terms, you are going to bias the judgments of the individual features.

From my perspective, if you want to get a good reading of your intuitions, you need to start with them. Once you have been decomposing the choice into its component dimensions and features, your first-impression intuition is going to be lost or at least distorted. Think of the exercise of flipping a coin to see what to do. You don't want to put yourself at the mercy of the way the coin bounces. The purpose of the coin flip is to gauge how you feel about the result—are you relieved or disappointed. That's how you can take stock of our intuitions.

What are the conditions for starting with intuitions or ending with them? Here are several dimensions to consider:

1. *What is your experience level?* If it is low, you should do it Kahneman's way because you don't have credible intuitions. Even if you have a lot of experience, you might still follow Kahneman's advice, but if the experience is low, then your intuition won't be very helpful, and you should bring in your intuitions at the end.
2. *How much time pressure are you facing?* If time is short (think of a firefighter), you won't be able to do the decomposition Kahneman recommends.
3. *How confident are you in the analytical framework?* If your dimensions are time-tested and have demonstrated their value, no problem. But if the dimensions are ones you created on the fly, that's a different story. Just being able to decompose a decision isn't going to necessarily help you. The dimensions may overlap. They may miss important aspects of the choice. They may blind you to issues that aren't reflected by your choice of dimensions.
4. *What kind of decision are you making?* For personnel selection decisions, I recommend going with Kahneman's approach. In my own career, I can think of a number of times that I went with my gut about hiring a candidate who turned out to be a disaster or discarding a candidate who turned out to be a star—working for someone else. These kinds of decisions are sometimes referred to as "tree felling" because once you make the choice, you're done. You don't start to cut down a tree and then change your mind after you've cut halfway through the trunk. In contrast, if you are making a "hedge-trimming" decision you can adjust and adapt depending on how you like the results. You may be running a restaurant and planning out the menu, but you will be watching what your customers like and what they aren't ordering. You will be changing the menu selections or descriptions or the way the dishes are prepared. Here, you are getting feedback and making discoveries. You don't want to be trapped or biased by the initial analyses.
5. *What kind of person are you?* If you are open-minded, you should be more likely to adapt and revise your views. On the other hand, if you tend to be definitive and resist changing your mind, then you should definitely postpone making an intuitive judgment. You don't want to fixate on that intuition.

6. *Is the situation stable?* If the conditions aren't changing very rapidly, then you can safely start with your analysis. If the situation is very fluid, then your analysis might become obsolete before you are finished.
7. *How clear are the goals?* If you are working with an ill-structured task and ill-defined goals (e.g., a wicked problem), then you will need to rely on your intuition to adapt as you learn more. Your initial analyses won't and shouldn't guide you for very long.
8. *Are you coordinating with others?* If so, they're likely to want some justification for your choice. Therefore, the analyses, based on decomposing the overall choice into smaller and more digestible chunks, are more likely to satisfy your team members than just saying, "This feels right to me."
9. *Can you put your intuition on hold?* With personnel selection decisions that might mean reviewing the credentials for each candidate and making assessments on the fine-grained evaluation features before you interview them, not after.

Where does this leave us? I think we can all agree on the value of objective data and the value of intuitions. Your decision about how to take these nine factors into account isn't going to be easy. The decision will take good judgment and careful analysis and experience and feedback. Hopefully, this essay has given you more to think about and more to analyze and has strengthened your intuitions.

—*May 30, 2018*

9.3 Know Yourself

To Know Ourselves Better, We Should Try to Know Others

We are often told to "know yourself." Different philosophers, religious leaders, and mental health specialists have given this advice. The ancient Greeks inscribed it on the Temple of Apollo at Delphi as a source of wisdom. Lao Tzu is quoted as saying, "He who knows others is wise. He who knows himself is enlightened."

But what does it mean to know yourself? Is it just a catchy phrase, or is there substance behind it? Perhaps we are considering a new type of insight, a means of discarding outmoded self-concepts and replacing them with ones that are more fitting. Let's distinguish the different facets of self-knowledge.

First, we might want to appreciate how we think and what is behind our beliefs. This is the facet I will explore in this piece, but before I do, I want to briefly list some of the other facets of self-knowledge.

Second, we might want to get a sense of our emotions. We might believe that we feel one way but may actually have different feelings. For example, when my mother-in-law Bessie died, I didn't feel any particular grief. I was fond of her, but she was old and in poor health. Her death wasn't a surprise. What was a surprise to me was a telephone call I made to put an announcement in the newspaper that Bessie had died—and without warning, I found myself choking up. There was an emotional reaction, even though I hadn't been aware of it.

Third, we might get a clearer idea of our goals. We might feel tormented by uncertainty, looking for clarity about what we really want.

Fourth, we might benefit from a deeper understanding of our strengths and our limitations. It is too easy to get swept away by overconfidence or to be discouraged by general feelings of inadequacy. We would do better if we could realistically assess our abilities and our weaknesses.

Fifth, we could get a better idea of the fears and attractions that govern our choices. We could appreciate their basis and even their origins so that we might prevent them from leading us to poor decisions.

Doubtless, there are other facets of self-knowledge. I just want to show that there are different varieties to be considered.

Now back to the first facet, the one I want to examine more closely: our beliefs. It is very easy to assume that other people think like us. When we size up situations, identify the causes of events, settle on a course of action, generate expectancies, we may suppose that others think in the same way and have the same mental models of how things work.

But I do a lot of scenario-based decision training, and I am struck by the differences in the way people think. In group sessions, one person will describe his/her understanding and then the next person will have a very different understanding of the same scenario. The third person will come up with something else entirely. Each person will have the same reaction: "I thought it was all so obvious; I never suspected there were so many other interpretations and analyses."

I speculate that there is value in discovering the ways our beliefs and thought processes differ from others, and also the similarities. There is value in discovering what is unique and what is common, in contrasting and comparing. We can strive to see the perspectives of others. We don't have to agree with them, but if we can start to understand them, we can put our own beliefs into perspective. We can better know ourselves by trying to know others.

—*December 1, 2015*

9.4 Are You Pursuing a Pipe Dream?

Bloom Where You Are Planted

High school and college graduation speeches often revolve around some variant of the advice to "follow your passion." The theme has enduring popularity because it sounds so liberating and affirming, and also because it is pretty much guaranteed to meet with audience approval. These speeches are a safe way to sound daring.

Unfortunately, the follow-your-passion plea may actually be poor advice, feeding into some destructive tendencies that new graduates should be trying to overcome.

Inexperience. Whose passion is it? The passion of a new high school graduate hopefully will change with age, experience, and maturity. Why would we want to encourage young people to fixate on childhood dreams that are likely to be unrealistic and, by definition, juvenile? Many new graduates have very restricted life experiences, so what career choices can they imagine? Becoming fashion models? Designing video games? Becoming a YouTube or TikTok star? Playing in a rock band? Parlaying their enjoyment of student plays into a career in theater or film?

Self-indulgence. The follow-your-passion message is self-centered—just the wrong message to beam to a population that already tends to be too self-indulgent. The follow-your-passion message is that what matters is your own satisfaction, not serving the needs of the community.

Cluelessness. Many young people don't know what their passion is. Yet they believe they are selling out if they choose paths that aren't their passion.

They wander through college and post-college unwilling to commit, waiting for the moment when their passion will become clear to them. Some of them wait a long time and never have that epiphany. They spend a lost decade in a twilight state, keeping their options open and rejecting one career path after another because they find some reason to doubt that it is their passion.

Financial irresponsibility. Society doesn't offer large rewards for self-indulgence. I suspect that the more high-paying jobs are ones for doing work that benefits others, not jobs that cater to narcissistic interests. A healthy society depends on citizens who cooperate, sacrifice, and try to help each other out. It depends on professions such as biomedical engineers, clinical nurse specialists, software architects, reservoir engineers, database administrators, information assurance analysts, accountants, occupational therapists, optometrists, and biochemists. We may enjoy the arts, but we really don't need an endless supply of artists, actors, and dancers—we appear well-stocked in these specialty areas.

Magical thinking. Let's not ignore the importance of luck. The graduation speakers encouraging young audiences to find their own path tend to be intelligent, persistent, and lucky. Their less fortunate counterparts rarely get invited to give motivational speeches. I am referring to those whose path ran into a brick wall and who persisted anyway because they didn't want to waste the time and energy they'd already expended. They found their passion, only to get trapped by it.

Perhaps we should be offering young graduates a different type of advice: bloom where you are planted. Learn to find ways to grow and thrive, even if the conditions aren't perfect. A friend of mine described how, late in his career, he was given an assignment typically reserved for those about to be pushed into retirement. He was disappointed—he wasn't ready to retire, and he had hoped for additional promotions and challenges. But then he remembered his mother's admonition to bloom where you are planted. He abandoned hopes for further advancement and plunged into his new work. Without having to worry about supervisor evaluations, he found that he could make some sweeping and necessary changes. He did an outstanding job, and to his surprise, he was promoted. But then, a few years later, he was again given a dreaded dead-end job. Same cycle of disappointment and acceptance and liberation. He again did an outstanding job. And again, an unexpected promotion.

Job and life satisfaction may depend less on finding one's passion than on making contributions and being valued members of worthwhile organizations. Too many graduates live in the purgatory of skeptically examining each career path to gauge whether this is their ideal. They might be better off learning to bloom where they are planted.

Still, we don't want to counsel anyone to stay stuck in a terrible situation, so even the advice to bloom where you are planted needs to be tempered. No one-liner is going to fit all situations. Job/career satisfaction will also depend on our intellectual and emotional strengths. It will depend on how our temperament fits the nature of the work, as well as on our relationships with our bosses and co-workers. Career choices aren't simple, which is why they shouldn't be guided by simplistic slogans.

—*June 1, 2014*

9.5 The Causal Landscape

A Way to Make Sense of a Multicause, Indeterminate World

When we hear that an acquaintance or a celebrity has died, one of our first questions is, What happened? We expect to get a clear and simple answer, just one or two words. Cancer. Heart attack. Car accident. Stroke. We can fit the reason into the distinct categories we have learned.

But further inspection often clouds the picture. Perhaps the dead person developed cancer after years of smoking and refused to see a physician until it was too late. Did the person die from cancer, unhealthy living habits, or obstinacy? A fatal heart attack can be traced to unhealthy diet, genetic tendency to high cholesterol, heavy smoking, lack of exercise, failure to adhere to a statin regimen, lack of friends, lack of spouse, depression, and many other factors that correlate with heart disease. We have come a long way from the one-to-two-word explanation of why people die.

The problem is that complex situations contain multiple causes for each effect—multiple paths, some intersecting, and multiple stations on each path. Yet we often want the simple one-to-two-word answer.

To compound this challenge, people want *definitive* one-to-two-word answers, as if life was a series of mechanical operations, and it was possible to affix blame and diagnose faults. If a copying machine jams, there is usually a mechanical reason—a sheet of paper may have gotten stuck in the assembly and once it is removed, the problem is solved. Mechanical problems like this are determinate; there is a cause, and it can be identified.

Yet most of our problems are not mechanical. They are not determinate. There is not a single cause. There are multiple, intersecting causes, and we may never uncover some of the most important ones. We live in a multi-cause, indeterminate world, and our attempts to understand why events occurred will usually be frustrating. We cannot expect specific single-cause, one-to-two-word answers.

Fortunately, I think there is a way to cope with all this complexity: the Causal Landscape. The concept of the Causal Landscape is to portray a wide array of causes, to help people escape from their single-cause determinate mindset but then highlight the few causes that matter the most. These are the causes that (a) contributed most heavily to the effect (if they hadn't occurred, neither would the effect) and (b) are the easiest to negate. When we want to take steps to prevent an adverse event, the highlighted nodes are the places to start working.

The Causal Landscape is a hybrid explanatory form that attempts to get the best of both worlds. It portrays the complex range and interconnection of causes but then it identifies a few of the most important causes. Without reducing some of the complexity, we'd be confused about how to act.

Consider the 1994 friendly fire incident in which two US Air Force F-15 fighter jets shot down two US Army Black Hawk helicopters in northern Iraq, killing 26 peacekeepers. That's right, the military shot down its own aircraft. The shootdown occurred in broad daylight, with no other aircraft around. The F-15s and the army helicopters were all being monitored by the same Airborne Warning and Control System (AWACS) airplane, which failed to prevent the fratricide. Scott Snook wrote a masterful analysis of the event in his 2002 book *Friendly Fire*, identifying a wide array of causes as shown in this diagram taken from his book (see figure 9.2). There are a lot of causes leading to the outcome at the bottom right—too many.

The next step to building a Causal Landscape is to assess each of causes on two dimensions mentioned above—how much the cause contributed to the outcome and how easy was it to negate the cause. Those causes scoring high on both dimensions are the ones to emphasize, as shown in figure 9.3.

The friendly fire incident illustrates what a Causal Landscape can look like. This Causal Landscape format may be useful for accident investigation in domains such as aviation and healthcare. More generally, it may help people gain insights about how to navigate the multiple causes for events they care about.

After I posted the initial essay on the Causal Landscape, I received a number of comments. Several psychotherapists suggested using the Causal

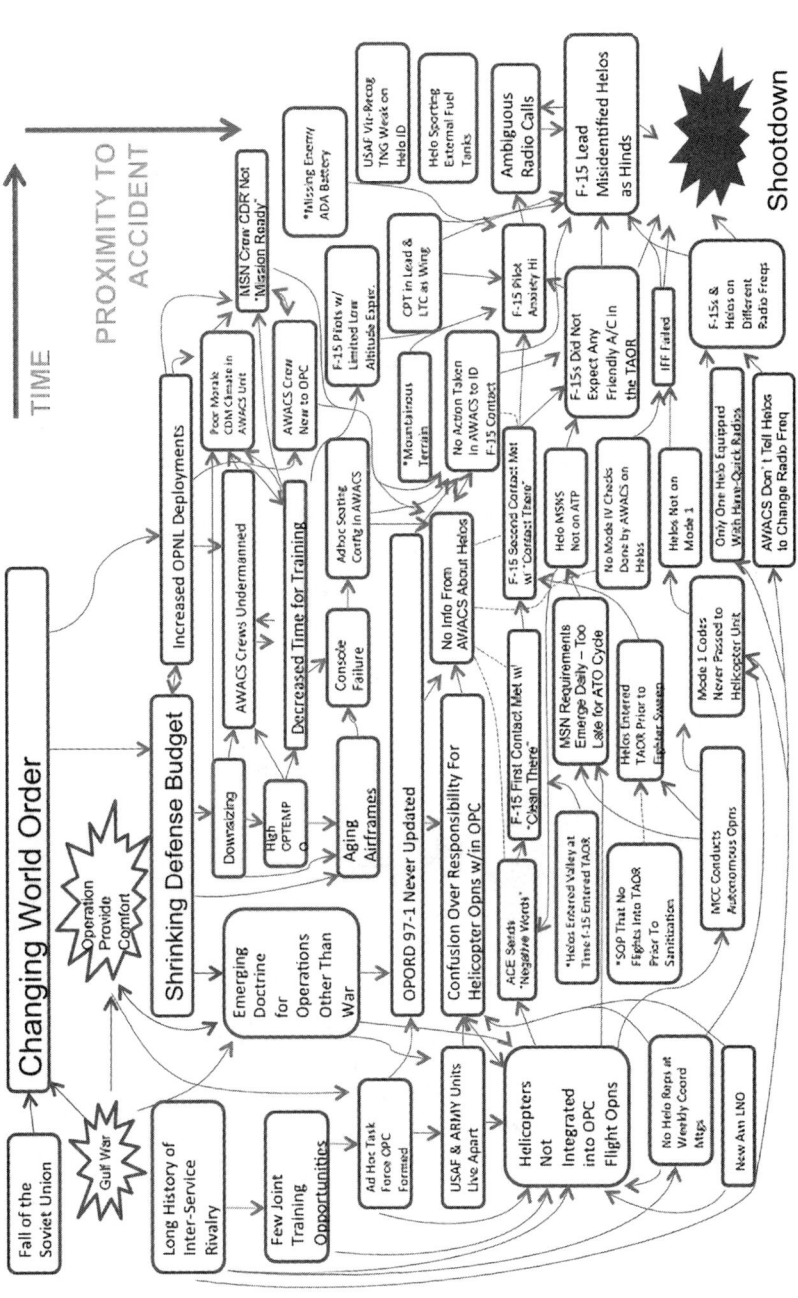

Figure 9.2

Snook's causal network for the Black Hawk shootdown.

Source: Reproduced with permission from Scott Snook, *Friendly Fire: The Accidental Shootdown of US Black Hawks over Northern Iraq* (Princeton, NJ: Princeton University Press, 2002).

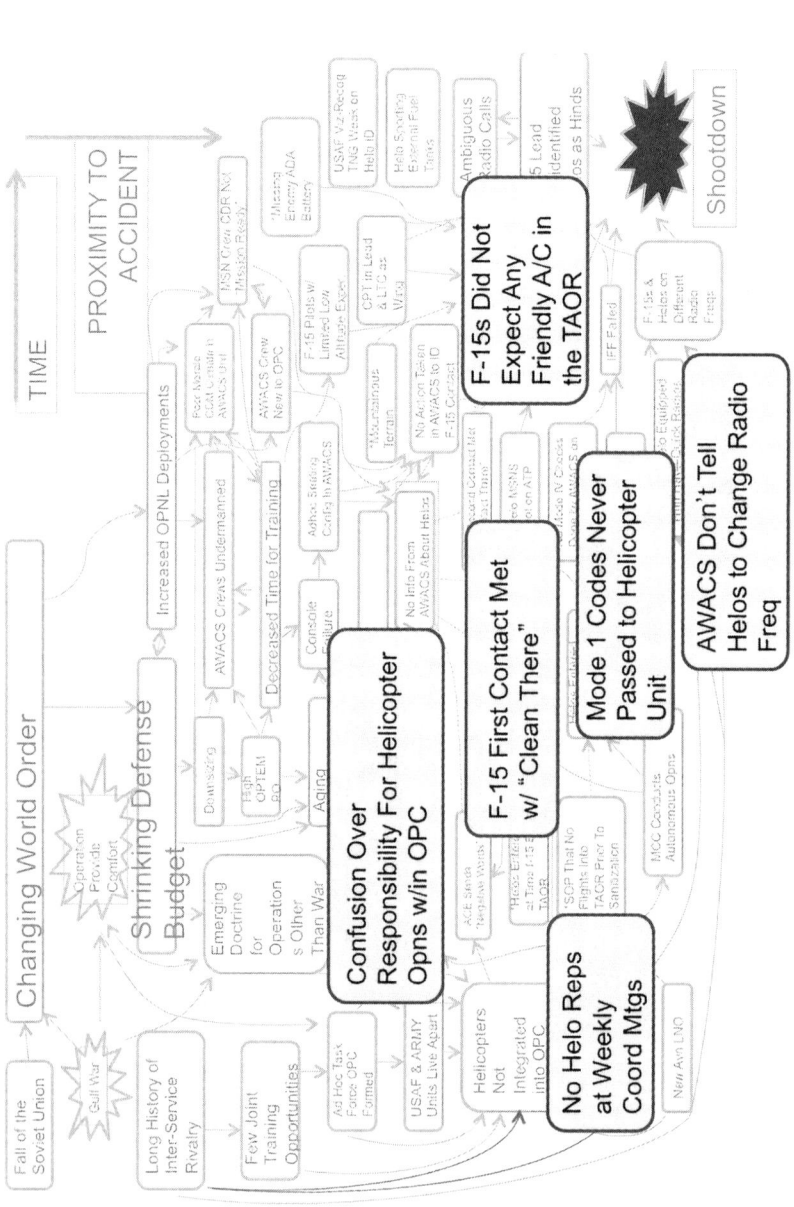

Figure 9.3

Snook's causal network highlighting the key nodes based on the scalar analysis.

Source: Reprinted with permission from Scott Snook, *Friendly Fire: The Accidental Shootdown of US Black Hawks over Northern Iraq* (Princeton, NJ: Princeton University Press, 2002).

Landscape with their clients. For example, a client seeking relief from anxiety might describe a range of conditions and triggers that provoke anxiety reactions, and this listing could be a starting point for reducing anxiety episodes in the future.

I received one comment from Scott Snook himself about the causes leading to the fratricide event in northern Iraq (Snook is a retired army colonel and currently is on the faculty of the Harvard Business School):

> I always struggle with this: How far up-stream do we swim? And what's the phenomenological distinction between "general states" that "set the conditions" which increase the likelihood of the event v. necessary conditions for the event to actually occur (counterfactual approach). In this piece you seem to take a more pragmatic approach: Which nodes could we have actually altered or reasonably done something about? If I were King for a day, I'd prefer to attack the deeper-rooted general conditions (e.g., Inter-service rivalry, few joint training exercises, etc.) that increased the likelihood of not only this particular accident, but also an entire family of others. (S. Snook, personal communication, April 23, 2014)

There are a few ways to direct the Causal Landscape forward, at preventing future accidents, not just backward at the previous accident.

One tactic is for the impact score to address the general type of problem, instead of being restricted to the current accident or outcome. Thus, a military planner can use the friendly fire tragedy to see if there is a way to improve coordination between army and air force. A psychotherapist can highlight the conditions and triggers that lead to a client's anxiety episodes.

Another tactic is to modify the reversibility score. The ease-of-change ratings can use a 4-point rating scale:

4 = Impossible to change. For the military shootdown incident, these factors would include the fall of the Soviet Union, which contributed to the tragedy but cannot be undone. Similarly, for anxious clients wanting to understand why they are so easily overwhelmed, causes such as childhood neglect and heredity may play a role but can't be undone.

3 = Very difficult to change. For the helicopter shootdown, that would include a shrinking defense budget. For the anxious client, it might include financial problems and chronic pain.

2 = Changeable with some effort. Snook mentions two things he would like to alter—interservice rivalry and few joint training exercises. Making these changes could prevent or reduce lots of different problems. The

benefits strongly outweigh the costs. Similarly, therapists might help anxious clients learn general strategies, such as coping skills.

1 = Simple to change. The shootdown would have been prevented if only the military did little things like arranging for helicopter representatives to attend the weekly coordination meetings. Simple fixes like this would have prevented the shootdown but wouldn't create more general benefits. Similarly, treating anxious clients with antianxiety medications is easy to implement but addresses only the immediate symptom.

In addition, we should probably distinguish *trigger* causes from *enabling* causes. A trigger cause is immediate and obvious, like dropping a lighted match onto a stack of newspapers and setting a house on fire. The lighted match is a trigger cause. The presence of oxygen in the house is an enabling cause. The trigger cause gets the attention but isn't always the best cause to address. Firefighters may spray foam on the fire to smother it—deprive it of oxygen. A psychotherapist may listen when a client complains that a recent arbitrary action by her domineering and insensitive husband made her feel helpless and anxious, but the therapist might want to spend time on an enabling cause—the client's inability to assert herself, which has played out with her husband, her daughter, and with colleagues at work.

As a final suggestion, we may sometimes find it useful to compare different Causal Landscapes. Thus, psychotherapists might contrast the Causal Landscape drawn up by a client with the therapist's own Causal Landscape for that client's difficulties. Or to compare the Causal Landscape a client generates at the start of a therapy program with one that the client produces after a few weeks.

These enhancements to the Causal Landscape retain the original goal of portraying a few actionable issues within the larger causal field. By expanding it in the ways described in this essay, hopefully, it will be more helpful in diagnosing problems and crafting plans.

—*April 22, 2014*

9.6 Why Did Hillary Lose the Election?

What Counts as a Useful Explanation?

The purpose of this essay is to examine what constitutes a useful explanation. I am using the recent presidential election as an illustration because it is so fresh in our memory, and so many commentaries have been written. The polls and the pundits predicted a Clinton victory, with a probability of 80 percent or higher at 8:00 p.m. eastern standard time when the voting ceased on the East Coast. Obviously, there was a lot of explaining to do.

I will be using the Causal Landscape as a means of sorting out the various reasons offered for the surprise outcome. The Causal Landscape has two phases. First, to provide perspective, it broadens the set of potential causes for an event, and in the second phase, it narrows to highlight the high-impact causes.

Note: This essay is not a political statement. It is not intended to be pro-Clinton or pro-Trump, and I have tried to be careful not to make any partisan statements. I simply want to use the election as an example of what we require in a causal explanation for an event—when we ask, "Why did that happen?"

Further, I am not attempting to catalog a comprehensive set of causes. I have collected a small number of causes for Clinton's defeat. I expect that most readers will be able to identify causes that I don't mention (see figure 9.4).

All I want to do is show that there were a number of reasons, rather than just one. This seems so obvious, but most of the accounts I have read zero in

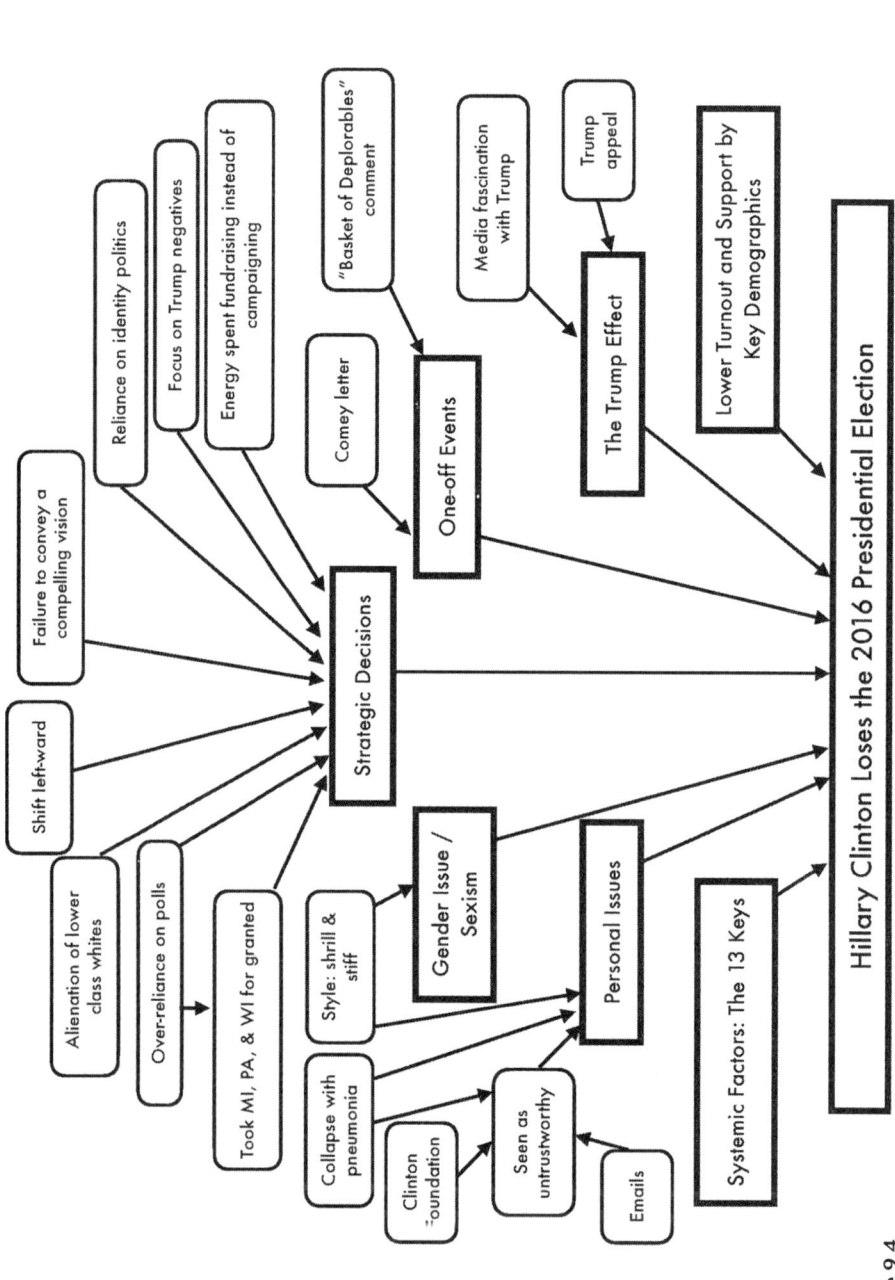

Figure 9.4
Causal Landscape of 2016 presidential election.

on a single cause for Clinton's defeat, which is a tendency Robert Hoffman and I encountered in our research on what constitutes an acceptable causal explanation (Hoffman et al. 2011). People like to have everything boiled down to a single cause, which is almost always a great oversimplification.

Now, some simplification is necessary. We would find it too overwhelming to deal with every possible cause for an event. The tendency to simplify is natural and is necessary. But at some point, useful simplification tips over into misleading oversimplification, and that's the problem I think we should try to avoid. In the case of the 2016 presidential election, boiling the explanation down into a single cause seems like just such an oversimplification. Presumably, the pundits know better and choose to oversimplify in order to convey a message more crisply, but they are doing a disservice to their readers, encouraging slogans rather than thoughtful analysis.

The Causal Landscape is a means of resisting the tendency to oversimplify. The first phase portrays a set of possible causes as a starting point, to get people out of the single-cause mindset. The diagram shows a Causal Landscape for explaining why Clinton lost the election.

We don't need to go into all the details shown in the diagram. Here are the primary causes I have culled from an unsystematic review of news commentaries. They are causes identified by experienced political analysts and published in opinion articles following the election. They are not causes that I generated myself.

Systemic factors, such as the 13 keys identified by Allan Lichtman for predicting presidential elections. These 13 keys include items such as the following:

- Having a party mandate. Did the incumbent party gain seats in the last midterm election?
- Is there a serious contest for the incumbent party nomination?
- Is the incumbent party candidate the sitting president?
- Has there been any major policy change (did the incumbent administration make major changes in national policy)?
- Social unrest.
- Foreign/military failure.
- Is the incumbent party candidate charismatic?
- Is the challenging party candidate charismatic?

Based on the full set of 13 keys, Lichtman bravely predicted a Trump victory in September 2016, relying on his model rather than on the prevailing wisdom.

Personal issues, especially the perception of untrustworthiness based on the classified emails in Clinton's private account and the concerns about influence-peddling using the Clinton Foundation, plus the secrecy surrounding Clinton's televised collapse, later attributed to pneumonia.

Gender issues/sexism that made some voters unwilling to choose a woman.

One-off events such as FBI Director Comey's letter just days before the election or Clinton's public comment that half of the Trump supporters belonged in a "basket of deplorables."

The Trump effect—the appeal he exerted, including the media fascination with him that allowed him to dominate the news coverage despite the Clinton campaign's much more effective fundraising.

A lower-than-expected turnout from groups such that had been expected to be strong Clinton supporters: Blacks and Hispanics, and a less-than-expected backing from women.

Strategic decisions the Clinton campaign made, such as, in retrospect, an overreliance on polls that led the campaign to take Michigan, Pennsylvania, and Wisconsin for granted; energy spent by Clinton in fundraising instead of campaigning; a failure to present a compelling vision, relying instead on reminding voters of Trump's negatives; a more leftist agenda adopted during the nomination process to fend off Bernie Sanders in the Democratic primaries; a heavy reliance on identity politics that excluded lower-class White voters and painted many of them as fitting into the basket of deplorables.

Some of these factors overlap. For example, I have listed the "basket of deplorables" issue as a one-off event, the comment itself, and as a strategic decision to distance the campaign from certain groups of voters.

As stated previously, this set of causes is not comprehensive, but it does show why any single explanation is inadequate. There were lots of reasons why the election swung in Trump's favor.

And, reiterating the point I made at the beginning, I do not intend this list of causal factors as a criticism of Hillary Clinton, the candidate for president. The list is intended to explore the reasons why Clinton lost an election that seemed within her grasp.

One of the problems with this type of analysis is that it can make Clinton's defeat seem inevitable, and it wasn't. This election was not a blowout on the order of Nixon versus McGovern or Reagan versus Mondale. At 7:59 p.m. Tuesday night, November 8, 2016, just before the election results started to be tabulated, we could have even more easily have prepared a Causal Landscape of why Trump lost, which was widely expected.

Causal Landscape diagrams include so many causes. If the Clinton campaign team wanted to imagine what it could have changed, the diagram can be overwhelming. Now we get to the second phase of the Causal Landscape: focusing on the highest payoff actions. In this phase, we ask two questions: Which of the causes shown in the diagram would have been the easiest to reverse, and which of the causes, if reversed, would have had the greatest impact? We make both of these estimates for each node in the diagram. Then we highlight the causes that were easiest to reverse and whose reversal might have tipped the outcome in favor of Clinton.

The next diagram shows my own judgments. (And I am not claiming any political sophistication—I am only illustrating how the process works; see figure 9.5.) I am suggesting four entries: Clinton's comment about the basket of deplorables and three of the Clinton campaign's strategic decisions.

The other influences, such as the systemic factors identified by Lichtman, perceptions of Clinton as untrustworthy, Clinton's gender, Trump's approach, all seem difficult if not impossible to alter.

Hillary Clinton has publicly blamed the Comey letter for stalling her momentum and costing her the election. But Diane Hessan, a polling expert who served the Clinton campaign by tracking 250 undecideds in swing states in the final months of the campaign, found that Clinton's remark about the "basket of deplorables" had a much stronger impact than the Comey statements.

In conclusion, all explanations are simplifications, but single-cause explanations seem to be oversimplifications that are unnecessarily misleading. The Causal Landscape seeks to portray a wide variety of causal factors, running the risk of presenting too much complexity. The next phase is to focus on the actionable explanations, running the causes through the filters of ease of reversal and likely impact. The goal is to establish a reasonable level

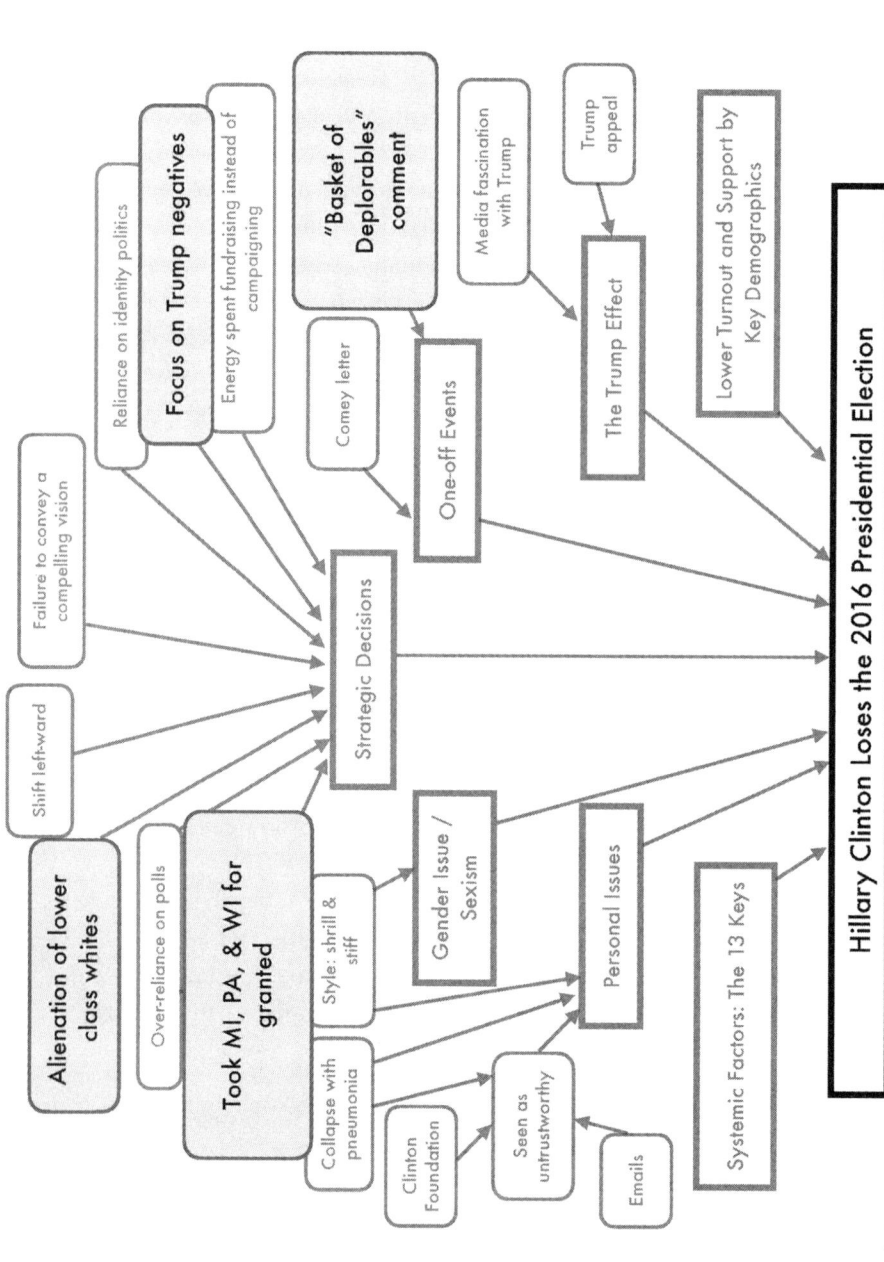

Figure 9.5
Causal Landscape with highlighted nodes.

of simplification. By highlighting these high-payoff entries within fields of influences, we can keep things in perspective.

If we can't be smarter in hindsight, it reflects badly on us. When political commentators resort to single-cause explanations, they are not doing us a service. Hopefully, we can use the election postmortems to learn how to simplify without oversimplifying.

—*December 6, 2016*

9.7 Is Wanting to Change Enough?

Designing for Sustained Adherence*

We all know how hard it can be to make a tough change—medication adherence and behavior change, in particular, are notoriously challenging. It's easy to wonder if it is even possible.

In this essay, we take a design thinking perspective and share tools with tactical implications for real adherence problems. (We define *adherence* as taking prescribed actions to gain the maximum benefit.)

This essay is about designing ways for patients to adhere to a medical regimen, but the lessons will resonate beyond healthcare to any situation calling for people to make lasting changes to their behavior.

Medication adherence is important for many reasons. An estimated 10 percent of all hospital admissions result from patients who fail to use their medications properly. In the United States, the cost of improper use of prescribed medications is over $100 billion per year (Viswanathan et al. 2012)

What can be done to help patients take their prescribed medications properly? We began studying this problem over a decade ago when we were both working at IDEO, the global design consultancy; we acknowledge the support and encouragement we received from the IDEO organization. We studied a wide range of conditions requiring different adherence tactics, ranging from HIV medications to weight-loss programs to multiple

---

*This essay was written by Devorah Klein, Marimo Consulting LLC, and Gretchen Wustrack, Curiosity Atlas. It is a response to questions I posed to them about what it takes to get people to change how they act and to sustain those changes.

sclerosis, rheumatoid arthritis, and erectile dysfunction (D. E. Klein, Wustrack, & Schwartz, 2006). We've also used these tools far beyond healthcare, in behavior changes in financial services, social engagement, and environmental stewardship.

We see medication adherence as depending on three dimensions:

- The elements acting on adherence
- The nature of the adherence journey for each patient
- The Adherence Loop

The elements of adherence

We have identified four elements that act on adherence: the individual (who they are, what has been their experience, what are their goals), the condition and how it affects the patient's life, the therapy (the regimen, the resources required, the duration), and the adherence network of friends, family, professionals, and institutions. These elements vary considerably for different patients and conditions and understanding that context is very helpful.

The adherence journey

The adherence journey consists of three phases: preparation, initiation, and maintenance.

The *preparation* phase includes the patient's understanding of the condition and its consequences (especially the consequences if untreated) and assessment of different treatment options, along with the type of commitment needed for each option.

If the patient is motivated to begin a course of treatment, she or he enters the *initiation* phase, which can include practical considerations, such as insurance coverage and travel schedules to see specialists but also logistic and practical issues, such as having a reliable supply of medications and the challenges of integrating the regimen into daily activities and into life-cycle events.

Once the patient gets to a steady state of following a regimen, he or she enters the *maintenance* phase, which depends on reliably following the established routines and also getting back on board after the inevitable

Is Wanting to Change Enough? 381

adherence failures. The maintenance phase includes wrestling with side effects and relapses. All three of these phases are marked by ups and downs as the patient's enthusiasm and commitment waxes and wanes.

The four elements play out differently for each patient and across the three phases.

The Adherence Loop

This loop has six components for the patient (see figure 9.6):

- Do you believe the therapy will work?
- Can you frame how the therapy (or proposed change) will help?
- Do you know how to use it?
- Can you prompt or cue action when needed?
- Do you have the resources to act at the different phases of the therapy journey?
- Is there a meaningful reward with feedback to reinforce action and strengthen belief?

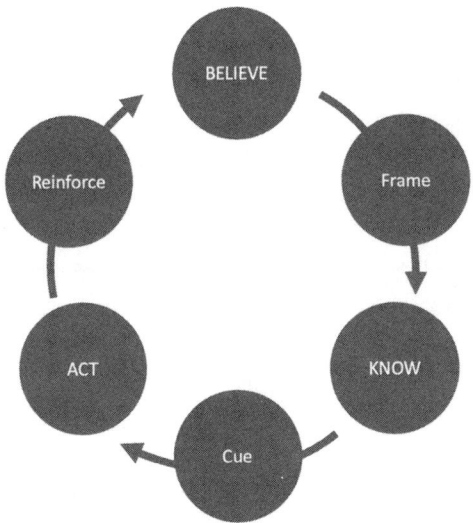

Figure 9.6
The Adherence Loop.
Source: Devorah Klein and Gretchen Wustrack, used with permission.

The *believe* component includes beliefs that you truly do have the condition, that you really want to change (as opposed to someone else telling you to change), that the therapy will help, and that you can be successful.

These beliefs are the core of the mental model that will underpin all that follows.

The *frame* component is how people build mental models or frameworks of how the change is going to help. While most people have some sort of mental model, it may or may not be accurate. The more accurate and complete the mental model, the more powerful a tool it is (H. A. Klein & Lippa, 2012). Particularly when people are under stress or need to make trade-offs in optimal ways, the validity of the mental model can help people make those trade-offs most optimally.

The *know* component covers the rules and procedures for following the regimen. It also includes knowledge of what to expect at different phases of the journey. Support here includes judging whether the patient is getting overloaded by information or determining that patients aren't getting the information they need or are getting misinformation.

However, knowing what to do is not enough—the patient will need *cues* and prompts to stay on course: to take doses at the right time. These prompts should fit comfortably within the patient's lifestyle schedules.

The *act* component refers to the resources the patient will need: physical, cognitive, emotional, social, and financial. Shortfalls in these resources will diminish the chances of successful adherence. Is the therapy physically hard to take—or is it socially hard because it is embarrassing or awkward?

On top of all this, patients should ideally be getting feedback to close the loop and *reinforce* and reward the beliefs and the motivations; ideally, this feedback would show immediate rather than delayed effects. Patients should get feedback on both each individual action and also the impact of the repeated actions over time. And the team should be alert to side effects.

Weight Watchers is an example of a very successful weight-loss program. It is instructive to use the Adherence Loop to make sense of all the aspects of Weight Watchers (see figure 9.7).

The six dimensions of adherence that we have described should enable healthcare personnel, as well as patients, to increase adherence success rates. In turn, that should give patients more confidence in the therapies they are using, increase revenues for businesses involved in supplying therapy materials, reduce costs overall for the healthcare system, and improve patient outcomes.

Is Wanting to Change Enough?

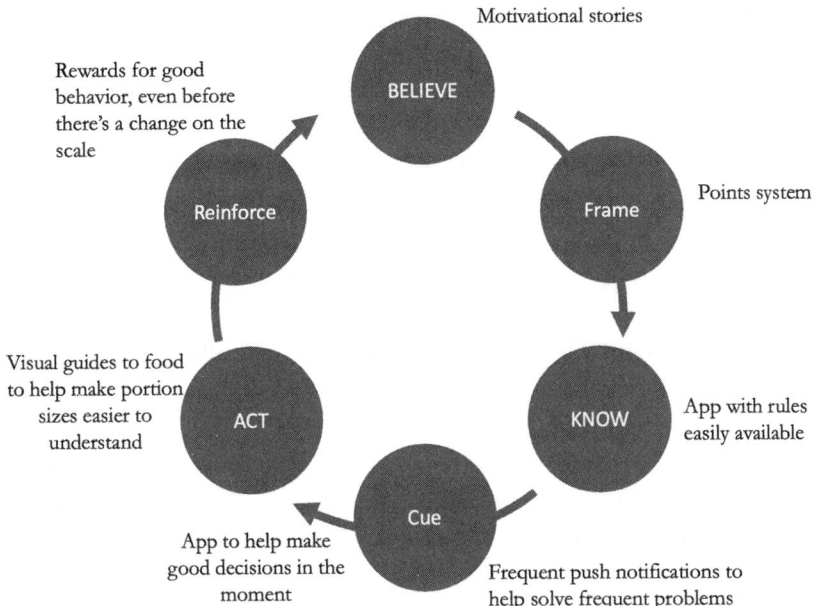

Figure 9.7
The Adherence Loop with Weight Watchers.
Source: Devorah Klein and Gretchen Wustrack, used with permission.

The goals for these tools are both descriptive, to help understand which parts of the loop are broken for a given adherence situation, but also generative. They were created to help design new interventions and suggest design principles:

BELIEVE: Get personal. Engage at life stage transitions when priorities and personal motivators change.

FRAME: Offer meaningful choice. Help people make trade-offs to find a lifestyle fit.

KNOW: Stage information. Provide the right information at the right time to ensure relevance and ease of comprehension.

CUE: Piggyback on patterns. Design systems that dovetail with people's existing daily, weekly, and monthly routines.

ACT: Tip the scales. Make the positive behavior more convenient, fun, or attractive than the negative behavior.

REINFORCE: Mind the gap. Provide immediate and tangible feedback, encouragement, or rewards for the new behavior.

Summary

We think the six dimensions will help both patients and providers identify and focus on the key adherence problems to solve. They should help providers better understand the role of individual differences and do a better job of finding analogous solutions in other domains. In addition, the six dimensions should help patients and providers better understand therapy or program profiles, identify and take advantage of support networks, and create solutions that work in everyday life.

Thus, the loop can help people determine the key adherence challenges to overcome. But the loop can be much more than that. It can also be a tool to help healthcare providers design solutions by pointing to the ways that patients are struggling and guiding the search for solutions. The output of the loop—a set of thoughtful designs focused on the biggest needs of the patients—has changed the way we approach adherence challenges. We hope it will help you as well.

—*September 20, 2019*

9.8 The Pre-mortem Method

A Practical Way to Do Risk Assessment

I developed the Pre-mortem method 30 years ago to help my company cut down on problems when we performed projects. We had no grand ambitions for the method. And yet, over the decades, the Pre-mortem method has kept getting more popular. It is used in corporate boardrooms, in wildland firefighting operations, in army programs, and on Wall Street. I have described the method in several books, *Streetlights and Shadows* and *The Power of Intuition*, and in a short article in the *Harvard Business Review*. The Pre-mortem method has been covered in a *Freakonomics* podcast and by Jason Zweig in his *Wall Street Journal* column.

Nobel laureates—Danny Kahneman and Richard Thaler—have encouraged people to use it. The Pre-mortem's appeal is that it is a risk assessment method that works.

Method. The Pre-mortem (figure 9.8) is simple to run and can take as little as 20–30 minutes. If you conduct the Pre-mortem in a kickoff meeting, with the team sitting around a table, the members have become familiar with the plan. Then you tell them that you are switching gears. You pretend you are looking into an imaginary, infallible crystal ball and—oh no! The plan you've just discussed has turned out to be a failure. A fiasco. That much is certain.

Next, you ask each team member to take two minutes to write down the reasons why the plan failed.

Once the two minutes are up, you go around the room asking each person to announce his/her top reason. Then on to the next person for a different

The PreMortem Method

Step 1: Prepare
Step 2: Imagine a fiasco
Step 3: Generate reasons for failure
 2 minutes to write these
Step 4: Consolidate the lists: Triple Filter
 Method —Impact, Reversibility,
 Likelihood
Step 5: "What can I do to reduce the
 chance of the fiasco?"
Step 6: Revisit the plan
Step 7: Periodically review the list

Figure 9.8
The Pre-mortem method.

item. You write their issues on a whiteboard, giving each person a chance to talk. You start with the team leader to set an example of being candid.

At the end, you have a list of showstoppers. The project leader and the team are now sensitized to things that can go wrong (Klein, 2007).

In contrast, the usual kickoff meeting might not even ask people to describe any concerns. Or the leader might ask, "Anyone see any problems?" There is silent pressure in these meetings not to surface doubts that might disturb the team's harmony. Team members might not even be able to think of any major problems.

The Pre-mortem reverses this dynamic—people show how smart they are by the quality of the issues that they raise. The crystal ball has shown a definite failure, and this changes everyone's mindset. Now your team members are drawing on their experience to imagine how this failure occurred.

Does it work?

Evaluation. Veinott, Klein, & Wiggins (2010) compared the Pre-mortem to other methods. We used 178 college students and posed a hypothetical situation in which a major epidemic was sweeping the country—an outbreak of H1N1 flu. (We were 10 years ahead of our time, showing the accuracy of our own crystal ball.) In this scenario, the university administrators had developed a plan for keeping the students safe while continuing operations, and the students had to critique that plan. Results: The students in the Pre-mortem condition showed the greatest reduction in (over)confidence, compared to simple critiques, or generating pros and cons.

Mistakes. Paul Sonkin, Paul Johnson, and I have identified some common mistakes people make in running a Pre-mortem: Asking the non-challenging question, "What can go wrong?" instead of using the crystal ball to affirm that the plan has been a disaster. Or allowing the team members to describe their items at a slow, leisurely pace rather than rapidly surveying them and keeping the energy high. Or letting one person, usually a senior team member, dominate the session by going through all the items on his/her list rather than taking turns going around the room.

Improvements. We've also made some changes over the years. To reduce discouragement, we now have the team look at the problem list and then take another two minutes for each member to identify actions s/he can take to address some of the items.

Benefits. The Pre-mortem method has additional benefits besides identifying trouble spots in a plan, reducing overconfidence, and promoting discoveries. The method can strengthen members' mental models as they hear from others. It can deepen the appreciation the team members have for each other as they hear ideas they hadn't thought of themselves. And it can help create a culture of candor and trust.

—*January 14, 2021*

9.9 The Decision Scorecard

Let's Evaluate Workers' Decisions Instead of Their Qualities

Personnel evaluations are one of the dreaded rituals of organizational life. They are usually frustrating, emotional, and de-motivating. In the guise of trying to offer helpful feedback and guidance for the future, the personnel evaluation typically provokes defensiveness and resistance. Instead of fostering closer bonds, the evaluation often results in hostility and loss of trust.

You can imagine my feelings when it came time to evaluate Corinne Wright, the CEO of my new ShadowBox company. She had been hired a year earlier, and this was going to be her first evaluation. During the year, we had had several informal feedback discussions, but there was no escaping it—the time had come for a formal review. I was definitely not enthusiastic about doing the review. Corinne was game but wary of how the session would go. We both knew the typical drill of reviewing previous goals and objectives and setting new objectives. We both knew that objectives change over the course of a year. Exhortations fade but criticisms don't fade—they often become more painful with time to mull them over, turning into grudges. Did I really have to go through this ritual with Corinne?

No, I didn't.

Out of desperation, I came up with a different approach. I asked Corinne to make a list of all the important decisions she had made during the year. I did the same—trying to remember the decisions she had managed. Next, we consolidated the two lists. And then we independently judged each decision. A double check (✓✓) for the decisions that had turned out really well. A single check (✓) for good decisions. An x (x) for decisions that had turned out badly. And a double x (xx) for the decisions we really regretted. A question mark (?) if we weren't sure of the quality or of the decision process.

We were careful to give good marks to decisions that had been correct at the time but didn't work out for reasons that couldn't be foreseen. And to give bad marks to ones which had, in retrospect, been poor decisions, even though we had been lucky and got a good outcome.

Then Corinne and I talked, face-to-face. We had a wonderful discussion. I learned a lot, and I think she did as well. We laughed a lot. We changed our ratings—both ways. The one decision that I thought was really poor (xx), I shifted to a single x. A few that Corinne had downrated herself, I convinced her to change because she was being too critical; I thought she made the right decisions, but they didn't turn out well for reasons that weren't her fault.

The conversation flowed in both directions. For one contentious decision, Corinne took the opportunity to explain why she felt I hadn't given her the support she wanted (and possibly deserved). It was important that I got that feedback.

When the meeting ended, and we had to attend to other scheduled activities, I think we both were sorry that we hadn't budgeted more time. Instead of feeling that we couldn't wait for this to end, we felt sorry that it had to end because it was so productive.

The overall result didn't matter as much as the conversation, but for those keeping score, Corinne's batting average was .667 after I made my initial ratings and .821 when we were done. Clearly, she had done a very good job.

Why did this performance evaluation go so well? One reason is that Corinne was so open and candid, so I give her a lot of the credit. But another reason is the format. Neither Corinne nor I took the comments personally. I think that the format highlighted the decisions, not the decision-maker, enabling us to be more objective and curious about each other's viewpoints. It was a nonpersonal personnel evaluation.

Perhaps we were lucky with this session. Or perhaps this might really be a more productive way to do evaluations, leading to better calibration of views at the end. It might help teams gain a better understanding of how they make decisions, using actual events—a sort of team introspection and lessons learned session rolled into one.

—*September 21, 2015*

9.10 Management by Discovery

Sometimes We Need to Give Up Our Original Goals

If you don't understand your destination, there's no telling where you might wind up. And since time is short and resources are limited, there's not much margin for wasted effort. Business leaders may have ambitious plans, but once the plans get the go-ahead, the program and project managers have to deliver within budget and schedule.

The standard game plan is to rely on some version of management by objectives: define the desired end state, then work backward to identify the necessary tasks, work out the schedule for each task, assign responsibilities to the team members, and get started.

If only the world was so cooperative. Unexpected events can throw even the most carefully defined plan into confusion. Skilled managers have to be able to adapt and perform trade-offs between different goals and constraints.

And then there is the challenge of wicked problems: goals and objectives that cannot be carefully defined in advance. Problems for which there are no "right" answers. Fixing the healthcare system in the United States is an example of a wicked problem because different stakeholders have competing needs and would argue about the merits and drawbacks of any proposed solution. Wicked problems can arise because not enough is known at the outset to specify all features of the goal, or because there is no optimal solution, or because of different stakeholder communities, or because a rapidly changing context is likely to render the original goals irrelevant.

Lower-level managers are usually given straightforward projects with clearly defined goals, but as they move to positions of greater authority, they are more likely to have to wrestle with wicked problems. Unfortunately, their previous success in tenaciously pursuing the initial goals may now get in their way because wicked problems demand that we revise, not our plans and tasks, but the goals themselves. Research has shown that most mid-level managers cling to their original goals even after it is clear to them that those goals are obsolete.

Here is where Management by Discovery (figure 9.9) comes into play. If the project or program is sufficiently important, the managers will have to start work even with goals that are somewhat vague. They are more likely to achieve an acceptable outcome if they can modify the goals along the way, making discoveries rather than rigidly clinging to the initial objectives.

The concept of Management by Discovery is that adaptive leaders and managers try to learn more about the goals even as they are pursuing them. Wicked problems won't clarify themselves. The only way to make progress is to gain insights about the goals by struggling, learning, and adapting. (Clayton Christensen, in *The Innovator's Dilemma* [2013], refers to this as discovery-based planning.) If the premise of Management by Discovery makes conventional managers uncomfortable, they should consider the software industry. After many years of cost overruns and rejected products, software firms pioneered techniques for rapid review and revision cycles to accommodate the discovery process.

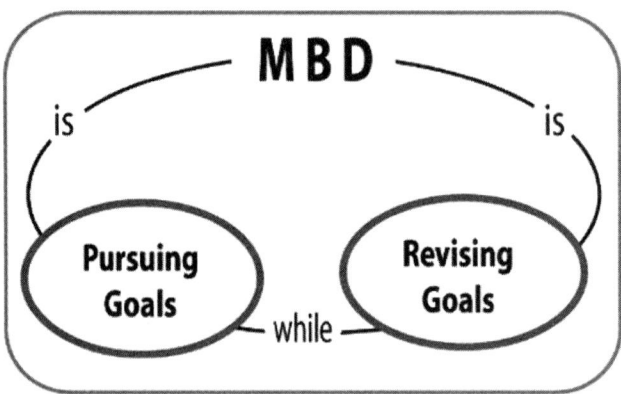

Figure 9.9
Management by Discovery.
Source: Gary Klein, *Streetlights and Shadows: Searching for the Keys to Adaptive Decision Making* (Cambridge, MA: MIT Press, 2009).

But other industries can't seem to break free from the traditional planning mindset. They rely on practices such as tying payments to the initial schedule and conducting progress reviews to measure cost and expenditures as specified in the original plan. These practices fit well-ordered tasks, but they become barriers to the insights and discoveries needed when facing wicked problems. I have described Management by Discovery in my book *Streetlights and Shadows* (Klein, 2009). And in my work on insights (e.g., *Seeing What Others Don't* [Klein, 2013]), the outcomes of insights are to change what we understand, what actions we can take, what we see, what we feel, and what we desire. Management by Discovery hits on this last component, gaining insights about what we desire.

—*October 12, 2014*

9.11 The Nine Levers Organizations Can Use for Better Performance

The Different Ways to Change Behaviors

When organizations want to make changes, they have a few options. I have identified nine of those options—we can think of these as levers we can use to gain impact.

First lever: Clarifying the goals. We can improve performance by clarifying the goals. Heath & Heath (2010) describe the SMART concept, goals that are specific, measurable, actionable, relevant, and timely. The previous essay described a Management by Discovery method to help people adapt their goals when working on wicked problems. Decision quality will improve with goals that are clearer or just more adapted to circumstances.

Second lever: Structuring the decision. We can find better ways to structure the choices we face. Thaler & Sunstein (2009) have described several ways to do this: setting the defaults (e.g., asking people to reject being an organ donor rather than asking if they were willing to donate an organ if they die in a car accident), setting the anchors (influencing people's estimates by providing more accurate anchors for them to adjust), minimizing loss so that you don't run into loss aversion (e.g., taking retirement investments out of future salary increases rather than out of the current salary), reducing options (because people grow frustrated when asked to choose between too many options). Heath and Heath have suggested other methods here. One is the use of sunk costs by giving people credit for partial fulfillment of a task even before they start. Dweck has shown the effect of priming the identity a person adopts, encouraging students to think of themselves as hard workers rather than as people who always ace tests, using a mental model of a brain as a muscle rather than a device with a fixed capacity. Along these lines, Heath and Heath talk about restructuring a person's identity by addressing three questions: Who am I? What kind of situation is this? What would someone like me do in this situation? For example, homeowners can be made to act in more civic-minded ways by helping them compare themselves to more civic-minded neighbors. This helps to shift their default position.

Third lever: Training. Principles of effective training are fairly well established. However, training is one of the most expensive levers to use. And in most situations, people don't have time for training. Therefore, we may want to turn to other methods, such as on-the-job learning (Fadde & Klein, 2010) in which people can use their job experiences to increase skills. The greater the skill level, the better the decision performance.

Fourth lever: Checklists. In many situations, job aids such as checklists can augment or substitute for training. Checklists are particularly valuable for procedural tasks, such as taking off in an airplane, which are easily disrupted in settings that are filled with interruptions. Gawande (2010) has described the different ways checklists can improve performance. However, checklists become less useful when the situation is more complex and ambiguous.

Fifth lever: Incentives. People should work harder to make better decisions if they receive the right incentives. The VIP treatment is to set incentives that are visible, immediate, and personal. Incentives are one of the most popular levers but are surprisingly ineffective in most situations because it is so difficult to link actions to outcomes. And if we provide very simple incentives, we run the risk of workers cutting corners so they can achieve the objective even if it means degrading performance overall.

Sixth lever: Behavioral engineering. Decision quality should improve if we design the options more cleverly, preventing mistakes rather than setting up rules and restrictions. Consider the way woodworking equipment such as power saws are designed with built-in safeguards so that people are less likely to lose fingers. Thoughtful design works better than posting notices about the dangers of power saws. It's more effective to move valuables out of reach than to tell a 1-year-old "No," when it crawls near something we want to protect.

Seventh lever: Selecting the right people. This is perhaps the most powerful lever but is the least understood and the most poorly applied. If we can find ways to select talented workers, we won't have to worry about training, incentives, clarifying goals, and so forth.

Eighth level: Information technology. People will do better if they have access to the information they need, but the technology has to be compatible with the way they make decisions. Militello and colleagues have described the principles of cognitive systems engineering (Militello, Lintern, Dominguez, & Klein, 2009).

Ninth lever: Designing better organizations. All of the other eight levers will depend on the organization and how it facilitates good decision-making or creates barriers to it. Dysfunctional organizations often emphasize error-free performance and rigid adherence to standards, even if these practices make it harder for workers to develop expertise. Or a dysfunctional organization may provide so little guidance that workers are confused and have trouble making any progress. Dysfunctional organizations may have rigid roles and functions that impede adaptation.

We don't have to be trapped by habits of using only one lever, such as training or incentives. Instead, we can be more adaptive by shifting to different levers and blends of several levers.

—*August 23, 2015*

9.12 Turning Policy into Practice

Merely Issuing Directives Isn't Enough

Organizations frequently issue policy statements about how people should carry out various activities. The policy statements are often carefully crafted, sometimes step-by-step instructions about how to do things. The military analog for these policy statements is a doctrine, the steps to be followed, and sometimes the order of those steps. The aviation community relies on checklists. The healthcare community compiles best practices.

These efforts provide valuable guidance. They also standardize the actions of different people, even people who may have never met, which improves coordination because everyone is intended to follow the same script. The efforts also provide quality control. There should be little debate about the benefits of these different kinds of policy statements. We should agree that in many situations, they are necessary.

However, they usually aren't sufficient. That's the argument I am making in this essay. Too many people and organizations believe that issuing a policy is all they have to do, a delusion that leads to disappointment, frustration, and recrimination when people fail to follow that policy as intended.

What's missing from the policy?

What's missing are the complexities and the contextual nuances that surround us. Attempts to capture these complexities and nuances in the policy rarely, if ever, succeed. The world has more variations than we can handle, more variations than we can imagine when we formulate the policy, and more variations that emerge after we formulate the policy as conditions evolve in unpredictable ways. Trying to capture these complexities and nuances is unlikely to succeed and often is counterproductive because the effort interferes with the clear message intended by the policy.

The other three quadrants

Part 2 includes an essay, "The Mental Model Matrix." We can apply that matrix to the challenge of getting policies implemented (see figure 9.10). The policy statement itself corresponds to the upper-left-hand quadrant, stating what is supposed to happen. The other three quadrants reflect the dilemmas that often arise.

People generating the policy often ignore the other three quadrants. The policy may well have limitations, which is the upper-right quadrant. Staff members will need the experience and skills to adapt the policy to different conditions, which is the lower-left-hand quadrant. And the policymakers can try to anticipate the ways people may become confused, the lower-right-hand quadrant.

Therefore, to increase the chances that a policy can be successfully carried out, the organization might want to consider these three other quadrants and think about tactics and interventions for each of them.

Scenarios

One strategy is to devise scenarios to help workers anticipate problems and adapt to them. The ShadowBox scenario method, described in part 2, can be used in this way, and there are obviously many other scenario techniques.

	Capabilities	Limitations
System	How the system works: Parts, connections, causal relationships, process control logic	How the system fails: Common breakdowns and limitations (e.g. boundary conditions)
User	How to make the system work: Detecting anomalies, appreciating the system's responsiveness, performing workarounds, and adaptations	How users get confused: The kinds of errors people are likely to make

Figure 9.10
Mental model matrix.
Source: Adapted from a chart by Joseph Borders.

Of course, organizations will not want to go through the effort of developing scenarios for each policy. In most cases, the payoff isn't sufficient to justify the costs and the time needed. Organizations should only take this extra step of augmenting policies with scenarios if they judge that the policy is sufficiently important and that noncompliance can have serious consequences. But there are easier strategies to use.

Patient discharge

Let's look at a simple example. A patient is about to be discharged from a hospital after a stay of several days. The discharge nurse carefully tells the patient the after-care regimen to be followed. Perhaps the discharge nurse has printed out the procedures the patient needs to follow.

Eisenberg & Mahar (2019) argue that this routine is not going to be sufficient. Merely issuing the directions, stating the policies, and handing off the printout doesn't ensure that the patient has grasped what needs to happen. The discharge nurse needs to go further, to judge whether the patient has understood what s/he is supposed to do.

And I would take this further. If the discharge nurse is serious about getting the policies followed, I would suggest anticipating the kinds of confusion that the patient might have. I suggest some simple scenarios to illustrate decisions the patient might face (e.g., "You are supposed to take this liquid medication every six hours. What are you going to do if you are at work and don't have a spoon available to measure the dose?"). The discharge nurse has the experience to understand common issues in the other three quadrants of the mental model matrix. The discharge nurse can use simple examples (mini-scenarios) to get the patient thinking about post-hospital care so that the recovery can go more smoothly and to reduce the chances of having to get readmitted.

Conclusion

Policies are often necessary but rarely sufficient. If organizations are serious about turning policies into practice, and if the policies are sufficiently important, then techniques such as scenarios, even simple ones, may have great value.

—*March 17, 2021*

9.13 The Difference-Makers

How Some Leaders Change Their Organization's Culture

Many organizations get stuck in counterproductive habits. These habits may build up gradually, without awareness, and after a while, they become the norm—the way the organization works. They become the status quo.

Mark Smith, the chief innovation officer at MedStar, has described the power of the status quo and how it blocks improvements. Staff members are so used to the status quo that they resist change because change is threatening, change is going to take more work, change is going to require people to adapt in ways they can't predict. Staff members feel secure that they know how to do their current jobs. Change guarantees insecurity.

Organizational leaders may try to explain the benefits of making alterations. They may state their values and desires for innovation. However, the status quo quietly defeats attempts at innovation.

Nevertheless, some leaders have been successful at overcoming the status quo. They have been able to make a lasting difference in an organization's culture. After I identified a few of these leaders, I wondered what their secret was. I didn't do any kind of exhaustive analysis, just a simple comparison to see what I could learn. I realize that these types of hindsight analyses are flawed in many ways. For example, any behaviors I flagged might also be found among leaders who failed to make a dent in their corporate culture. And besides, I only looked at four individuals. Therefore, I'm not promising any cures for the status quo barrier. I am just sharing my speculations, based on my attempt to uncover a useful culture-change method.

I did spot one common strategy. But before I describe it, I want to introduce you to four people I consider difference-makers: Rooster Schmidle, John Mattingly, Alan Mulally, and Judith Goodhand.

Robert "Rooster" Schmidle is a Marine Corps fighter pilot. (For some reason, military pilots have to have colorful nicknames, and Schmidle's orange-red hair earned him his.) I met Rooster about 20 years ago when he was a lieutenant colonel (he is now a lieutenant general, with a PhD in philosophy to boot). I was observing a high-visibility marine exercise called Hunter-Warrior, designed to evaluate the use of digital technology to radically shorten the chain of command and the reaction time of field units. The exercise was due to start in just a few weeks, but the staff members weren't close to being ready. The previous executive officer had just gotten fired for ineffectiveness. Everyone was bracing himself/herself for a disaster. Then Schmidle appeared, the new executive officer. And he was like a force of nature.

The command post was filled with marines sitting at workstations, passively receiving and sending messages. That didn't suit Schmidle. He walked over to one marine and had him send a message. Then he made that marine stand up and walk over to the person in the back of the room who was receiving the message—they had never met before. Schmidle had them discuss what the message meant, and why it was important. Then Schmidle had the second marine send his own message, and they all walked over to the marine who received that one. This drill continued until everyone had a turn. In short order, everyone in the command post had a feeling for how they all needed to work together. Schmidle never gave any speeches about coordination or teamwork. He simply made sure that the marines knew who was sending and receiving the different messages. Hunter-Warrior turned out to be a great success, helping the Marine Corps transition to the age of information technology.

John Mattingly was commissioner of the Administration for Children's Services for New York City. His organization of caseworkers make some of the toughest decisions I have observed—whether to remove a child at risk from its mother or leave the family intact and risk further damage. I got to know John in 2011 when I was doing a project on caseworker decision-making. I learned how John and his deputy Jan Flory introduced several exciting innovations—the one I am including here was to require a team decision-making (TDM) meeting with the family, caseworker, supervisor, and facilitator to make decisions about a child's safety before removing a child with placement in a foster family. These meetings involved the family in critical decisions about their children and changed the way these decisions were traditionally made. But how could Mattingly be sure that the caseworkers would arrange these TDM meetings? Mattingly found a simple strategy. He informed the legal staff that they should not process any requests for removing a child unless a TDM meeting had been held. And that did the trick. He had built a "firewall." In short order, the TDM meetings became standard—the new status quo.

Alan Mulally was the executive vice president at Boeing and then the CEO of Ford Motor Company. As Bryce Hoffman tells the story in his 2012 book *American Icon*, Mulally stepped in as Ford Motors was in crisis. The company lost $6 billion in the third quarter of 2006, even before the 2007–2008 recession. A culture of entitlement had resulted in inflated salaries and benefits, and a self-promoting mindset that put individual advancement over the needs of the company. Executives jockeyed for political power while relying on their staff members to get the work done. Mulally introduced a number of reforms but one of them seems particularly relevant to cultural change. At his first meeting with his senior executives, just a few weeks after he arrived, Mulally explained that at these weekly meetings, an executive could bring assistants, but the assistants weren't allowed to speak during the meeting. Previously, the executives relied on their assistants to respond to tough questions. No longer. Now each executive was expected to know the answers, if not that week, then at the next week's meeting. A wave of discomfort spread over the room. It is one thing to talk about accountability, but this new rule was a way to enforce accountability.

In 1992, a new director, Judith Goodhand, was appointed for the Cuyahoga County Department of Children and Family Services in Cleveland, Ohio. (I heard about Goodhand from Pat Rideout, one of Goodhand's successors.) The department, in response to a crisis, had newly been created as a separate child welfare agency (vs. a division of a larger department), and Goodhand was its first leader. One of the earliest problems she encountered was the fact that many children needing to enter care had no identified placement at the end of the workday. Some even spent the night in the agency's building as they waited for a foster home to be identified. Goodhand was concerned at what seemed to be the lack of a sense of urgency about this problem and was dismayed to watch her staff head home for the night while children, recently taken away from their parents and likely fearful and traumatized, were sleeping in an office building. She felt that if she was going to change the agency culture from staff "just putting in the hours" to a culture of advocating for the children, this was a good place to start.

Therefore, she instituted a new and simple policy: none of the senior staff members could go home as long as there was a single child left in the building waiting for a placement.

Needless to say, this simple intervention resulted in a dramatic change, as all eyes were on the children who had not yet been placed. It took only a few days before there were no more children sleeping in the agency's office building.

What struck me most forcefully about these four examples was that each one introduced a *minimal intervention*. Undoubtedly, other factors came into play, such as charisma and trust. However, these leaders didn't try to rely on personal attributes. They wanted to rapidly achieve a lasting cultural change, a shift in mindsets, and they did it by introducing a novel activity. Schmidle spent an hour or so walking marines around the command center so they could understand how they fit into the mission. Mattingly built a small firewall to prevent caseworkers from backsliding and skipping the team decision meetings. Mulally ensured that his executives mastered the details of their units. Goodhand made sure her top staff personally felt the urgency of getting all children safe placements.

As I see it, these difference-makers (a) were aware that the status quo wasn't acceptable, (b) diagnosed how the culture needed to change, and (c) designed a minimal intervention, a leverage point, that would not only interfere with the status quo but would make it difficult to later return to the dysfunctional status quo. The difference-makers were all behavioral engineers.

Speeches, lectures, values statements, all have limited impact. What counts is finding a way to block the status quo so that it doesn't block you.

—*August 10, 2016*

9.14 Reflections

Naturalistic Decision Making (NDM) is not an academic discipline. It does have many adherents within universities, but it emerged and has primarily taken root in applied settings as a basis for action—for training decision-making skills and achieving higher levels of expertise, for designing systems that strengthen rather than compromise expertise, for organizational interventions that seek to promote expertise instead of fixating on ways to reduce errors.

Part 9 offered different ideas for putting NDM to work. It suggested several tools and tactics that serve as examples of what might be done. Essay 9.1 set the stage by listing 42 tools and methods. These fell into 9 categories: knowledge elicitation tools, methods for specifying and representing cognitive requirements for tasks, training approaches, system design approaches, techniques for evaluation, teamwork aids, risk assessment methods, measurement techniques, and conceptual models for different aspects of cognition. If you are looking for an NDM method to help accomplish a given task, this compilation seems like a good place to get started. But this essay was just a listing. The remaining essays in this part offered more details about a few of the specific tools and methods.

Some of these tools and methods were aimed at improving decision-making and intuitions—when to consult your intuition, for example, contrasting Kahneman's recommendations with my own. Another essay unpacked what it means to know yourself; once we move beyond the cliché, self-knowledge turns out to be trickier than you might have imagined and depends on our ability to understand others.

The essay about pursuing a pipe dream has turned out to be fairly controversial. It took aim at a commonplace staple of graduation ceremonies, the tendency of speakers to exhort the new graduates to follow their passion. Perhaps that exhortation is not such a great idea.

Part 9 described the Causal Landscape method, which is a way to escape from oversimplified explanations without running into the morass of under simplifying. The Causal Landscape achieves this goal by including a wide array of causes for an outcome (thereby countering the tendency to consider only a single cause) and then prioritizing the causes that are easiest to reverse and whose reversal will likely have the greatest impact (thereby providing a practical agenda for action). It may sound reasonable, but don't fool yourself. Look back on the essay about why Hillary Clinton lost the 2016 election. Many, perhaps most people, have a favorite theory—in essence, a single and preferred cause. As I introduced more and more contributing causes in this essay, what was your reaction? I suspect many readers felt some frustration. The additional causes were getting in the way of their favorite theory. That reaction illustrates our tendency to prefer a single cause even though intellectually we may know that several causes were involved. And that's why we can benefit from methods like the Causal Landscape to drag us out of this single-cause mindset.

Part 9 also took up the thorny problem of how to make changes that will last. Not short-term fixes that quickly fade away but long-term enduring changes. Essay 9.7 centered on medication adherence, but the approach should generally apply to situations in which people want to make lasting modifications to their behavior. The adherence model relies on our beliefs that the changes will work, knowledge for carrying out the changes, and resources, prompts, and rewards to sustain the actions.

Part 9 also examined tools and methods for the team and organizational level, not the individual level. Essay 9.8 described the Pre-mortem method and some common mistakes organizations make in conducting Pre-mortems—mistakes that I think can greatly reduce the impact of a Pre-mortem session. One mistake is to simply ask, "What can go wrong?" instead of establishing the mindset that the plan has failed. It may seem like a minor difference, but research we have done suggests that it can matter a lot.

Part 9 introduced the idea of a Decision Scorecard for personnel evaluations—changing the conversation from objectives and behaviors and outcomes to a chance for the supervisor and subordinate to reflect on tough choices the subordinate made during the previous year so the two of them can jointly consider what was learned from these choices.

Reflections

Part 9 presented a Management by Discovery approach. Standard management tactics seek to identify the objectives of a project and the steps that are planned to achieve those objectives. If the project addresses wicked problems, and many projects do, then the objectives are likely to change as the team gains insights into what they really need to accomplish. Therefore, a Management by Discovery mindset should be more effective than a mindset that locks managers into the initial understanding of the goals.

Essay 9.11 listed nine general strategies that organizations can use to change performance. There is nothing particularly insightful in this essay except that it might help shake leaders and managers out of some of their routines and their automatic reliance on only a few of these levers, like training and incentives. There are more options than many people imagine.

Part 9 explored the challenge of turning policy into practice. Too often, upper management thinks that merely by issuing directives—policy statements—they can accomplish their objectives. That's just wishful thinking. A lot of extra work is needed to help people adapt to different contexts and constraints to carry out the policy effectively. If organizations are serious about their policies, this kind of work may be essential.

The last essay in this part is a change of pace and is also intended as an inspiration. Having tools and tactics isn't enough. We also need individuals who can put these tools and tactics into play. "The Difference-Makers" told the story of four individuals who were able to achieve significant and enduring change. So we see that it is possible to have an impact, we see that individual qualities of leadership and vision can contribute to this impact, and perhaps we can be inspired to use our abilities to see cognition and to deploy the sources of power to make a difference ourselves.

Afterword

The nine parts of this book contained a lot of ideas. However, my overall goal was not to present ideas but to help you see cognition more readily and more clearly. I wanted you, at this point, to better appreciate the cognitive dimension and why it is so important yet at the same time why it is so invisible. I wanted you to become attuned to the cognitive challenges that are routinely missed by organizations.

Do you think that has happened? Are you perceiving situations differently than before you started reading? Are you noticing things you might have missed previously? Are you asking better questions, deeper questions, more useful questions? Are you more skilled at appreciating the perspectives that others bring to a situation?

I hope so. And I acknowledge that these are hard questions. It's difficult to recapture what you were capable of before.

At the least, this book should serve as a starting point, guiding you in the direction of becoming attuned to the cognitive dimension even as others are captured by the observable events and the explicit statements being made. Best wishes on your explorations as you accumulate experiences and stories of your own.

The nine parts of the book contain more than 80 essays, but if we step back from the essays, we can see a progression. From this vantage point at the end of the book, we can see that narrative arc more clearly. The book started with a description of the cognitive dimension and its different facets. Then, to sharpen this description, the next part contrasted the cognitive dimension with the conventional analytical account, showing how they differed and suggesting some of the limitations of that conventional account. Next, we explored some of the downsides of the conventional analytical account by examining how it influences work on artificial intelligence systems by inadequately valuing our expertise and explaining why we need technologies that support our expertise rather than interfere with it.

And that raises the question of what we mean by expertise, so part 5 explores some of the characteristics of expertise that need to be augmented instead of compromised. One aspect of expertise is to enhance insights and discoveries, which is the topic of part 6. But how do we strengthen expertise and foster insights? That's the issue covered in part 7 on training. Further, we need to promote the expertise of others, not only ourselves or our subordinates—we need to take the perspectives of others into account, which is explored in part 8. Finally, part 9 wraps up all of these issues by describing a variety of tools and tactics that can improve individual and team and organizational performance.

With such a range of topics, it is inevitable that you have found yourself disagreeing with some of my assertions and arguments. That's only natural. These disagreements may be useful for helping you sharpen your own views. And I suspect that you found more to agree with than disagree with. At the very least, the essays should have helped you expand your views and your mental models.

I also want to assure you that I have not intended these essays to be provocative, to make claims merely to get an emotional reaction from readers. The essays may seem contrarian to some readers because I do not share the dominant perspective about the primacy of analytical, context-free rationality. I view that perspective as a rationalist fever dream that sometimes appears very attractive but is limited in many ways. So the essays are reflecting a sincere and authentic difference in perspective.

That's another objective of the essays—to demonstrate that there is an alternative perspective, to articulate that perspective, and to explore its implications. Readers should have a sense of how this cognitive perspective, this Naturalistic Decision Making perspective, might possibly have a greater value and stronger utility and more direct application than the purely analytical perspective. At this point, readers may sense how this cognitive perspective might help researchers and practitioners and society.

This collection of essays can serve as an invitation to readers, whether or not they are researchers, to align with the cognitive perspective, or perhaps only to inspect it further, or at least to apply any aspects of it that might be valuable and meaningful to them.

Acknowledgments

This section of a book is an opportunity for the author to express gratitude to everyone who made a contribution to its writing. But we can also look at this section as a form of causal landscape (see essay 9.5), capturing those who played a role in the final outcome and, to some extent, describing the nature and magnitude of their contribution through the expressions of appreciation.

For *Snapshots of the Mind*, the contributors cover a wide spectrum given the large number of essays and the time period of their composition—almost a decade, from 2013 to 2022.

My greatest thanks go to my daughter, Devorah Klein, who suggested this book in the first place. She urged me to collect the essays I had written for my *Psychology Today* blog and publish them as a book. Devorah also made many other contributions and you will find her name again below, but without her suggestion and encouragement there would be no book.

I also want to thank John Mahaney and his colleagues at PublicAffairs books for arranging for me to have a *Psychology Today* blog in the first place. The initial idea was to use the essays I posted to attract more readers to my previous book, *Seeing What Others Don't: The Remarkable Ways We Gain Insights* (2013), and my initial essays were about the nature of insights. But then I started branching out and writing essays about other topics related to cognitive psychology, and then finally, essays about anything that interested me, from railroad accidents to teaching, sports, and career counseling for recent graduates.

Devon Frye, my editor at *Psychology Today*, has been very helpful and patient as I drew on my blog essays to populate this book.

Phil Laughlin is my editor at the MIT Press, and he deserves major credit for agreeing to publish this book and then providing invaluable advice in organizing it and turning an assemblage of essays into what could pass as a coherent story. Phil also was the driving force behind the additional essays I wrote to introduce the book and each section, and then to reflect on what we can take away from the sections. Phil is responsible for the final shape that this book has taken. He also arranged for four reviewers to provide their reactions to an earlier draft. I never found out their names, but they should know how helpful I found their comments and recommendations.

Deborah Cantor-Adams was my production editor at the MIT Press. I have dealt with a number of different editors for my previous five books, not always happily, but Deborah was wonderful to work with. I think I am done writing books, but if I could be assured that Deborah would do the editing I might reconsider.

For the preparation of the book, turning the essays from an online blog into a coherent volume, I depended on Adam Zaremsky, my colleague at ShadowBox LLC, the company I founded in 2014. Adam simply did everything that I needed and anticipated things I hadn't even thought about. He was always on schedule and often ahead of schedule, sometimes hurrying me along. I was very lucky to have his help.

Kari Hoy, another colleague at ShadowBox LLC, provided a complete editing of the book at the earliest stage, and made important contributions.

Many of the graphics in this book were designed by my friend Michael Fleishman. We have worked together for over 30 years and I have valued his creativity and skills. I should also mention David Sweeney, who prepared the very first diagram of the cognitive sources of power, shown in essay 2.2.

Next in our informal causal landscape, come all those who contributed to specific essays, either by writing the essays or by collaborating with me on them: Herb Bell, Ron Besuijen, Joseph Borders, Devorah Klein, Shane Mueller, John Schmitt, Ben Shneiderman, and Gretchen Wustrack. Along with these authors and coauthors I want to acknowledge friends and colleagues who made significant contributions to individual essays: Lorenzo Barberis Canonico, Sterling Chamberlain, Lia DiBello, Terry Fairbanks, Bill Ferguson, Trevor Hadley, Neil Hintze, Robert Hoffman, Peter Kamstra, Dennis Klein, Rebecca Klein, Dave Lehman, Barbara Mellers, Andrew Mills, Shawna Perry, Jan Maarten Schraagen, Scott Snook, Phil Tetlock, and Corinne Wright.

Somewhere in here I should thank Danny Kahneman. For almost 20 years we have had an adversarial collaboration that I think we both find productive. Danny will hate most of these essays if he ever reads them (which I hope he does not). His contribution to the book is that, knowing that he might read them, I have tried to be more fair and even-handed in my comments than I might otherwise have been.

One of the primary themes of this book is the importance of the field of Naturalistic Decision Making, and I want to thank Judith Orasanu, who sponsored and guided the original work. I also want to thank the current core members of the NDM movement: Joseph Borders, Cindy Dominguez, Rhona Flin, Julie Gore, Robert Hoffman, Rob Hutton, Laura Militello, Brian Moon, Neelam Naikur, Emilie Roth, John Schmitt, Jan Maarten Schraagen, Joel Suss, Paul Ward, William Wong, and David Woods. I also want to acknowledge the contributions to the NDM movement made by Mary Omodei, who, sadly, passed away in 2021.

I greatly appreciate my colleagues at ShadowBox LLC for their support and also for their conceptual contributions, their constructive disagreements and recommendations, for their willingness to be sounding boards for different ideas I have entertained: Joseph Borders, Kari Hoy, Reza Jalaeian, Laura Militello, Emily Newsome, John Schmitt, Adam Zaremsky, and fellow travelers Emily Fine and Devorah Klein.

Should I call out my grandchildren, Jacob Lawlor, Ruth Judson, Jonathan Lawlor, and Harold Judson? They didn't make any direct contributions—the oldest is only 11—but they provided me with an endless and enjoyable set of distractions and emotional connections as I prepared this manuscript. I almost included an essay on what I learned playing online chess with each of them during the pandemic.

Finally, I want to acknowledge my wife, Helen, for her complete support all through our marriage, her patience, the enjoyment of working with her as a colleague and collaborator, her wisdom, and her love. Many years ago someone asked me what attracted me to Helen and after a moment's thought, I answered, "I like to make her laugh." I still try.

References

Ariely, D., & Jones, S. (2008). *Predictably irrational*. New York: Harper Audio.

Arkes, H. (1981). Impediments to accurate clinical judgment and possible ways to minimize their impact. *Journal of Consulting and Clinical Psychology, 49*, 323–330.

Balogh, E. P., Miller, B. T., & Ball, J. R. (2015). *Improving diagnosis in health care*. Washington, D.C.: National Academies Press

Barra, A. (2011, September 27). The many problems with "Moneyball." *The Atlantic*.

Beach, L. R. (2019). *The structure of conscious experience*. Newcastle upon Tyne, UK: Cambridge Scholars Publishing.

Berg, N., & Gigerenzer, G. (2010). As-if behavioral economics: Neoclassical economics in disguise? *History of Economic Ideas, 18*(1), 133–166.

Bonde, A. (2013, October 18). Defining small data [blog]. Retrieved from https://smalldatagroup.com/2013/10/18/defining-small-data.

Borders, J., Klein, G., & Besuijen, R. (2019, June). An operational account of mental models: A pilot study. In *Proceedings of the 2019 International Conference on Naturalistic Decision Making*, San Francisco, CA.

Boser, U. (2019). What do teachers know about the science of learning? The Learning Agency, Washington, DC. Retrieved from https://www.the-learning-agency.com/insights/what-do-teachers-know-about-the-science-of-learning.

Brafman, O., & Brafman, R. (2008). *Sway: The irresistible pull of irrational behavior*. New York: Doubleday.

Chi, M. T. H., Roy, M., & Hausmann, R. G. M. (2008). Observing tutorial dialogues collaboratively: Insights about human tutoring effectiveness from vicarious learning. *Cognitive Science, 32*, 301–341.

Chi, M. T. H., Siler, S., & Jeong, H. (2004). Can tutors monitor student's understanding accurately? *Cognitive and Instruction, 22*, 363–387.

Chi, M. T. H., & Wylie, R. (2014). The ICAP framework: Linking cognitive engagement to active learning outcomes. *Educational Psychologist, 49*(4), 219–243.

Chinn, C. A., & Brewer, W. F. (1993). The role of anomalous data in knowledge acquisition: A Theoretical framework and implications for science instruction. *Review of Educational Research, 63*(1), 1–49.

Christensen, C. M. (2013). *The innovator's dilemma: When new technologies cause great firms to fail*. Boston, MA: Harvard Business Review Press.

Coffield, F., Moseley, D., Hall, E., & Ecclestone, K. (2004). *Learning styles and pedagogy in post-16 learning: A systematic review*. London: Learning and Skills Research Center. Retrieved from https://www.voced.edu.au/content/ngv%3A13692.

Cohen, M., Freeman, J. T., & Thompson, B. (1997). Training the naturalistic decision maker. In C. E. Zsambok & G. Klein (Eds.), *Naturalistic decision making* (pp. 257–268). Mahwah, NJ: Erlbaum.

Crispen, P., & Hoffman, R. R. (2016). How many experts?, *IEEE Intelligent Systems* (November/December), 56–62.

Crosskerry, P. (2003). The importance of cognitive errors in diagnosis and strategies to minimize them. *Academic Medicine, 78*, 75–780.

Dawes, R. (2001). *Everyday irrationality: How pseudo-scientists, lunatics, and the rest of us systematically fail to think rationally*. Boulder, CO: Westview.

De Keyser, V., & Woods, D. D. (1990). Fixation errors: Failures to revise situation assessment in dynamic and risky systems." In A. Colombo & A. Bustamante (Eds.), *Systems reliability assessment* (pp. 231–251). Dordrecht: Springer.

Devine, P. G., Hirt, E. R., & Gehrke. E. M. (1990). Diagnostic and confirmation strategies in trait hypothesis testing. *Journal of Personality and Social Psychology, 58*, 952–963.

Dweck, C. S. (2006). *Mindset: The new psychology of success*. New York: Random House Digital, Inc.

Eisenberg, E. M., & Mahar, S. E. (2019). *Stop wasting words: Leading through conscious communication*. Charleston, SC: Advantage Press.

Ericsson, K. A., Hoffman, R. R., Kozbelt, A., & Williams, A. M. (Eds.). (2018). *The Cambridge handbook of expertise and expert performance*. Cambridge: Cambridge University Press.

Eyal, T., Steffel, J., & Epley, N. (2018). Perspective mistaking: Accurately understanding the mind of another requires getting perspective, not taking perspective. *Journal of Personality and Social Psychology, 114*, 547–571.

Fadde, P. J., & Klein, G. (2010). Deliberate performance: Accelerating expertise in natural settings. *Performance Improvement, 49*(9), 5–14.

References

Fadde, P. J., & Klein, G. (2012). Accelerating expertise using action learning activities. *Cognitive Technology, 17*(1), 11–18.

Feltovich, P. J., Coulson, R. L., & Spiro, R. J. (2001). Learners' (mis)understanding of important and difficult concepts: A challenge to smart machines in education. In K. D. Forbus & P. J. Feltovich (Eds.), *Smart machines in education* (pp. 349–375). Cambridge, MA: MIT Press.

Feltovich, P. J., Hoffman, R. R., Woods, D., & Roesler, A. (2004). Keeping it too simple: How the reductive tendency affects cognitive engineering. *IEEE Intelligent Systems, 19*(3), 90–94.

Fischhoff, B., & Beyth-Marom, R. (1983). Hypothesis evaluation from a Bayesian perspective. *Psychological Review, 90*, 239–260.

Frazier, I. (2013, May 13). Form and fungus. *The New Yorker*.

Fugelsang, J. A., Stein, C. B., Green, A. E., & Dunbar, K. N. (2004). Theory and data interactions of the scientific mind: Evidence from the molecular and the cognitive laboratory. *Canadian Journal of Experimental Psychology, 58*, 86–95.

Gawande, A. (2010). *The checklist manifesto*. New York: Picadur.

Gigerenzer, G. (2019). Expert intuition is not rational choice. *American Journal of Psychology, 132*, 475–480.

Gigerenzer, G. (2022). *How to stay smart in a smart world*. Cambridge, MA: MIT Press.

Gladwell, M. (2014, March 31). Sacred and profane: How not to negotiate with believers. *The New Yorker*.

Gopher, D., Weil, M., & Bareket, T. (1994). Transfer of skill from a computer game trainer to flight. *Human Factors, 36*, 387–405.

Griggs, R. A., & Cox, J. R. (1982). The elusive thematic-materials effect in Wason's selection task. *British Journal of Psychology, 73*, 407–420.

Hall, K. G., Domingues, D. A., & Cavazos, R. (1994). Contextual interference effects with skilled baseball players. *Perceptual and Motor Skills, 78*(3), 835–841. Retrieved from https://doi.org/10.1177/003151259407800331.

Halpern, D. F. (2007). The nature and nurture of critical thinking. In R. J. Sternberg, H. L. Roediger III, & D. F. Halpern (Eds.), *Critical thinking in psychology* (pp. 1–14). New York: Cambridge University Press.

Heath, C., & Heath, D. (2010). *Switch: How to change things when change is hard*. New York: Crown.

Higgins, T. R., Staszewski, J., Herman, H., Flanigan, V., Falmier, O., & Hancock, R. A. (2008). *Warfighter research in mine detection: Improved clutter rejection with the An/PSS-14*. Land Mine Detection Research Center Report, Lincoln University.

Hoffman, B. G. (2012). *American icon: Alan Mulally and the fight to save Ford Motor Company*. New York: Three Rivers Press.

Hoffman, R., Klein, G., & Miller, J. (2011). Naturalistic investigations and models of reasoning about complex indeterminate causation. *Information Knowledge Systems Management, 10*(1–4), 397–425.

Hoffman, R. R., Mueller, S. T., Klein, G., & Litman, L. (2018). *Metrics for Explainable AI: Challenges and prospects* (Technical report, Explainable AI Program, DARPA). Washington, DC: DARPA. Retrieved from https://arxiv.org/abs/1812.04608.

Hoffman, R. R., Ward, P., Feltovich, P. J., DiBello, L., Fiore, S. M., & Andrews, D. (2014). *Accelerated expertise: Training for high proficiency in a complex world*. New York: Psychology Press.

Johnson, S. (2010). *Where good ideas come from: The natural history of innovation*. New York: Penguin.

Jones, R. V. (1978). *The wizard war: British scientific intelligence, 1939–1945*. New York: Coward, McCann & Geoghegan.

Kahneman, D. (2011). *Thinking fast and slow*. New York: Farrar, Straus and Giroux.

Kahneman, D., & Frederick, S. (2002). Representativeness revisited: Attribute substitution in intuitive judgment. In T. Gilovich, D. Griffin, & D. Kahneman (Eds.), *Heuristics and biases: The psychology of intuitive judgment* (pp. 49–81). Cambridge: Cambridge University Press.

Kahneman, D., & Klein, G. (2009). Conditions for intuitive expertise: A failure to disagree. *American Psychologist, 64*(6), 515.

Kahneman, D., & Tversky, A. (1972). Subjective probability: A judgment of representativeness. *Cognitive Psychology, 3*, 30–454.

Kiefer, C. F., & Constable, M. (2013). *The art of insight: How to have more aha! moments*. Oakland, CA: Berrett-Koehler Publishers.

Klayman, J., & Ha, Y.-W. (1987). Confirmation, disconfirmation, and information in hypothesis testing. *Psychological Review, 94*, 211–228.

Klein, D. E., Woods, D. D., Klein, G., & Perry, S. J. (2016). Can we trust best practices? Six cognitive challenges of evidence-based approaches. *Journal of Cognitive Engineering and Decision Making*, 10(3), 244–254.

Klein, D. E., Woods, D., Klein, G., & Perry, S. (2018). EBM: rationalist fever dreams. *Journal of Cognitive Engineering and Decision Making, 12*(3), 227–230.

Klein, D. E., Wustrack, G., & Schwartz, A. (2006). Medication adherence: Many conditions, a common problem. *Proceedings of the 50th Annual Meeting of the Human*

Factors and Ergonomics Society, San Francisco (pp. 1088–1092). Santa Monica, CA: Human Factors and Ergonomics Society.

Klein, G. A. (1993). A recognition-primed decision (RPD) model of rapid decision making. In G. A. Klein, J. Orasanu, R. Calderwood, & C. E. Zsambok (Eds.), *Decision making in action: Models and methods* (pp. 138–147). Norwood, NJ: Ablex.

Klein, G. (1998/2017). *Sources of power: How people make decisions.* Cambridge, MA: MIT Press.

Klein, G. (2007). Performing a project premortem. *Harvard Business Review, 85*(9), 18–19.

Klein, G. (2008). Naturalistic decision making. *Human Factors, 50*(3), 456–460.

Klein, G. (2009). *Streetlights and shadows: Searching for the keys to adaptive decision making.* Cambridge, MA: MIT Press.

Klein, G. (2011). Critical thoughts about critical thinking. *Theoretical Issues in Ergonomics Science, 12*(3), 210–224.

Klein, G. (2013). *Seeing what others don't: The remarkable ways we gain insights.* New York: Public Affairs.

Klein, G., & Borders, J. (2016). The ShadowBox approach to cognitive skills training. *Journal of Cognitive Engineering and Decision Making, 10,* 268–280.

Klein, G., Calderwood, R., & Clinton-Cirocco, A. (1986/2010). Rapid decision making on the fire ground: The original study plus a postscript. *Journal of Cognitive Engineering and Decision Making, 4*(3), 186–209.

Klein, G., Feltovich, P. J., Bradshaw, J. M., & Woods, D. D. (2005). Common ground and coordination in joint activity. In W. B. Rouse, & K. R. Boff (Eds.), *Organizational simulation* (pp. 139–184). New York: Wiley.

Klein, G. A., & Hoffman, R. R. (1992). Seeing the invisible: Perceptual-cognitive aspects of expertise. In M. Rabinowitz (Ed.), *Cognitive science foundations of instruction* (pp. 203–226). Mahwah, NJ: Erlbaum.

Klein, G., Hoffman, R. R., & Mueller, S. T. (2020). *Scorecard for self-explaining capabilities of AI systems* (Technical report, Explainable AI Program, DARPA). Washington, DC: DARPA.

Klein, G., & Jarosz, A. (2011). A naturalistic study of insight. *Journal of Cognitive Engineering and Decision Making, 5*(4), 335–351.

Klein, G., & Militello, L. (2004). The knowledge audit as a method for cognitive task analysis. In H. Montgomery, R. Lipshitz, & B. Brehmer (Eds.), *How professionals make decisions* (pp. 335–342). Mahwah, NJ: Erlbaum.

Klein, G., Moon, B., & Hoffman, R. R. (2006). Making sense of sensemaking 2: A macrocognitive model. *IEEE Intelligent Systems, 21*(5), 88–92.

Klein, G., Phillips, J. K., Rall, E. L., & Peluso, D. A. (2007). A data-frame theory of sensemaking. In R. R. Hoffman (Ed.), *Expertise out of context: Proceedings of the 6th International Conference on Naturalistic Decision Making, January 2007* (pp. 113–155). New York: Erlbaum.

Klein, G., Pliske, R. M., Crandall, B., & Woods, D. (2005). Problem detection. *Cognition, Technology, and Work, 7*, 14–28.

Klein, G., Ross, K. G., Moon, B. M., Klein, D. E., Hoffman, R. R., & Hollnagel, E. (2003). Macrocognition. *IEEE Intelligent Systems, 18*(3), 81–85.

Klein, G., Shneiderman, B., Hoffman, R. R., & Ford, K. M. (2017). Why expertise matters: A response to the challenges. *IEEE Intelligent Systems, 32*(6), 67–73.

Klein, G., Shneiderman, B., Hoffman, R. R., & Wears, R. L. (2018). The "war" on expertise: Five communities that seek to discredit experts. In P. Ward, J. M. Schraagen, J. Gore, & E. M. Roth (Eds.), *The Oxford handbook of expertise* (pp. 1158–1191). New York: Oxford University Press.

Klein, G. A., Wolf, S., Militello, L., & Zsambok, C. (1995). Characteristics of skilled option generation in chess. *Organizational Behavior and Human Decision Processes, 62*(1), 63–69.

Klein, H. A., & Lippa, K. D. (2012). Assuming control after system failure: Type II diabetes self-management. *Cognition, Technology & Work, 14*(3), 243–251.

Kontzer, T. (2016). Deep learning drops error rate for breast cancer diagnoses by 85%. Retrieved from Nvidia blog: https://blogs.nvidia.com/blog/2016/09/19/deeplearning-breast-cancer-diagnosis.

Kornell, N., & Bjork, R. A. (2008). Learning concepts and categories: Is spacing the "enemy of induction"? *Psychological Science, 19*(6), 585–592. Retrieved from https://doi.org/10.1111/j.1467-9280.2008.02127.x.

Kotovsky, K., Hayes, J. R., & Simon, H. A. (1985). Why are some problems hard? Evidence from Tower of Hanoi. *Cognitive Psychology, 17*, 248–294.

Kounios, J., & Beeman, M. (2009). The aha! moment: The cognitive neuroscience of insight. *Current Directions in Psychological Science 18*(4), 210–216.

Kunda, Z. (1999). *Social cognition: Making sense of people*. Cambridge, MA: MIT Press.

Kurzweil, R. (2005). *The singularity is near: When humans transcend biology*. New York: Viking Press.

Langer, E. J. (2014). *Mindfulness*. Boston: Da Capo Lifelong Books.

References

Lanir, Z. (1986). *Fundamental surprise*. Eugene, OR: Decision Research.

Lewis, M. (2004). *Moneyball: The art of winning an unfair game*. W. W. Norton.

Lichtenstein, S., Slovic, P., Fischhoff, B., Layman, M., & Combs, B. (1978). Judged frequency of lethal events. *Journal of Experimental Psychology: Human Learning and Memory, 4*, 551–578.

Lilienfeld, S. O., Ammirati, R., & Landfield, K. (2009). Giving debiasing away: Can psychological research on correcting cognitive errors promote human welfare?, *Perspectives on Psychological Science, 4*, 390–398.

Lindstrom, M. (2016). *Small data: The tiny clues that uncover huge trends*. New York: St. Martin's Press.

Loewenstein, G. (1994). The psychology of curiosity: A review and reinterpretation. *Psychological Bulletin, 116*, 75–98.

Lopes, L. L. (1991). The rhetoric of irrationality. *Theory & Psychology, 1*(1), 65–82.

Marcus, G. (2018). Deep learning: A critical appraisal. Retrieved from https://arxiv.org/abs/1801.00631.

Mauboussin, M. J. (2012). *Think twice: Harnessing the power of counterintuition*. Brighton, MA: Harvard Business Review Press.

McDaniel, M. A., & Butler, A. C. (2011). A contextual framework for understanding when difficulties are desirable. In A. S. Benjamin (Ed.), *Successful remembering and successful forgetting: A festschrift in honor of Robert A. Bjork* (pp. 175–198). New York: Psychology Press.

McNeil, B. J., Pauker, S. G., Sox, H. C. Jr., & Tversky, A. (1982). On the elicitation of preferences for alternative therapies. *New England Journal of Medicine, 306*(21), 1259–1262.

Meehl, P. E. (1954). *Clinical versus statistical prediction: A theoretical analysis and a review of the evidence*. Minneapolis: University of Minnesota Press.

Militello, L. G., & Hutton, R. J. B. (1998). Applied cognitive task analysis (ACTA): A practitioner's toolkit for understanding cognitive task demands. *Ergonomics, 41*, 1618–1641.

Militello, L. G., Lintem, G., Dominguez, C. O., & Klein, G. (2009). Cognitive systems engineering for system design. *INCOSE INSIGHT, 12*(1), 11–14.

Minsky, M. (1988). *The society of mind*. New York: Simon and Schuster.

Mueller, J. S., Melwani, S. & Goncalo, J. A. (2012). The bias against creativity: Why people desire but reject creative ideas. *Psychological Science, 23*(1), 13–17.

Mueller, S. T., & Klein, G. (2011). Improving users' mental models of intelligent software tools. *IEEE Intelligent Systems 26*(2), 77–83.

Mumaw, R. J., Roth, E. M., Vicente, K. J., & Burns, C. M. (2000). There is more to monitoring a nuclear power plant than meets the eye. *Human Factors, 42*(1), 36–55.

National Assessment of Education Progress. (1983). *A nation at risk*. US Government Printing Office, Washington, DC.

National Transportation Safety Board. (2016). *Railroad accident report: Derailment of Amtrak passenger train 188, Philadelphia, PA, May 12, 2015* (NTSB/RAR-16/02, PB2016-103218).

O'Donnell, R. D., Moise, M., & Schmidt, R. (2004). *Comprehensive computerized cognitive assessment battery* (Final Report for the Office of Naval Research under contract N00140-01-M-0064).

Pashler, H., McDaniel, M., Rohrer, D., & Bjork, R. (2009). Learning styles: Concepts and evidence. *Psychological Science in the Public Interest, 9*(3), 105–119.

Perrow, C. (1984). *Normal accidents: Living with high-risk technologies*. New York: Basic Books.

Pines, J. M. (2006). Confirmation bias in emergency medicine. *Academic Emergency Medicine, 13*, 90–94.

Polanyi, M. (1958). *Personal knowledge*. Chicago: University of Chicago Press.

Rohrer, D., Dedrick, R. F., & Stershic, S. (2015). Interleaved practice improves mathematics learning. *Journal of Educational Psychology, 107*(3), 900–908. Retrieved from https://doi.org/10.1037/edu0000001.

Rosenberg, L., Willcox, G., Halabi, S., Lungren, M., Baltaxe, D., & Lyons, M. (2018). Artificial swarm intelligence employed to amplify diagnostic accuracy in radiology. Paper presented at IEMCON 2018: 9th Annual Information Technology, Electronics, and Mobile Communication Conference.

Rouse, W. B., & Morris, N. M. (1986). On looking into the black box: Prospects and limits in the search for mental models. *Psychological Bulletin, 100*(3), 349–363.

Schmidt, R. A., & Wulf, G. (1997). Continuous concurrent feedback degrades skill learning: Implications for training and simulation. *Human Factors, 39*(4), 509–525.

Seligman, M., & Csikszentmihalyi, M. (2000). Positive psychology. An introduction. *The American Psychologist, 55*(1), 5–14.

Shaer, M. (2016, January 31). The wreck of Amtrak 188. *The New York Times Magazine*, 49–55.

Shanteau, J. (1992). Competence in experts: The role of task characteristics. *Organizational Behavior and Human Decision Processes, 53*, 252–262.

Shanteau, J. (2015). Why task domains (still) matter for understanding expertise. *Journal of Applied Research in Memory and Cognition, 4*, 169–175.

Siddiqui, G. (2018, October 15). Why doctors reject tools that make their job easier. *Scientific American*, Observations Newsletter.

Simon, H. A. (1975). The functional equivalence of problem solving skills. *Cognitive Psychology, 7*, 268–288.

Smith, P. (2018). Making brittle technologies useful. In P. J. Smith & R. R. Hoffman (Eds.), *Cognitive systems engineering: The future of a changing world*. Boca Raton, FL: CRC Press.

Snook, S. A. (2002). *Friendly fire: The accidental shootdown of US Black Hawks over Northern Iraq*. Princeton, NJ: Princeton University Press.

Stanton, D. (2009). *Horse soldiers: The extraordinary story of a band of US soldiers who rode to victory in Afghanistan*. New York: Scribner.

Staszewski, J. (2004). Models of expertise as blueprints for cognitive engineering: Applications to landmine detection. *Proceedings of the 48th Annual Meeting of the Human Factors and Ergonomics Society, New Orleans, LA, September 20–24, 2004*. Santa Monica: Human Factors and Ergonomics Society.

Taleb, N. N. (2007). *The black swan: The impact of the highly improbable*. New York: Random House.

Tetlock, P. E. (2005). *Expert local judgment: How good is it? How can we know?* Princeton, NJ: Princeton University Press.

Tetlock, P. E., & Gardner, D. (2016). *Superforecasting: The art and science of prediction*. New York: Random House.

Thaler, R. H., & Sunstein, C. R. (2009). *Nudge: Improving decisions about health, wealth, and happiness*. New York: Penguin.

TNTP. (2018). The opportunity myth: What students can show us about how school is letting them down—and how to fix it. Retrieved from https://tntp.org/assets/documents/TNTP_The-Opportunity-Myth_Web.pdf.

Trope, Y., & Bassok, M. (1982). Confirmatory and diagnosing strategies in social information gathering. *Journal of Personality and Social Psychology, 43*, 22–34.

Tversky, A., & Kahneman, D. (1971). Belief in the law of small numbers. *Psychological Bulletin, 76*(2), 105–110.

Tversky, A., & Kahneman, D. (1974). Judgment under uncertainty: Heuristics and biases. *Science, 185*(4157), 1124–1131.

Van Hecke, M. L. (2009). *Blind spots: Why smart people do dumb things*. Amherst, NY: Prometheus Books.

Veinott, B., Klein, G., & Wiggins, S. (2010). Evaluating the effectiveness of the premortem technique on plan confidence. In S. French, B. M. Tomaszewski, & C. W.

Zobel (Eds.), *Proceedings of the 7th International ISCRAM Conference, Seattle, May 2010*, 1–29.

Vinge, V. (1993). The coming technological singularity: How to survive in the post-human era. Paper presented at the VISION-21 Symposium, March 30–31.

Viswanathan, M., Golin, C. E., Jones, C. D., Ashok, M., Blalock, S. J., Wines, R. C., Coker-Schwimmer, E. J., Rosen, D. L., Sista, P., & Lohr, K. N. (2012). Interventions to improve adherence to self-administered medications for chronic diseases in the United States: A systematic review. *Annals of Internal Medicine, 157*, 785–795.

Wallas, G. (1926). *The art of thought*. London: Jonathan Cape.

Walters, K. (1994). *Re-thinking reason: New perspectives in critical thinking*. Albany: SUNY Press.

Wang, D., Khosla, A., Gargeya, R., Irshad, H., & Beck, A. H. (2016). Deep learning for identifying metastatic breast cancer. Retrieved from arXiv:1606.05718.

Ward, P., Gore, J., Hutton, R., Conway, G., & Robert, H. (2018). Adaptive skill as the conditio sine qua non of expertise. *Journal of Applied Research in Memory and Cognition, 7*(1), 35–50. Retrieved from https://doi.org/10.1016/j.jarmac.2018.01.009.

Wason, P. C. (1960). On the failure to eliminate hypotheses in a conceptual task. *The Quarterly Journal of Experimental Psychology, 12*, 129–140.

Wason, P. C. (1968). Reasoning about a rule. *The Quarterly Journal of Experimental Psychology, 20*, 273–281.

Willingham, D. T., Hughes, E. M., & Dobolyi, D. G. (2015). The scientific status of learning styles theories. *Teaching of Psychology, 42*(3), 266–271. doi: 10.1177/0098628315589505.

Woodruff, P. (2006). *First democracy: The challenge of an ancient idea*. New York: Oxford University Press.

Woods, D. D., & Sarter, N. (2000). Learning from automation surprises and going sour accidents. In N. Sarter and R. Amalberti (Eds.), *Cognitive engineering in the aviation domain* (pp. 327–353). Mahwah, NJ: Erlbaum.

Index

Note: Page numbers in *italic type* indicate illustrations.

Active mindset, 171, 208, 229–230, 234, 241. *See also* Mindset shifts
Adaptability, 14, 296
Adaptation skills, 182–183
Adaptive Expertise, 182–183
Adherence, 379–384
Adherence Loop, 381–383, *381*, *383*
Administration for Children's Services, New York, 404–405
After-Action Review, 271, 272
AIQ. *See* Artificial Intelligence Quotient
Air Force Research Lab (AFRL), 143, 245
Air France 447, 107–108
Alexa, 105
Algorithms, 11, 43–44, 60, 81, 83, 99, 103, 104, 122–123, 141, 155, 163, 193
Ambiguity, 5, 9, 19, 32, 42–44, 51, 54, 69–70, 76, 100, 131, 138, 161–163, 170, 237, 279, 281, 283, 284, 301, 308, 332, 351, 396
Amtrak, 100, 111–114, *112*
Anomalies, 74–75, 78–79, 82, 116, 165–167, 212, 234, 236
Anticipatory thinking (AT), 1, 14, 17, 169–171, 187, 229, 271
Arkes, H., 70
Army Research Institute, 21

Artificial intelligence (AI). *See also* Explainable AI
 cognition compared to, 11, 15, 99, 104–105, 121–125, 193–194
 critiques of, 99–100, 163
 expertise challenged by, 6, 99, 153–155, 158, 163
 human partnering with, 154–155
 RPD model, 31
 the singularity, 100, 121, 123–124, *124*
 Tower of Hanoi puzzle, 11
Artificial Intelligence Quotient (AIQ), 101, 141–143, 147
Assumptions, 23, 77, 203, 204–205, 211–212, 223, 226, –230
Astrology, 187–188
AT. *See* Anticipatory thinking
ATF. *See* Bureau of Alcohol, Tobacco, and Firearms
Attention management, 281

Ball, Deborah, 274, 276, 277
Baseball, 57–61
Bayer, Eben, 213
Bayesian statistics, 47, 51, 53, 82
BBN/Raytheon project, 243
Beach, L. R., 81
Beathard, C. J., 85–86

Beeman, Mark, 225
Behavioral engineering, 396
Beliefs, decision-making role of, 25–26, 203, 204, 234, 337
Berg, N., 159
Berlin Wall, fall of, 340
Berners-Lee, Tim, 127–128
Best practices, 45, 182
Besuijen, Ron, 25, 182, 272
Beville Engineering, 272
Beyth-Marom, R., 71
Biases. *See also* Confirmation bias; Heuristics and Biases (HB) community; Judgment biases
  critiques of explanations based on, 44, 54, 96
  in HB framework, 49–52
  heuristics in relation to, 53, 159
  popular attention to, 17, 42, 69
Big Data, 100, 115–120, 131, 146, 163, 340
Big-picture perspective, 271
Black Hawk shootdown, 366, *367*, *368*, 369–370
Black swan events, 339–341
Blockbuster, 115
Bob Newhart Show, The (television show), 322
Boeing 737 MAX, 123
Bonde, A., 134
Borders, Joseph, 25, 158, 182, 272
Boser, U., 253
Bostian, Brandon, 111–114
Brainstorming, 203, 204
Branch Davidians, 314
Breakout (game), 139
Breakthroughs, 225–227, 239–241
Brewer, W. F., 74, 78
Brexit, 132
Britain, 177–179
Buehler, Walker, 61–62
Buffalo Bill (television show), 321–323

Building block approach, 254
Bureau of Alcohol, Tobacco, and Firearms (ATF), 314

Camera grips, 321–323
Causal Landscape, 350, 365–376, 408
Causal reasoning/relationships, 115, 134, 139, 146, 166, 169–170, 187, 203, 204, 293, 350, 365–376, 408
Center for Operator Performance, 25
Centers for Disease Control and Prevention, 340
Central Intelligence Agency (CIA), 131, 217–218
Chamberlain, Sterling, 263
Change, creating lasting, 379–384
Checklists, 44, 45, 51, 60, 87, 103, 123, 209, 396
Chess, 31, 101, 137–139, 163, 199–200, 239
Chi, Micki, 259–261, 305
Child protective services, 35, 122, 174–175, 209, 286, 404–405
China, 131–132
Chinn, C. A., 74, 78
Christensen, Clayton, 392
Churchill, Winston, 89, 177
Clinton, Hillary, 350, 371–377, 408
Closure, danger of, 171
Cognition and cognitive dimension. *See also* Sources of power, knowledge and abilities as
  AI compared to, 11, 15, 99, 104–105, 121–125, 193–194
  definition and nature of, 1, 9, 15, 41
  positive vs. negative views of, 44–45, 48, 50, 87–89, 99, 200, *200*, 247, 285
  seeing, 1, 4–5, 41, 193, 199, 249, 307, 347
  training appropriate for, 249–250
  training scenarios based on, 283–284
Cognitive analysis, 117–120
Cognitive Audit, 279–281, 283

Index

Cognitive challenges
  anticipation of, 4, 14
  conditions creating, 21, *22*
  examples of, 284
  presentation of, in training, 279–281, 283–284
  studying the, 40
  welcoming, 299–300
Cognitive Engineering and Decision Making Technical Group, 21–22
Cohen, M., 77, 79
Coincidences, 203, 204, 209, 229, 234
Coleman, Dabney, 321
Comey, James, 374, 375
Commonalities, 244. *See also* Pattern matching
Common ground, 105, 281, 283, 308–310, 331–333, 336
Communication
  breakdowns, 331–333
  dispute resolution, 335–337
  skills, 182
Complacency, 170, 230, 340
Complexity, 19, 23, 32, 42, 44, 47–48, 50, 51, 76–77, 95, 110, 163, 169, 170, 199, 209, 236, 243, 269, 284, 301, 308, 344, 350, 365–366, 375, 396, 399
Computer science, 161, 163
Conceptual skills, –182
Confirmation bias, 45, 65–72, 75–76. *See also* Fixation
Conflict resolution, 335–337
Conflicts, 236–237
Confusion
  clarification of language and communication, 331–333
  decision-making in context of, 55, 69, 95, 104, 199
  in mental models, 11, 26–27, 108, 111, 113, 190
  as resource for insights, 230, 244

Connections, 23, 55, 88, 157, 165, 169, 209, 212, 226, 229–230, 234, 240, 247, 276
Consistency, 51
Constable, M., 225
Contradictions, 23, 169, 212, 226, 227, 230, 234, 240, 247, 276–277
Contrasts, 244
Controlled experiments. *See* Experiments
Coordination, 281, 308
Correction paths, 78, 169, 201, 212, 223, 226, 229–231, 247
Correlation, 55, 134, 139, 146, 203, 204
Counterfactuals, 186, 290, 369
COVID-19 pandemic, 150, 183, 339–341, 348
Cox, J. R., 67–68
Creative desperation, –239–240
Creativity, 104, 186, 207–208, 344
Crick, Francis, 217–218
Crispen, P., 185
Critical thinking, 23, 207–210, 223, 234, 247, 301–303
Crosskerry, P., 77
Crystal ball method, 77
Csikszentmihaly, Mihaly, 48
Cuban Missile Crisis, 187, 217–218
Curiosity. *See also* Exploration
  anomaly detection, 166
  critical thinking, 209
  dispute resolution, 335–336
  encouragement of, by trainers/supervisors, 269, 277, 291
  obstacles to, 76, 290–291, 295
  overcoming fixation/impasses through, 78–79, 241, 272
  psychological power of, 289
  of trainers/supervisors, 237, 268
  as trait of experts, 194
  triggers for, 289–290, *290*
  as valuable cognitive trait, 15, 17, 171, 234

Cuyahoga County Department of Children and Family Services, Cleveland, Ohio, 405

Damon, Matt, 311, 328
Darwin, Charles, 31, 212, 217
Data and information. *See also* Big Data; Small Data
 anomalous, 74–75, 78
 confirmation bias and, 65
 decision-making role of, 22–23, 96
 experts' use of, 134–135, 163
 insights in relation to, 115–120, 134, 146
 missing, 131, 135, 166
 smoothing, 110
Davis, Geena, 321
Decision-making
 analytical/mechanical approaches to, 4, 7, 22–23, 29, 43–44, 51, 81–83, 97, 99–100, 165–167, 209
 conditions of, 21, *22*
 confirmation bias and, 68–69
 critiques of, 17, 41–97
 human capabilities in, 17, 23
 intractable situations in, 46, 91–93
 intuition's place in, 355–358
 NDM approach, 10, 21–23
 performance improvement components, *200*
 personnel evaluations based on, 389–390
 positive vs. negative approaches to, 44–45, 48, 50, 87–89, 99, 200, *200*, 247, *344*
 recent discoveries in, 22–23, 39–40, 203–204
 in risk management, 4
 RPD model, 29–32
 teamwork, 327–329
 time constraints, 29
Decision Research, 161–162, 193
Deep learning, 139, 155

Defective thinkers, 76
Defense Advanced Research Projects Agency (DARPA), 141, 243
De Keyser, V., 74
De minimus explanations, 167
Dentists, 182
Dewey, John, 273
Diagnostic errors, 72–79, 170
DiBello, Lia, 263
Difference-makers, 403–406
Differential diagnosis, 77
Disagreements, 335–337
Discoveries. *See also* Insights; Speculative thinking
 expertise linked to, 183
 good performance involves, 23, 50, 76–77, 88
 management based on, 391–393
 obstacles to, 208
 opportunities for, 117, 137, 199–201, 233–237, *236*
 source of, 61
 training- and education-related, 243–245, 269–270, 274, 277
 using data for, 135
Discovery Platforms, 243–245, 248
Dispute resolution, 335–337
DNA, 217–219
Doctors. *See* Physicians
Dodge, Wagner, 226, 239–241
Dominguez, Cindy, 353
Dreamy states, 223, 225–227, 230, 248
Duncker, Karl, 53
Dweck, Carol, 285, 287–288, 295, 306, 395

Education. *See* Training
Eisenberg, E. M., 401
Elis, Steffan, 273
Epley, N., 313–317
Ericsson, K. A., 51
Error reduction, 23, 44–46, 49–50, 76–77, 85–89, 96, 200, 247, 285,

Index

344–345, 348. *See also* Mistakes, sensationalizing of
Evaluation, vs. training, 250, 257–258, 268, 270, 297
Everest (movie), 328–329
Evidence-Based Medicine, 149–150
Evidence-Based Practices, 161, 163, 193
Evolution, 212, 217
Examples, for communication clarification, 332–333
Exceptions, 244
Expectancies, 82, 135, 151, 163, 166–167, 173–175, 284, 289. *See also* Unexpected situations
Experience
 anomaly detection, 166
 confirmation bias and, 69–71
 gaps in, 131, 135, 166, 173–175
 "job as performed" mindset, 113
 NDM approach, 21
 RPD model, 31
 value of, 2–4, 203, 204
Experiential education, 273, 276
Experiments, controlled/laboratory, 22, 44, 82, 161, 163, 203, 205, 223
Expert-Eyes approach, 34–35
Experts and expertise, 149–195
 adaptive, 182–183
 advice from, 294–295
 AI's challenge to, 6, 99, 153–155, 158, 163
 anomalies as resource for, 82, 165–167
 anticipatory thinking, 169–171
 attitudes and behaviors conducive to, 251, 270–272, 293–297
 automation in relation to, 104, 106, 110, 114, 122–125, 158, 163
 characteristics/aspects of, 1, 4, 22, 103–105, 151, 185–188
 conditions for developing, 159–160
 costs associated with, 122–123
 COVID-19 challenges for, 149–150
 data as used by, 134–135, 163
 decline of, 101, 122–125, 145
 devaluing of, 6, 23, 44, 51, 57, 59–60, 99, 123, 150–151, 153–155, 157–164, *162*, 193–194, 249
 forecasting, 160
 fractionated, 181
 increases of, 122
 mental models, 123, 135, 166, 182, 185, 193
 noticing gaps or missing data, 173–175
 obsolete instances, 124
 opportunity detection, 177–179
 perspective taking, 189–191
 popular conception of, 150
 skill portfolio account, 151, 181–183
 tacit knowledge, 15, 22, 51, 151, 185, 194, 249, 268–269, 293–297
 training tool based on, 33–34
 value of, 6, 23, 41, 157
Explainable AI (XAI), 101, 141, 243
Explanations
 focused, 269
 useful, 365–377, 408
Exploration, 69, 72, 76, 188, 229, 234, 235, 245, 253, 258, 270, 274, 277, 283, 295, 297. *See also* Curiosity
Eyal, T., 313–317

Failures, learning from, 222, 233, 296. *See also* Limitations and failures, anticipation of or response to
Falsification, 31, 66, 69, 71, 186
Federal Bureau of Investigation (FBI), 117, 314
Federal Railroad Administration, 113
Feedback, 276, 293–294, 317
Feltovich, P. J., 74, 170
Ferguson, Bill, 243–245
Field studies, 31. *See also* Naturalistic inquiry
Fischer, Bobby, and Fischer Random Chess, 137–138
Fischhoff, B., 71

Fixation, 45, 50, 72–79, 170, 219, 271–272. *See also* Confirmation bias
Fleishman, Michael, 18
Flory, Jan, 404
Focused explanations, 269
Fonda, Henry, 336
Football, 46, 85–86
Ford Motor Company, 405
Fractionated expertise, 181
France, 132
Franklin, Rosalind, 219
Frazier, Ian, 213
Frederick, S., 81
Fredkin's paradox, 91
Friendly fire, 366, *367*, *368*, 369–370
Frontier thinking, 100, 104–105, 146. *See also* Speculative thinking

Gaps in experience or expectations, 131, 135, 166, 173–175, 284, 289–290
Gardner, D., 60, 160
Gawande, A., 396
Generic questions, 77
Germany, 177–179
Gigerenzer, G., 32, 100, 159
Gladwell, Malcolm, 134, 314
Glaser, Robert, 273
Go, 101, 137–139, 163
Goal recursion strategy, 39
Goncalo, J. A., 344
Goodhand, Judith, 405–406
Good Strangers, 286–287
Google, 101, 105, 146, 344
Google Flu Trends, 163
Google Translate, 104
Gore, Julie, 353
GPS systems, 100, 101, 113
Graduation speeches, 361–363
Griggs, R. A., 67–68

Ha, Y.-W., 69–70
Hadley, Trevor, 131–132

Hall, Rob, 328–329
Hausman, R. G. M., 259–261
HB. *See* Heuristics and Biases (HB) community
Heath, C., 395–396
Heath, D., 395–396
Helicopters, 63, 108–110, 366
Hessan, Diane, 375
Heuristics. *See also* Heuristics and Biases (HB) community
 biases in relation to, 53, 159
 confirmation bias and, 76
 examples of, 53
 speculative likened to, 54–55
 subconscious vs. conscious use of, 55
 value of, 45, 47, 50, 53–55, 96, 159
Heuristics and Biases (HB) community, 44, 47–53, 70, 81, 95, 157–159, 161, 162, 193
Hints, 77–78, 241
Hintze, Neil, 33–34
Hitler, Adolf, 75, 151, 177
Hoffman, Bryce, 405
Hoffman, Robert, 123, 141–142, 185, 187, 243, 293, 353, 373
Holmes, Sherlock (literary figure), 173–174
Human Factors and Ergonomics Society, 22
Hunter-Warrior exercise, 404
Hussein, Saddam, 132–133, 146
Huxley, T. H., 217
Hyperlinks, 101, 127–129
Hypothesis generation, 70
Hypothesis testing, 272

IBM Watson, 121
IDEO, 350, 379
Ignorance. *See* Stupidity
Illusory correlation, 55
Impasses, 203, 204, 211–212, 223, 226, 239–241

Improv Chess, 137–139, 199–200
Improvisation, 101, 137–139, 183, 186, 210, 235–236, 267, 280
Incubation, 211, 223, 225–227, 248
Information. *See* Data and information
Information overload, 284
Insights, 197–248. *See also* Discoveries; Speculative thinking
  attitudes and behaviors conducive to, 78, 117–118, 198–199, 225–248, 275, 276–277
  bias imputed to, 47
  critical thinking, 207–210
  data in relation to, 115–120, 134, 146
  defined, 274
  error-phobia as hindrance to, 86–89
  forms of, 211–214
  obstacles to, 86–89, 115–116, 217–219, *218*, 239–241, 247
  organizations resistant to, 203–204, 343–345, 348
  popular conceptions of, 203–205, 221–223, 233
  scientific, 215–216
  teaching in relation to, 250, 273–278
  value of, 48
Insight Stance, 233–237, 248, 277
Intelligent technology, 107, 145–146, 193, 194
Intentions, 61–63
Intuitions, 50, 77, 355–358
Irrationality, 17, 47, 54
Israel Defense Forces (IDF), 170, 355–356

James, Bill, 60
JDM. *See* Judgment and Decision Making (JDM) community
Jeopardy! (television show), 163
"Job as performed" mindset, 113
Johnson, Paul, 387
Johnson, Steven, 221, 229

Jones, R. V., 177–179, 194
Judgment and Decision Making (JDM) community, 44, 69, 95, 158
Judgment biases, 81, 159

Kahneman, Danny, 47, 49–50, 53–55, 81, 157–159, 162, 181, 183, 185, 186, 349, 355–357, 385, 407
Kamstra, Peter, 1–4
Kennedy, John F., 187
Kent, Sherman, 217–218
Khrushchev, Nikita, 217–218
Kiefer, C. F., 225
Klayman, J., 69–70
Klein, Dennis, 321–323
Klein, Devorah, 5, 34, 43, 150, 185, 325–326, 350, 353
Klein, G., 158–159, 181, 182, 183, 187, 386
Klein, Helen, 27, 286, 325
Klein, Rebecca, 62–63, 325–326
Knowledge Audit, 279–281
Knowledge shields, 74–75, 170, 276
Koresh, David, 314
Kounios, John, 225
Kriegspiel, 138
Kurzweil, Ray, 121–123
Kuwait, 132–133

Laboratory experiments. *See* Experiments
Langer, E. J., 229
Language, breakdowns in, 331–333
Lanir, Zvi, 170
Lao Tzu, 359
Laplace, Pierre-Simon, 54
Larry Sanders Show, The (television show), 322
Laughlin, Phil, 5
Leadership, difference-making, 403–406
Learning, 250, 259–261
Learning styles, 253–254
Lehmann, Dave, 263

Leverage points, 79, 178–179, 234, 240, 351, 395–397
Lewis, Michael, *Moneyball*, 45, 57–60
Libya, 132
Lichtenstein, S., 54
Lichtman, Allan, 373–374
Lilienfeld, S. O., 70
Limitations and failures, anticipation of or response to, 26–27, 110–113, 142, 171, 187, 244, 266. *See also* Failures, learning from
Lindstrom, Martin, 134
Loewenstein, G., 289–290

Machine learning, 6, 104, 137, 139, 141, 201, 243
Machines, for making humans smarter, 100, 101, 103–106, 125, 129, 141–143, 145, 155. *See also* System design and operation
Mahar, S. E., 401
Malthus, Thomas Robert, 212
Management by Discovery, 210, 391–393, *392*, 395, 409
Management skills, 182
Maneuver Warfare movement, 301, 303
Marcus, G., 139
Marine Corps Gazette, 281, 301
Martian, The (movie), 311, 328, 347
Mattingly, John, 404–405
McCone, John, 217–218
McNeil, B. J., 157
Medication adherence, 379–380
MedStar, 79, 403
Meehl, Paul, 51, 158
Mellers, Barbara, 160
Melwani, S., 344
Mental models
  of AI systems, 142
  anomalous data, 116
  anticipatory thinking, 169
  experts' repertoire of, 123, 135, 166, 182, 185, 193
  flaws in, 39, 275
  matrix, *26*, 182, *400*
  overview of, 25–27
  of systems' strengths and limitations, 142
  as tacit knowledge, 118–119, 187
  trying to comprehend another's, 118–119, *118*, 237
Mental simulation, 29–31, 39
Militello, Laura, 353, 397
Mills, Andrew, 38–39
Mind reading. *See* Perspective taking
Mindset shifts. *See also* Active mindset
  for anticipatory thinking, 171
  to cognitive dimension, 15
  from criticism to curiosity, 268
  for diagnosticians, 79
  from explaining to discovering, 269–270
  importance of underlying mindsets, 285–288
  from "job as envisioned" to "job as performed," 113
  from passive to active, 226, 229
  from procedural to problem-solving or investigative, 194, 209, 268–269, 295–296, 301–303
  resulting from experience, 14
  training-related, 250–251, 266–272, 280, 285–288, 301–303
Mining training exercise, 263–266, *265*
Minsky, Marvin, 91–92
Missing data. *See* Gaps in experience or expectations
Mistakes, sensationalizing of, 46, 85–86. *See also* Error reduction
Moon, Brian, 353
Mueller, J. S., 344
Mueller, Shane, 141–142, 201, 243, 245
Mulally, Alan, 405
Mumaw, R. J., 26
Mushrooms, 212–213

Index

Naikar, Neelam, 353
National Academy of Engineering, 128
National Transportation and Safety Board (NTSB), 111
Nation at Risk, A, 207
Naturalistic Decision Making (NDM), 10, 17, 21–23, 37, 42, 44, 72, 95, 197, 247, 349, 353–354, 407, 412
Naturalistic inquiry, 21, 23, 42, 52, 97. *See also* Field studies
NDM. *See* Naturalistic Decision Making
Netflix, 115
Neural networks, 104, 139, 141
Newell, Alan, 53
Newsome, Emily, 286
9-dot puzzle, 211, *211*, *214*, 226
9/11 attacks, 108, 116, 146, 340
Noble, Ed, 269
Numbers and statistics
  anomalies from perspective of, 82, 165–166
  in baseball, 45, 57–60
  effectiveness and trustworthiness of, 45
  experts' judgments contrasted with, 45, 51, 58–60
  limitations of, 61–63

Oakland Athletics, 57
On-the-job learning, 396
Open-mindedness, 76, 222, 233
Opportunities, 177–179, 229
Orasanu, Judith, 21
Organizations
  cultivation of insights by, 236–237
  design of, 397
  difference-making leaders, 403–406
  error reduction favored over increasing insights, 86–89, 200, 208, 285, 344–345, 348
  guidelines for change, 395–397
  Management by Discovery, 391–393, 395
  policy into practice, 399–401
  Pre-mortem method, 385–387
  resistant to insights, 203–204, 343–345, 348
  rigidity of, 43
  technological solutions favored by, 100–101, 122–125
  training mistakes, 270
  vetting of information by, 340–341
Originality, 186
Ostroff, Dan, 127
Outliers, 82, 95, 165–166
Overconfidence, 17, 157, 170, 266, 290, 329, 360, 387
Oversimplification, 43, 170, 373, 375, 377, 408

Panel operators. *See* Petrochemical plant operators
Pattern matching, 29–31, 165, 244
Patton, George S., 319
Perceptual discrimination, 281
Perceptual-motor skills, 181–182
Perfection trap, 344
Perrow, C., 167
Perry, Shawna, 43, 198–199
Personnel evaluations, 389–390
Perspective taking
  cultivating, 317–319, 325–326, 347
  dispute resolution, 335–337
  effectiveness of, 313–316, 318
  hindsight, 271
  seeing cognition in others, 307, 347
  self-knowledge through, 359–360
  teamwork, 308, 319
  trainers'/supervisors' need for, 190
  viewpoints of others, 14, 307–308
Petrochemical plant operators, 25, 122, 158, 187, 189–190, 197–198, 257–258
Physicians, 65, 71, 78, 122, 149, 153–155, 170, 198–199, 332–333
Piaget, Jean, 274

Pines, J. M., 65
Pitt, Brad, 57
Plato, *Euthyphro*, 332–333
Police officers, 286–287, 300
Policy into practice, 399–401
Polya, George, 55
Popper, Karl, 274
Positive psychology, 48
Positive test strategy, 69–70
Predictability, 281, 308, 343
Pre-mortem method, 230, 350, 385–387
Probability theory, 53–54
Problem-Based Learning, 273
Problem detection and diagnosis, 14, 23, 166, 209, 281, 284
Problem-solving, 171, 178, 286–287
Procedures, 44, 45, 51, 209, 249–250, 254, 268–269, 279, 280, 286–287, 295–296
Procter & Gamble (P&G), 117–119
Progress reviews, 236–237
Psychoeducation, 70

Question asking, 240–241, 302

Ralston, Aron, 239–241
RAND Corporation, 138
Rational choice theory, 31–32
Rationalist approaches. *See* Decision-making: analytical/mechanical approaches to
Rationalist fever dreams, 7, 43–45, 83, 95, 97, 99, 412
Recognition-Primed Decision (RPD) model, 10, 29–32, *30*, 55, 193, 356
Recursion, 11. *See also* Goal recursion strategy
Reliability, 186, 188
Repetition, 254
Representations, 244
Resnick, Lauren, 273

Responsibility, 105
Rideout, Pat, 405
Rio Tinto, 263
Risk assessment and management, 1, 4, 14, 55, 209, 229, 279, 327–329, 343, 354, 385–387
Rivera, Mariano, 58–59
Rock climbing, 178–179
Rock fishing, 1–4, *2*
Rodgers, Aaron, 85
Role reversals, 318
Rommel, Erwin, 319
Roth, Emilie, 353
Rothman, Jay, 337
Rowing, 62–63
Roy, M., 259–261
RPD. *See* Recognition-Primed Decision (RPD) model

Sanders, Bernie, 374
Scenarios, 14–15, 25, 33–34, 197, 250–251, 257–258, 263–266, 281, 283–284, 301–303, 318, 335, 360, 400–401
Schmidle, Robert "Rooster," 404
Schmitt, John, 301–302
Schraagen, Jan Maarten, 353
Science, process of, 215–216
Scouts, baseball, 58–60
Seattle Fire Department, 33
Second singularity, 101, 121–125, *124*, 145
Self-explaining, 259–261
Self-knowledge, 359–360
Seligman, Martin, 48
Sensemaking, 17, 74–75, 166–167
ShadowBox, 10, 13, 33–35, 193, 279–280, 283, 293, 318, 335, 389, 400–401
Shanteau, James, 181, 183, 185, 188
Shneiderman, Ben, 100, 101, 123, 127–128, 138
Showstoppers, 92–93

Shuttling, 244
Siddiqui, G., 155
Simon, Herbert, 39, 53, 55
Singularity, 100, 121, 123–124, *124*.
    See also Second singularity
Siri, 105, 128
Skill portfolios, 151, 181–183
Sleep. *See* Dreamy states
Small Data, 101, 131–135, 146
Smith, Mark, 79, 403
Smoothing data, 110
Snap back, 79
Snook, Scott, 366–369
Social engagement, 105
Social psychology, 193
Sociology, 161, 162–163
Socrates, 207, 332–333
Sonkin, Paul, 387
Sources of power, knowledge and abilities as, 17–19, *18*, *19*, 42, 44
Speculative thinking, 197–248. *See also* Discoveries; Frontier thinking; Insights
    chess, 137
    as cognitive source of power, 146
    confirmation bias and, 70, 72
    heuristics likened to, 54–55
    as human capability, 199
    insights encouraged by, 234
Sports. *See* Baseball; Football
Stalin, Joseph, 75
Standard operating procedures, 182
Stanton, Doug, 108–109
Staszewski, Jim, 159
Statistics. *See* Numbers and statistics
Steffel, J., 313–317
Stories, for communication clarification, 332–333
Strobhar, Dave, 272
Stupidity, adopting perspective of, 151, 189–191
Subconscious. *See* Dreamy states

Substitution bias, 81–83
Sullenberger, Chesley Burnett "Sully" (airline pilot), 103, 105
Sunstein, Cass, 395
Surprises. *See* Anomalies; Unexpected situations
Swarm intelligence, 155
Sweeney, David, 17
Swirl, 221–222
System 1/System 2, 30, 81, 208
System design and operation, 25–26, 107–110, 113. *See also* Machines, for making humans smarter
Systems integration, 13–15

Tacit knowledge
    acquisition of, 158, 249
    aspects of, 186–187, 280, 293, *294*
    cultivating, 249, 268–269, 293–297
    eliciting, 146
    of experts, 15, 22, 51, 151, 185, 194, 268–269, 293–297
    explicit vs., *294*
    mental models as, 119
Tactical Decision Games (TDGs), 281, 301–303
Taleb, N. N., 339–340
Teaching. *See* Training
Teamwork
    conditions for, 281, 308
    decision strategies, 327–329
    perspective taking, 308, 319
Temple of Apollo, Delphi, 359
Tetlock, Phil, 60, 160, 194
Thaler, Richard, 385, 395
Thinking. *See* Cognition and cognitive dimension
Time pressure, 17, 21, 29, 31, 50, 73, 263, 284, 357
Tower of Hanoi puzzle, 10–11, 37–40, *38*
Toyota, 133–134, 146
Trade-offs, 14, 280

Training, 249–306
  curiosity, 289–291
  developing scenarios, 283–284
  evaluation vs., 250, 257–258, 268, 270, 297
  for expertise, 293–297
  importance of, 396
  insight-centered, 250, 273–278
  mindset shifts, 250–251, 262–272, 280, 285–288, 301–303
  misconceptions about, 253–255
  motivation in, 263–266
  perspective taking, 317–319
  presenting cognitive challenges, 279–281
  tips for effective, 267–272, 275–284
  US Marine Corps, 301–303
  value of, 250, 259–261
  welcoming challenges in, 299–300
Triple Path model of insight, 211–212, *212*, 223
Trump, Donald, 374
Tversky, Amos, 47, 49–50, 53–55, 157, 162
12 Angry Men (movie), 336
Two-string problem, 240, 241

Uncertainty, 1, 17, 21, 23, 29, 37, 47, 50, 69, 81, 87, 138, 170, 208, 223, 279, 281, 283, 284, 301, 343–345, 359
Unexpected situations, 26, 108–110, 113, 123, 138, 169–171, 199
United Kingdom, 132
Unlearning, 275
US Army, 159
US intelligence community, 132–133
US Marine Corps, 251, 301–303, 318, 404
US Special Forces, 108–109

Vagabonding, 75
Veinott, B., 386

Via, Lisa, 272
Vinge, Vernor, 121
VisiCalc, 344
V-1 rockets, 151, 177–179, 194

Wallas, Graham, 211–213, 225
Walters, Kerry, 207
Wang, D., 154
Ward, P., 182, 186
Wason, Peter, 66–68, 71
Watson, James, 217–219
Weather forecasting, 110
Weight Watchers, 382–383, *383*
Wicked problems, 22, 76, 163, 205, 209, 351, 358, 391–393, 395, 409
Wiggins, S., 386
Wikipedia, 101, 105, 134, 146, 208
Wilson, Joe, 116
Woodruff, Paul, 335
Woods, Dave, 43, 69, 74
Workarounds, 26, 272, 280–281
Workplace Technology Research Inc. (WTRI), 263–266
Workstations, 203, 205
World Health Organization, 340
World War II, 151, 177–179
World Wide Web, 128
Wright, Corinne, 389
WTRI. *See* Workplace Technology Research Inc.
Wustrack, Gretchen, 350
Wylie, R., 260

XAI. *See* Explainable AI
Xerox, 116, 344

Yom Kippur War, 170, 340

Zaremsky, Adam, 353
Zone of Indifference, 92–93, *92*
Zweig, Jason, 385